ELISABETH VREEDE

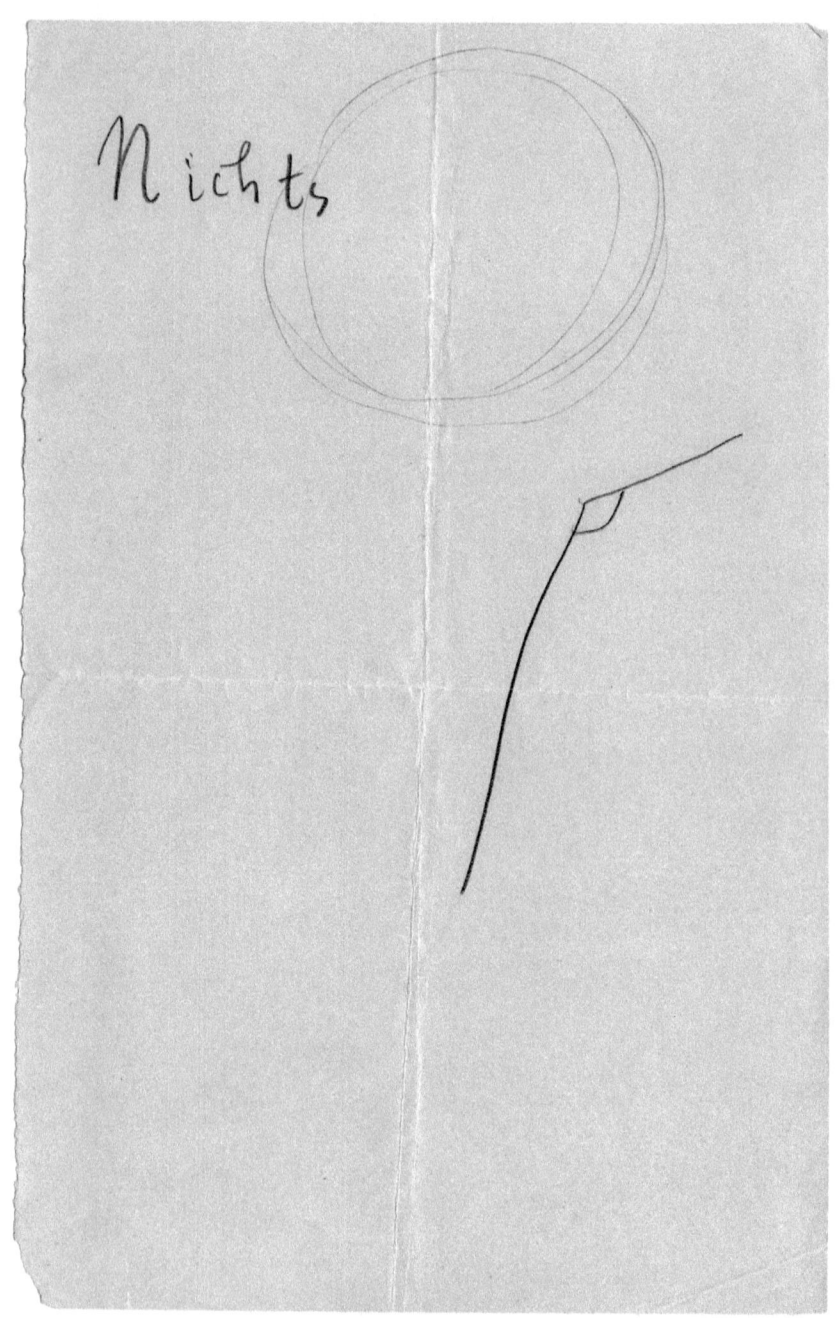

"Nothingness," by Rudolf Steiner

Elisabeth Vreede

Adversity, Resilience and Spiritual Science

Peter Selg

SteinerBooks | 2017

SteinerBooks
An imprint of Anthroposophic Press, Inc.
610 Main St., Great Barrington, MA 01230
www.steinerbooks.org

Translated by Marsha Post

Copyright © 2017 by Peter Selg. All rights reserved. No part of this publication may be reproduced, stored in a retrieval system, or transmitted, in any form or by any means, electronic, mechanical, photocopying, recording, or otherwise, without the prior written permission of the publisher.

Originally published in German as
Elisabeth Vreede: 1879–1943
(Verlag des Ita Wegman Instituts, 2009)
Design: Jens Jensen

Library of Congress Control Number: 2017953366

ISBN: 978-1-621482-00-0 (paperback)
ISBN: 978-1-62148-201-7 (ebook)

Contents

Foreword vii

1. "All of Heaven seemed to be called down" (1879–1913)
   The Way to Rudolf Steiner 1

2. "Dr. Steiner was very pleased with my lectures" (1914–1923)
   Dornach 41

3. "Tested to the ultimate degree" (1924–1925)
   The Christmas Conference and the Esoteric Executive Council   79

4. "Executive Council's Idylls" (1925–1935)
   The Decade after Rudolf Steiner's Death 111

5. "May soul live in this house" (1935–1943)
   The Final Years 169

APPENDICES:

Elisabeth Vreede:
The Christmas and Michael Impulses:
Lecture at the Opening of the Second Goetheanum
Dornach, October 2, 1928 207

Elisabeth Vreede:
Isis–Sophia
Christmas Essay, 1928 229

Bibliography 243

Notes 245

"The being Anthroposophy—I myself have always felt it to be a spiritual being brought newly into existence by Rudolf Steiner, as it were, the first hierarchical being brought into existence by human beings; totally young, a being that must first develop further through our collaborative effort, as 'knowledge community,' and with the collaboration of its Creator from the spiritual world."
—Elisabeth Vreede [1]

Foreword

> "*Fräulein Vreede is one of those who best understands my lectures.*"
> —RUDOLF STEINER[2]

In the thirty-third anniversary year of the death of the Dutch anthroposophist and astronomer, Dr. Elisabeth Vreede (1879–1943), the doctor and close colleague of Ita Wegman, Madeleine van Deventer, published a small anthology with recollections of various people who wanted to snatch an image of Vreede from oblivion. "Out of consideration that Elisabeth Vreede today, as during her life, has remained unknown to most people," per van Deventer in 1976,[3] she set about to publish the recollections in Natura Verlag in Arlesheim. Dora Krück von Poturzyn, who had known Vreede well and who also wrote a contribution for the book, recalled that Elisabeth Vreede was aware of the oblivion dynamic of her person already during her lifetime. "'It will not be long until one has forgotten me,' she said to friends in her refreshing, unsentimental manner."[4]

With their recollection work, van Deventer and Krück von Poturzyn did not turn first to past companions on their paths and to opponents, but to the future generations. They did not strive to produce a biographical presentation and a thorough documentation, but an imagination or memory of Vreede as possibility of inner relationships, a memorial stressing the future. People like van Deventer and Krück von Poturzyn who really knew Vreede—at least initially—had also recognized and had no doubt that there would come to her an acknowledgment of her substantial significance for the progress of the anthroposophic movement. Elisabeth Vreede was—and is—a very effective individuality; forgetting her existence, however, complicates the possibilities of the dead to be able to help fully support the earthly efforts for the future of the anthroposophical Spiritual Science. When the following generations pass Vreede by, they miss out on a source of spiritual help that should be taken seriously, according to van Deventer.

~

Ita Wegman's biographer, Emmanuel Zeylmanns van Emmichoven, said in an interview:

> I have the strongest memories of Vreede: above all, how she was a guest with us in class [of the Waldorf school]; or how she sat with a wooden countenance at our table in our home. I had a very strong connection with her after her death. I believe that she was spiritually very honest.... She was unrelentingly truthful with regard to herself and to all other anthroposophists, and to Anthroposophy itself, even to the point of sacrificing herself. That is the character of the consciousness soul. With Vreede I had the deepest experience of the consciousness soul.[5]

Emmanuel Zeylmans was only a child when he saw Elisabeth Vreede; her being remained close to him also in later decades in his difficult works and studies—"...the deepest experiences of the consciousness soul."

Elisabeth Vreede was extraordinarily awake, quick to comprehend and had a spiritualized intellect. According to Dora Krück von Poturzyn, she was, as a person, of "unrelenting simplicity."[6] Nat Schatborn-Lievegoed wrote, "One could always be sure that her statements were accurate and well substantiated. One felt that what she said is true. She walked and stood calmly, resting within herself. She was well dressed, simply and tastefully. She looked upon one in her calm and friendly way."[7]

Van Deventer spoke of an "ancient element of truth" in Vreede's being.[8] This "ancient element of truth" found its way into modernity, into the epoch of the consciousness soul and that selflessness of "I," the significance of which Rudolf Steiner repeatedly drew attention,[9] the selflessness that remained a definite rarity in the anthroposophical leadership circle. Vreede never pushed into the foreground; she was powerful, but undemanding and modest. She rested within herself, had tremendous spiritual gifts and went through a school for natural science. She was educated philosophically and heard not only a majority of Rudolf Steiner's lectures, but retained these livingly in her magnificent memory. Elisabeth Vreede was not only one of the best authorities in Anthroposophy—in the content and circumstances of the origin of Rudolf Steiner's research—but handled it with her schooled power of judgment, as much of her words and deeds show.

Otfried Doerfler wrote accurately about Vreede's presentations of "The Bodhisattva Question in the History of the Anthroposophical Society": "Over the course of decades much has been written about the being of Rudolf Steiner. Only very little of it shows the care and clarity that the presentation by Elisabeth Vreede shows." The knowledge about Rudolf Steiner, but also the loyalty to Anthroposophy, was engraved into Vreede, into her destiny and being. Dealing with her was not only easy—per Dora Krück von Poturzyn, Vreede was a "touchstone" for many people, "insofar as loyalty to Anthroposophy lived in them." Krück von Poturzyn wrote further: "This alone was what counted for Elisabeth Vreede. As delicate as she appeared, as undemanding and loving as she was, she was a rock on which one could build."[11]

Why such a person with these special qualities could succumb to far-reaching oblivion is not easy to understand, particularly since the anthroposophical community, during Rudolf Steiner's lifetime and especially in the decades after his death, had only a limited number of highly gifted persons. It was stressed repeatedly that the forgetting of Vreede lay in the circumstances of her incarnation. Madeline van Deventer wrote, "It was not easy to reach the innermost common determining character of Elisabeth Vreede's nature. She was shy and spoke very seldom about herself and her innermost experience."[12] Rudolf Steiner, according to Elisabeth Knottenbelt, evidently said, *"This individuality wished not to be known."*[13] Vreede supposedly incarnated too early so that she could be present for the development of Anthroposophy at the beginning of the twentieth century. This was at the expense of the circle of people in her destiny—her old relationships and friends. For that reason she had few close relationships and was often overlooked; even in the train or streetcar where the conductor ignored her. Further, it was reported with regard to the deeper signature of her biography that Elisabeth Vreede never saw an accident or was involved in one. She was often away and traveled to many countries—in a not so harmless way—from Turkey to Egypt. However, nothing ever happened to her or her fellow travelers. Vreede told her sometimes-companion, Charlotte Fiechter, that she was a talisman for others. "She used to say, 'As long as they travel with me, nothing will happen to them.'"[14] Van Deventer said that Vreede also spoke about this with Rudolf Steiner. "As she spoke to Rudolf Steiner one time about this peculiarity, he told her that this is substantiated deep in her destiny; it is connected with the manner of her death in an earlier life. At that time she died in a natural catastrophe. He also named the people with whom she had died."[15]

Accordingly, through Rudolf Steiner, Elisabeth Vreede knew some things about the special circumstances of her earthly life. He also spoke with her once—according to Willy Sucher—about (very possibly) her last incarnation as a leading person of the Temple community, with a difficult, terrible destiny.[16] In a lecture Elisabeth Vreede said about the spiritual teacher:

> He answered questions put to him, especially in private conversations, very differently—I mean, as regards the concreteness, the positivity of the answer, and so on. He went now and then, one wants to say, amazingly far; and one can have the impression that it basically pleased him when, so to speak, he was presented with

the karmic opportunity to say more about some things than was possible in the general lectures.[17]

At the same time it is not to be overlooked that Elisabeth Vreede's being forgotten is founded also on completely different circumstances. These have little to do with her old destiny and the specific conditions of her incarnation around and after 1879, but in contrast, it has much to do with her biography in the twentieth century. The decline of the Dornach Executive Council and the Anthroposophical Society in the first decade after Rudolf Steiner's death and the actual expulsion of people like Ita Wegman and Elisabeth Vreede remained in no way without consequences. Rather, it all determined, and still determines, the further history, in broad strokes but also with respect to single individualities. (In April 1935, as is known, Ita Wegman and Elisabeth Vreede were relieved of their positions and these were never officially restored.) A large part of Vreede's literary estate was lost; among the things lost was her private correspondence that was everything but "impersonal," but was written in an extremely soulful and original manner. The small residual, mostly in the Dutch language, is distributed among various places and archives.

No biography or comprehensive tribute to her work was ever written. There was also no detailed examination of the reproaches and accusations raised against her in Dornach that led her to her expulsion. Documentation such as Emmanuel Zeylmans von Emmichoven wrote and published as a private individual for Ita Wegman does not exist for Elisabeth Vreede. Nevertheless, she not only deserved it but the Anthroposophical Society also owed it to her in a certain sense. One can have the justified opinion that there are things to do that are more urgent than producing historical documents of the events of the 1920s and '30s in Dornach. On the other hand, the question remains as to how to handle the injustice that happened and how to do justice to an individuality such as Elisabeth Vreede while avoiding the corresponding challenges. To fulfill them is complicated and possible only under demanding prerequisites. To interpret the failure to remember Elisabeth Vreede as merely a matter of destiny is perhaps a bit justified, however, but threatens to lose sight of other issues.

~

In the introduction to her Memorial volume in 1976, Madeline van Deventer wrote:

> We stand at the beginning of a second thirty-three year period after her earthly life. Will her individuality now take the opportunity to work into the views of people and thus to overcome the tragedy that she had to experience in life: that her work would bear no fruit? And will a generation have grown up that is capable and prepared to work from her spirit? It would be a great gain for the progress of our work. For it is a significant individuality who now enters a new phase of effectiveness.[18]

In 1976, seven years before her death, Madeline van Deventer had hope for the future. The willingness and capability to work from the spirit of the individuality of Elisabeth Vreede meant Vreede's spiritual behavior that was on the level of the consciousness soul but also her work on the topic of a spiritual-scientific astronomy or astrosophy. Vreede wrote in an essay, *"Today's Spiritual Science wants to understand human life through living knowledge working in from the universe."*[19] On this basis, Rudolf Steiner also developed his esoteric courses for medical students and doctors.[20] Van Deventer knew the relevance of these courses; she had helped organize them and participated in them.[21] Rudolf Steiner emphasized in his first—very first!—"Leading Thought": "Anthroposophy is a path of knowledge that wants to leads the spiritual in the human being to the spiritual in the cosmos."[22] In this respect, as leader of the Mathematics–Astronomy Section at the Goetheanum, Elisabeth Vreede was of a high-ranking significance. Nevertheless, Lili Kolisko, whose difficult destiny is equal to that of Elisabeth ("Lili") Vreede's in every way, wrote in an accurate summary of Vreede's anthroposophical biography:

Elisabeth Vreede, PhD, was a member of the Executive Council, on whose opinion one laid very little—one could almost say, absolutely no—value. This was in spite of the fact that Dr. Steiner introduced her in the Christmas Conference with the following words: "Likewise, a very long-time member is the person I now mean and who was proven, right down to the last detail, to be the most loyal coworker here and with whom you really can also agree to the very last detail: Fräulein Dr. Lili Vreede."[23]

~

One might ask whether much, or even anything, decisive has happened for Elisabeth Vreede since Madeline van Deventer's extraordinary Memorial volume in 1976. In 1980 a new edition of her main literary work *Astronomy and Anthroposophy*, as well as her essays *Astrology and Anthroposophy* were published in Dornach by the Verlag am Goetheanum. In 1989, Thomas Meyer published for the first time (through Perseus Verlag, Basel) Vreede's bodhisattva lectures with extensive commentary. Seven years later (1996), a beautiful edition of the collection of essays *Geschichte und Phänomene der Astronomie* (History and phenomena of astronomy) was published, again by Verlag am Goetheanum, as the first of four announced volumes from the scientific estate ("Essays–Lectures–Reports").[24]

In 2001, Ranatus Ziegler dedicated a noteworthy chapter to Elisabeth Vreede in his work *Biographien und Bibliographien. Mitarbeitende und Mitwirkende an der Matematisch-Astronomischen Sektion am Goetheanum* (Biographies and bibliographies. Colleagues and coworkers in the Mathematics–Astronomy Section of the Goetheanum). Ziegler also wrote the article on Elisabeth Vreede in the anthology, *Anthroposophie im 20 Jahrhundert* (Anthroposophy in the twentieth century), edited by Bodo von Plato. At Christmas 2003 the Swiss National Society of the Anthroposophical Society published a special brochure on Elisabeth Vreede, with contributions by many authors (*Besinnung auf Elisabeth Vreede* [Reflections on Elisabeth Vreede]).

Also in 2003, Hans Peter van Manen published, for the "Anthroposophical Association in Holland," the small work *"Elisabeth Vreede.*

Enkle brieven uit 1943" (Elisabeth Vreede: Some letters of 1943). In contrast, in 2007 the Executive Council of the Clinic-Therapeutic Institute in Arlesheim disposed of "Haus Vreede" that was designed by Rudolf Steiner and provided with a Foundation Stone. She lived and worked in this house for over two decades. It is no longer owned by anthroposophists. And in an edition of the weekly *Das Goetheanum* that came out on August 28, 2009, three days before the sixty-sixth anniversary of Elisabeth Vreede's death, and had the theme of "Starry World" (in "International Year of Astronomy 2009"), not one word was mentioned about Dr. Vreede, the Dornach leader in this field who was so highly valued by Rudolf Steiner. And this was not out of any bad intention.[25] To answer Madeline van Deventer's question in the positive is not easy based on this background, and a corresponding departure hardly appears to be in view, despite the publication of individual writings.

Based on this, for the sixty-sixth anniversary of Elisabeth Vreede's death—at the end of the second thirty-three-year cycle—this present book shall follow on van Deventer's initiative. It seemed thereby essential to bring out a number of life attitudes and motives of Elisabeth Vreede that continue to have an effect and that characterized her biography in the nineteenth and twentieth centuries. Vreede's handling of difficult things also belongs to these attitudes and motives, especially within the Anthroposophical Society. If one studies the corresponding events, the impression can arise that Elisabeth Vreede was the main sacrifice or the main bearer of the suffering of the society's tragedy and expulsions of 1935 in the Dornach Executive Council, more so than Ita Wegman, who drew to herself the greatest, most aggressive and blindest criticism. However, Ita Wegman continued to run, also after April 14, 1935, her clinic extremely well; remained in contact with therapeutic and curative institutes; and continued her international income and forms of work that were centered on her or were connected with her.

After 1935, from Arlesheim, she led the Medical Section of the Goetheanum, though not in an official capacity. In contrast, Elisabeth

Vreede's loss was almost total. She had to give up everything: the position on the Executive Council; the Mathematics–Astronomy Section; the Rudolf Steiner Archive at the Goetheanum that she built, financed and managed; the planetarium and more—her entire professional existence. That Vreede understood how to handle it is more than impressive and reveals the greatness of her individuality that knew the hard strokes of destiny and was able to integrate them into her path of development. A knowledgeable man, Emanuel Zeylmans van Emmichoven, wrote, "One can have the impression that she was the most learned, cultured one on the Executive Council."[26]

A comprehensive presentation of the crisis in the history of the Anthroposophical Society has not been written even today. It is, however, an absolute urgent necessity of the future—with the inclusion of perspectives of all of the central participants and the extensive documents of all of the archives.[27] This book merely presents a few of Elisabeth Vreede's experiences—events in her life, experiences and sufferings—as a memorial. The difficult years in Dornach are part of Vreede's biographical path and must be included in this presentation. There is a widespread tendency to consider this part of anthroposophical history, because of its accumulated suffering and because of the changed circumstances of the times, as being over, finished. Contrary to this, it is necessary to recognize that the experiences with Rudolf Steiner and in the anthroposophical community belong to the decisive, further effective forces of such a vita and individuality like that of Elisabeth Vreede—in light and darkness; the easy and the difficult. I hope that one day someone takes up the initiative to develop and bring into the open the biography of Elisabeth Vreede and her mathematics and astronomic work in all detail—the way Emanuel Zeylmans van Emmichoven did for Ita Wegman. "The time is long / Yet there comes to pass / What is true" (Friedrich Hölderlin).

For the right to look at and take into account and publish documents that concern Elisabeth Vreede, I thank especially Ineke and Frau Lutters (Estate of Elisabeth Vreede in the Library of the Dutch

National Society, The Hague); further, Uwe Werner (Archive at the Goetheanum) and Walter Kugler (Rudolf Steiner Archive, Dornach). I am also grateful to Gunhild Pörksen (Ita Wegman Archive) for her support with the research.

Peter Selg
Walcheren, Holland
August 31, 2009

I

"All of Heaven seemed to be called down"
(1879–1913)

The Way to Rudolf Steiner

"When the teacher knows the mathematical truths and passes them on to the student, then the student no longer needs a belief in authority. Then he or she sees the mathematical truths through their own correctness, and needs nothing else than to see them correctly. It is no different with the whole esoteric development in the Rosicrucian sense. The teacher is the friend, the advisor, who lives through the occult experiences first and then allows the student to live them."
—Rudolf Steiner[28]

Elisabeth Vreede in her parents' home (undated)

Elisabeth Vreede (née Jacoba Elisabeth Vreede) came to Earth on July 16, 1879, the second of four children of a prominent old Dutch family of a significant lineage. Her parents were theosophists, and many theosophical meetings were held in their house in The Hague. Henry Steele Olcott, President of the Theosophical Society, visited there, and later Rudolf Steiner came for conversations, lectures, and esoteric lessons. Elisabeth Vreede's father, Henrik Vreede (1847–1933), was a wealthy scholar of jurisprudence who was Director of "De Nederlandsche Bank des Vos te 's-Gravenhage." Her mother, Jacoba Elisabeth Schill (1853–1925), who grew up in Dutch India, engaged herself socially in many ways. She took on joint responsibility for the Theosophical and Anthroposophical Societies in Holland quite early, and became the branch leader in The Hague as of 1913. She was described as a still and kind, but also a very active woman. A few years before her death Rudolf Steiner was able to give her essential information about her earlier incarnations.[30]

Elisabeth Vreede was a delicate, fine-boned child who impressed people with her powers of attention and memory. She learned a great deal very quickly by heart and seldom forgot it again; hers was an astonishing intelligence and an extraordinary talent for understanding and memory. Her parents held the beginning of her schooling back a year out of concern for her accelerated intellectual development; this did her no favor, because Elisabeth Vreede was not only the oldest child in her class, but she was also the best in all the subjects and far beyond the others, without exerting any effort. She was often alone and had no friends; her talents and the questions she was living with were very different, falling outside the scope of the community. When her older brother Adriaan received a gift of four books by the French astronomer, Camille Flammarion, she taught herself French, in order to read these volumes. "From the expectation to find within those worlds, from which...the human individuality descends and to which this child had a very special, mysterious relationship, she taught herself French in order to be able to read this work" (Ernst Bindel).[31]

As early as when she was attending the gymnasium, Elisabeth accompanied her parents to many countries; among these was Switzerland, where she would live from age thirty-five years on. When she was sixteen years old she learned Goethe's Faust I and II by heart.

~

After her *Abitur* (final exam following the completion of secondary education), Elisabeth Vreede began her university studies in Leiden. She registered for mathematics, astronomy, and philosophy; it was an unusual educational track for a woman at that time. Among her studies—she studied quite energetically—were the lectures and works of Hegel, whose "enormously disciplined thinking" (Steiner)[32] made a profound impression on her. Elisabeth Vreede also learned Sanskrit and Pali, to understand and penetrate the mathematics of the ancient Indians better. She was seeking the ancient, cosmic mystery-knowledge of the human being and the human being's relationship to present-day thinking in science and philosophy. None of this hindered her from joining the executive council of a student association or from taking part in the founding of a womens' rowing club. She was independent, practical and self-conscious—a woman of the modern age. After completing her university studies, Elisabeth Vreede taught mathematics several years at an upper school for girls. It is not known where or how she lived during these years.

Elisabeth joined the Theosophical Society, to which her parents belonged, when she was twenty-one years old. Although she did this of her own accord, her motivation was ambivalent and, in the end, reluctant.

> Something in me rebelled against it all the more vehemently, as I had the feeling that even the most intense rejection does not help you; a force that is stronger than you are in your usual consciousness

"All of Heaven seemed to be called down" (1879–1913)

Elisabeth Vreede in her youth

is sending you into it (Theosophical Society). I knew such forces in my life, but I was not accustomed to have them place me into something unfathomable.³³

The destiny–will sphere of (her) biography was awakened and demanded its due. Being placed "into something unfathomable" was alien to Elisabeth Vreede's nature; she was a person for whom clarity and knowledge were most important of all. Nevertheless, she took the step of joining in 1900, one year after the end of Kali Yuga, the Dark Ages in occult tradition.

Elisabeth Vreede never wrote about how she experienced the Theosophical Society in her parents' home. She did meet people there who were impressive, cultivated, charismatic and elegant; there were possibly others, however, who appealed to her less. The Theosophical Society was founded in 1875 in New York City; whether it held the future within it was very likely questionable to Elisabeth Vreede.

Three years after joining the Theosophical Society she heard Rudolf Steiner speak at a conference in London (July 1903).

> I will never forget the impression the first meeting with Rudolf Steiner made on me. The meeting was about to begin as a man entered the hall; he was dark, slender, of an upright posture, gaunt, and wore a long, almost priestly black coat. His countenance was full of inner fire; he exhibited intense attention and a fully controlled will. This is the image that rises from my memory. I was so impressed that I poked my neighbor and said, "Look—who is that coming in there?!"³⁴

Elisabeth Vreede reported the powerful impression Rudolf Steiner made on her—his unusual spiritual energy so different from that within the Theosophical Society: "a countenance full of fire, the most intense attention, and controlled will." She did not like the extraordinary forcefulness that was connected with Steiner's lecture, the "power of the temperament.... It was as if he wanted to communicate to the world the strength and significance of his mission in every sentence; from the black hair flying around his small head to

"All of Heaven seemed to be called down" (1879–1913)

Elisabeth Vreede, undated

the remarkably animated gestures of his hands and arms, and with the immensely emphatic nature of his words he appeared to make himself into the physical embodiment of what he had to say."[35] Elisabeth Vreede conceded that Rudolf Steiner had a "commanding power of speaking that he allowed to take hold of his essentially delicate physical nature."[36] She was more alienated than impressed by this power. The teachers of wisdom in the ancient East had spoken and written differently, as well as Hegel in his peaceful style of expression. Colonel Olcott was an old and wise person; Annie Besant was smart, peaceful, and exemplary, in control of form in speech and in writing. The fire, power of will, and impulsive style of Rudolf Steiner's lectures were very different from those of the others, though his presentation, too, showed clear composition. Elisabeth Vreede was also irritated partially by the content of the lectures themselves. Rudolf Steiner spoke of the spiritual task of Central Europe and Germany, and Elisabeth Vreede listened skeptically. Very little good had come from Germany in the recent decades, and the times of Hegel, Fichte, and Schelling were long gone. What Steiner said came across to Elisabeth Vreede as "nationalistic."[37]

One year later, in the summer of 1904, she attended another lecture by Rudolf Steiner at the Congress of the European Section of the Theosophical Society. This time Steiner spoke in Holland (Amsterdam) at the Congress Section for Philosophy on "Mathematics and Occultism,"[38] a theme that concerned her like no other. Again, however, Elisabeth found it difficult to deal with what she heard.

> I could not hear this lecture either; I could not understand it. Neither the materialistic thought habits of my youth nor the university studies, nor the way of thinking I had become acquainted with in the Theosophical Society allowed a possibility of experiencing the spiritual meaning of his words; they remained mere words to me.[39]

Elisabeth Vreede named the "thought habits" of her youth, her university studies, and the theosophy she had come to know up to that point; these three ways of thinking were not very compatible, although

"All of Heaven seemed to be called down" (1879–1913)

Rudolf Steiner, 1905

quite a few theosophists tried to incorporate contemporary materialism and atomism in their worldview. *What* Rudolf Steiner taught and *how* he taught it were completely different from these ways of thinking. He was no doubt a scientific thinker, but Vreede found it difficult to perceive the spiritual meaning of his words.

In a personal consultation in Amsterdam Rudolf Steiner expressed to the young, twenty-five-year-old woman how much he valued the fact that she was studying mathematics and astronomy and encouraged her to continue with these studies. ("She was somewhat ashamed of studying such a banal subject and when she told him she was studying mathematics, he answered that mathematical thinking is the best preparation for Spiritual Science."[40]) Elisabeth Vreede never said whether or not she articulated her difficulties with his lectures in this conversation. Rudolf Steiner valued critical, awake, honest people and would have in no way experienced Vreede's judgment with indignation. Most likely she kept her concerns and questions to herself; she probably wanted to hear more from him and read, in order to attain more clarity. It was remarkable that Rudolf Steiner spoke precisely about mathematics in Amsterdam; and he was without a doubt quite aware of her. "Rudolf Steiner asked her many years later if she still knew what dress she wore at that time [in Amsterdam]. As she, surprised, said no, he responded with, 'but I still know, a green one'" (Bindel).[41]

⁓

Elisabeth Vreede found the spiritual meaning in Rudolf Steiner's words in the next years that followed. She read his essays on the soul-spiritual development of the human being that were brought out as a series titled *Wie erlangt man Erkenntnisse der höhern Welten* (in English, *How to Know Higher Worlds*). Rudolf Steiner published these essays himself in a theosophical magazine in 1904 and 1905. "What was said here about entering into the spiritual world and the deep, inner way to lead the human being to spiritual knowledge,"[42] made a lasting impression on Vreede. She realized that Rudolf Steiner taught a Rosicrucian path in a methodical, systematic, "deeply inner" way. Elisabeth Vreede began doing his exercises and experienced that they led her further, as did his next lectures. In May and June 1906 she attended a theosophical event in Paris where Rudolf Steiner spoke in not fewer than eighteen lectures about a new cosmology based on Spiritual Science. Twelve months later at Whitsun 1907, Vreede attended the Congress of the Theosophical Society in Munich. Immediately following the Congress she heard Steiner's lecture cycle titled *The Theosophy of the Rosicrucians,* which meant a great deal to her. "Through these [lectures]…the dissatisfaction I had always experienced in the theosophical doctrine was fully overcome. What one could understand and accept scientifically was given there. Spiritual knowledge fulfilled the yearning for the spiritual."[43]

Elisabeth Vreede wrote in an autobiographical retrospective of her long and painful path to a fruitful uniting of academic science with spiritual knowledge.[44] It held true in the general and in the specific way that the posited task of spiritual-scientifically imbued astronomy and cosmology was great, and its achievement belonged to the future; although Steiner had already shown numerous perspectives and details of such work early on.

The fact that Vreede developed a deepened connection to Rudolf Steiner and Anthroposophy through his Rosicrucian lectures of 1907 is of spiritual-historical significance. The following year in his lectures to members of the Theosophical Society, in which he went into details of Rosicrucianism, Steiner reported repeatedly that, as early as the Middle Ages, Christian Rosenkreutz took into account the coming development of science in the nineteenth and twentieth centuries. That means, he prepared a form of spiritual knowledge that could meet the demands of the coming time and the circumstances of the development of consciousness. "The Rosicrucians had to work for an age that must think mathematically. They had to prepare in this sense and had, therefore, to be, for the most part, misunderstood."[45] Steiner characterized Christian Rosenkreutz as an individuality "who set the tone in a certain way for the way and manner by which, in

Wie erlangt man Erkenntnisse der höheren Welten.

Von Dr. Rudolf Steiner.

Es schlummern in jedem Menschen Fähigkeiten, durch die er sich Erkenntnisse über höhere Welten erwerben kann. Der Mystiker, der Gnostiker, der Theosoph sprechen von einer Seelen- und einer Geisterwelt, die für ihn ebenso vorhanden sind wie diejenige, die man mit physischen Augen sehen, mit physischen Händen betasten kann. Sein Zuhörer darf sich in jedem Augenblicke sagen: wovon dieser spricht, kann ich auch erfahren, wenn ich gewisse Kräfte in mir entwickele, die heute noch in mir schlummern. Es kann sich nur darum handeln, wie man es anzufangen hat, um solche Fähigkeiten in sich zu entwickeln. Dazu können nur diejenigen Anleitung geben, die schon in sich solche Kräfte haben. Es hat, seit es ein Menschengeschlecht gibt, auch immer Schulen gegeben, in denen solche, die höhere Fähigkeiten hatten, denen Anleitung gaben, die ebensolche Fähigkeiten suchten. Man nennt solche Schulen Geheimschulen; und der Unterricht, welcher da erteilt wird, heißt geheimwissenschaftlicher, oder okkulter Unterricht. Eine solche Bezeichnung erweckt naturgemäß Mißverständnis. Wer sie hört, kann leicht zu dem Glauben verführt werden, daß diejenigen, die in solchen Schulen tätig sind, eine besonders bevorzugte Menschenklasse darstellen wollen, die willkürlich ihr Wissen den Mitmenschen vorenthält. Ja, man denkt wohl auch, daß vielleicht überhaupt nichts erhebliches hinter solchem Wissen stecke. Denn, wenn es ein wahres Wissen wäre — so ist man versucht zu denken — so brauchte man daraus kein Geheimnis zu machen:

man könnte es öffentlich mitteilen und die Vorteile davon allen Menschen zugänglich machen.

Diejenigen, welche in die Natur des Geheimwissens eingeweiht sind, wundern sich nicht im geringsten darüber, daß die Uneingeweihten so denken. Worin das Geheimnis der Einweihung besteht, kann nur derjenige verstehen, der selbst diese Einweihung in die höheren Geheimnisse des Daseins bis zu einem gewissen Grade erfahren hat. Nun kann man fragen: wie soll denn der Uneingeweihte überhaupt irgend ein menschliches Interesse an dem sogenannten Geheimwissen unter solchen Umständen erlangen? Wie und warum soll er etwas suchen, von dessen Natur er sich doch gar keine Vorstellung machen kann? Aber schon einer solchen Frage liegt eine ganz irrtümliche Vorstellung von dem Wesen des Geheimwissens zugrunde. In Wahrheit verhält es sich mit dem Geheimwissen nämlich doch nicht anders, als mit allem übrigen Wissen und Können des Menschen. Dieses Geheimwissen ist für den Durchschnittsmenschen in keiner anderen Beziehung ein Geheimnis, als warum das Schreiben für den ein Geheimnis ist, der es nicht gelernt hat. Und wie jeder schreiben lernen kann, der die rechten Wege dazu wählt, so kann jeder ein Geheimschüler, ja ein Geheimlehrer werden, der die entsprechenden Wege dazu sucht. Nur in einer Hinsicht liegen die Verhältnisse hier noch anders als beim äußeren Wissen und Können. Es kann jemandem durch Armut, durch die Kulturverhältnisse, in die er hineingeboren ist, die Möglichkeit fehlen,

1

the approaching new phase for humanity, an illumined, knowing spirit could develop a relationship to the spiritual world."[46] "The Rosicrucians had to prepare a science through which they could let their wisdom flow gradually into the world."[47] In a detailed presentation of these connections (Budapest, June 3, 1909, two years after the Munich Congress) Rudolf Steiner would say:

> It was Christian Rosenkreutz who could say in the clearest sense that we have received in the mysteries knowledge of the suprasensory, a treasure of wisdom. Let us use it so that we may hope to do in the future what was done in the past; that we send out from our schools mature individuals who have learned and have seen the mysteries of the primal cosmic wisdom to teach others. This old method of spreading the original, primal wisdom should be continued, but also something else must be prepared. He [Christian Rosenkreutz] was able to say to himself that a great many people would come who would ask for the original wisdom. We could communicate these in the form we have for this now. Acceptance of our communications, however, would depend on a high degree of faith and recognition of our authority; and these will disappear more and more in humanity. The more the power of judgment increases in human beings, the less they will believe the teachers the way they did earlier. Belief and trust were the prerequisites for the earlier form of communication. Now one must say that people will come who want to test for themselves what is communicated. These people will say that they want to use the same logical understanding they use in observing the sense world also for what we say to them. They admit that something other than this kind of understanding is necessary for research of the spiritual, but they still want to test it with the thinking used for the sense world. For this reason, it was necessary in the beginning of our age to pour the primal world wisdom into new forms. That was the work of the Rosicrucians. They had to form the original wisdom in such a way that it would gradually be adapted to the modern mind and soul.[48]

Rudolf Steiner's own work was connected with this historically, as Elisabeth Vreede saw ever more clearly. From Steiner's early Rosicrucian lectures she experienced something decisive for her path of development and her further destiny. "One could understand scientifically and accept what was offered there; the yearning for the spiritual found its fulfillment in spiritual knowledge." Rudolf Steiner said in 1907 in Munich that "Rosicrucian theosophy" can be understood in all its details, principally through human thinking. It is accessible to human contemplation; and it is in agreement with the development of natural science, though not with the formation of hypotheses of natural science. "A correct understanding of modern science (understanding free of all abstract theories and materialistic fantasies, standing strictly on the basis of the facts and not going beyond them) delivers the proof precisely from science, bit-by-bit, for the Rosicrucian truths."[49] Rudolf Steiner did not speak about these connections but showed their sense and content in anthropological and cosmological orientation, in the decisive turning to tasks for civilization, to the demands of the present time. Steiner said that Rosicrucian theosophy strives toward a knowledge that "one can use," that can directly influence practical life; it can enter into the active work life.

> Rosicrucian wisdom must not stream only into the head, nor into the heart, but also into the hand, into our manual skills, into our daily actions. It does not take effect as sentimental sympathy; it is the acquisition, by strenuous effort, of faculties enabling us to work for the wellbeing of humanity. Suppose some society was to arise that had only brotherhood as its aim, that it did nothing but preach brotherhood. That would not be Rosicrucianism, for the Rosicrucians say: Imagine someone lying in the road with a broken leg. If fourteen people stand around him in pity but not one of them is able to help, the whole fourteen together are of less importance than a fifteenth who comes, perhaps without any sentimentality at all, but is able to, and actually does, deal with the broken leg.
>
> The Rosicrucian attitude is that what counts is practical knowledge that can take hold of and intervene effectively in life. Rosicrucian wisdom considers repeated talk about pity and sympathy has an element of danger in it; for continual harping on sympathy denotes a kind of astral sensuality. Sensuality on the physical plane has the same nature as a constant wish to feel but never to know on the astral plane. Knowledge capable of taking

"All of Heaven seemed to be called down" (1879–1913)

Entry ticket for the cycle "About the Initiation" (Munich, 1912)

effect in practical life—not in a materialistic sense, of course, but because it is brought down from the spiritual worlds—this is what enables us to work effectively. Harmony flows of itself from knowing that the world must progress; it flows all the more surely because it arises quite naturally from knowledge. You could say of people who know how to deal with a broken leg but fail to do so that they neglect the sufferer because they dislike people. Such a thing would be possible in the case of knowledge pertaining only to the physical plane, but it would not be possible for spiritual knowledge. There is no spiritual knowledge that would refrain from entering practical life.[50]

Elisabeth Vreede was of an intellectual and spiritual nature at the beginning of the twentieth century; and yet at the same time she was at home in practical life, unlike many theosophists. She became a mathematics teacher to help genuinely developing human beings, and not just to have a job in the field of science. She heard in Rudolf Steiner's *Rosicrucian Wisdom* lectures (CW 99) not only about the nature of the human being and the world, but also about the revelation that could be easily followed—that modern Spiritual Science is an instrument that will be created for future culture. Modern Theosophy, according to Steiner, has a great cultural task, too, in advancing natural-scientific thinking and transforming it. "Today Spiritual Science is being taught because people will need these teachings in the future, because they must be introduced into the process of humanity's development."[51]

~

In 1908, Rudolf Steiner undertook his first significant lecture tour in Holland. From this time on Elisabeth Vreede attended nearly all of his lectures. She traveled with him like only a few others did, among whom was Marie von Sivers. She wrote at the end of her life appropriately, "On the whole, no one besides Frau Dr. Steiner was able to hear as many lectures as I did."[52] Her financial independence and lack of familial and personal attachments (after her teaching duties) made it possible for Vreede to participate; and beyond this, her receptivity and ability to understand also made it possible. Andrej Belyj wrote generally in an autobiographical description about the effort involved in making Steiner's lectures one's own for a person like Elisabeth Vreede.

> The ability to endure the cascade of lectures (for the public; for members; courses; and other that was personal) developed as the result of a special learning process. We learn to hear or sense the main theme and to follow all the modulations of it through the various tones of voice, according to whichever country or city (the lectures were given in). He spoke differently for the Swiss than for the Finns; differently for the Swedes; differently for the Germans. He spoke differently, according to the city; he spoke differently in Cologne than in Berlin; he spoke differently in Berlin than in Munich. The kernel of the theme changed not only in the geographic horizontal, but also in the vertical (if we may express it thus), because the content was formed anew for each human being, for the anthroposophists, or an esoteric group. The theme was handled differently in the Class Lessons than in a lecture for members (of the Anthroposophical Society) and quite differently than a lecture given at a conference. Many people cannot understand why we would follow Steiner from city to city. I can say for my part that listening to the lectures conveyed an insight into the theme, not through *what* was said but through *how* it was said... I learned that the initial formulation of the question was developed differently later in every city and for every audience. After our ear became accustomed to the technique of the formulation of the question, we could also hear the most hidden overtones of the public lectures.... To hear him speak several times a week, to be there for the birth of various themes and their counterpoints, and then not to follow him outside of Dornach to Basel or Zürich would be quite impossible for a person with a highly developed ear for the lectures. You could go without the personal conversations with the Doctor and even temporarily without studying his works; you needed only to listen to him and you found yourself in a true universality in which the ear, the attention, and the flexibility of view were trained. Listening was not a passive faculty; with increasing experience the student faced ever-new tasks for the activation of his or her ability to take in.... The Doctor required our collaboration; our attention worked with him.[53]

In this way Elisabeth Vreede followed Rudolf Steiner's lectures for almost two decades of his life.

She was accepted early (1908 at the latest) into the Esoteric School and experienced Steiner as her personal teacher who gave her mantras and exercises. Esoteric ritual lessons were held in her parents' home (among others). Rudolf Steiner said in 1907 in Munich that the Rosicrucian pupil does not live with belief in an authority; rather the pupil has the same relation to the teacher as a student of mathematics has to the person who is able to lead him or her into the secrets of this science. "The teacher is the friend, the counselor, one who has already lived through esoteric experiences and now helps the pupils do so for themselves."[54]

~

As Elisabeth Vreede advanced to a closer relationship to Rudolf Steiner's lectures cycles (1906 to 1907), his central themes were on the evolution of the world and humanity. His book *Theosophy: An Introduction to the Spiritual Processes in Human Life and in the Cosmos* (CW 9) was published in May 1904. He had already announced by that time that he would issue a comprehensive continuation of the description of the cosmology. "A second volume of my *Theosophy*, which will appear soon, will cover the cosmology" (June 9, 1904).[55] Steiner developed the contents for his book *An Outline of Esoteric Science* (CW 13, finally published in 1910) beforehand in lectures of extraordinary significance in *The Spiritual Hierarchies and the Physical World* (CW 110), the Düsseldorf course. Elisabeth Vreede was present also at these lectures; she was receptive and inwardly moved. Later she wrote, "This [lecture] cycle made an overwhelming impression."[56] Ernst Bindel added to what Vreede had told about her experiences of the Düsseldorf course and an Esoteric Lesson, explaining: "She felt herself to be detached from the whole earthly surroundings and walked as if in a dream."[57] When she was thirty years old (in the human biography termed the *Sun-birth*), she met Rudolf Steiner as an initiate who was indeed a

"All of Heaven seemed to be called down" (1879–1913)

Abend: 1.) Rückschau. Vom Abend zu Morgen.

2.) Blau des Himmels mit vielen Sternen:

Fromm und ehrfürchtig
Sende ahnend in Raumesweiten
Meine Seele den fühlenden Blick
Aufnehme dieser Blick
Und sende in meines Herzens Tiefen
Licht Liebe Leben
Aus Geisteswelten
 (Seelenruhe)

Morgen:
☩
Was in diesem Sinnbild
Zu mir spricht
Der Welten hoher Geist
Erfülle meine Seele
Zu aller Zeit
In allen Lebenslagen
Mit Licht, Liebe Leben
 (Seelenruhe) –

6 Nebenübungen. –

Rudolf Steiner: Meditation (estate of Elisabeth Vreede)

"friend and counselor who has already lived through it and lets her, the pupil, do for herself." He described the creation of the Earth and the human being through the working of the beings of the hierarchies. He described it from the inner perspective of these beings themselves (*The Spiritual Hierarchies and the Physical World.*

In his introduction to the course in Düsseldorf, Rudolf Steiner went into the history of the knowledge that was kept hidden a long time in the mystery centers. Now at the beginning of the Michael Age this knowledge would gradually have to become openly accessible. ("In the course of these lectures, however, it will become clear that what was kept alive in small circles must today penetrate into the masses of humanity to a greater extent than before."[58]) The primordial holy wisdom that lived in the ancient, high cultures was preserved at the beginning of the new age as the secret of the new mysteries in smaller circles by such esoterically minded groups as the Brotherhoods of the Holy Grail and of the Rose Cross, in order that it become open to humanity at the end of the Dark Ages. With regard to the spiritual hierarchies, in the open lecture of his Düsseldorf course Rudolf Steiner spoke about the knowledge of cosmology as cosmology that still existed of not only in the high spiritual culture of India, but also in the School of Paul.

> When the Rishis spoke of spiritual hierarchies, their words expressed what Greek and Roman wisdom expressed in their ascending universe of Moon, Mercury, Mars, Venus, Jupiter, and Saturn. Dionysius, the pupil of St. Paul, had in mind the same worlds the Rishis spoke of. Dionysius clearly wished to emphasize that he was referring to spiritual matters. So, he deliberately chose words he knew would be taken spiritually—that is, he spoke of Angels, Archangels, Archai, Powers, Mights, Dominions, Thrones, Cherubim and Seraphim. The people had completely forgotten what they once knew. If the connection between the terminology of Dionysius the Areopagite and the Rishi's had been understood, one would have known that the "Moon" the Rishi's referred to, and the "angelic realm" in other mysteries are one and the same thing. One might have heard the word *Mercury* on the one hand,

and the word *Archangel*, on the other, and would have known that they are one and the same. *Archai* and *Venus* refer to the same realm, as do *Sun* and *Powers*. On hearing the word *Mars*, one would have had the feeling of rising to the *Mights*. The word *Dominions* in the school of Dionysius corresponds to Jupiter, and the term *Saturn* to the Thrones.

In wider circles, this knowledge had disappeared and was no longer known. As science became more and more materialistic, the old names, which had once denoted spiritual realities, remained. But now increasingly they applied only to matter. In contrast to this materialistic stream, there did exist a spiritual stream that referred to Archangels, Angels, and so on. But this stream had lost the connection with the physical expression of these spiritual beings. Thus, we see how primeval cosmic wisdom penetrated into the school founded by St. Paul through Dionysius and how it is a question now of permeating new-found knowledge with the spiritual impulse of the past. Indeed, it is the task of Spiritual Science, or Anthroposophy, to renew the bond between the physical and the spiritual, between the world of the Earth and the spiritual hierarchies. For the spiritual aspect of knowledge must always remain incomprehensible to those who do not know the true origin of ideas about the outer world.[61]

~

As with all of his lectures on cosmogony in 1909, his Düsseldorf lectures were Christological.[62] Rudolf Steiner showed in his Outline of Esoteric Science, as well as in the preparatory lectures, that the Christ-being was, and is, the central working principle in the evolution of the Earth and of humanity. Therein lay a significant point of separation from the theosophical Eastern character; it was a departure from the Theosophical Society in its old form and also from Annie Besant, its President. Rudolf Steiner's Christ-doctrine and his proclamation of the etheric reappearance of the Christ-being (which Steiner began in a decisive manner in 1910), was different from what was stressed by Besant and Adyar, the Indian Center of the Theosophical Society. There the physical reincarnation of the world teacher Christ was spoken of and the search for his embodiment had begun years

Die Geheimwissenschaft im Umriss.

Von

Dr. Rudolf Steiner.

Leipzig
Verlag von Max Altmann
1910

First edition of Die Geheimwissenschaft im Umriss, *1910*
(An Outline of Esoteric Science)

earlier, which led to discovering Krishnamurthi. Already at the time of the Munich Congress in 1907 Rudolf Steiner separated his Esoteric School from that of Annie Besant[63] and asked his pupils to choose which way they wanted to go:

> The Eastern school is being led by Mrs. Annie Besant, and those who feel more attracted to her in their hearts can no longer remain in our school. People should sound exactly their hearts longing to discover which way they are being led. At the head of our Western school there are two Masters: the Master Jesus and the Master Christian Rosenkreutz. And they lead us along two paths: the Christian and the Christian–Rosicrucian way. The Great White Lodge leads all spiritual movements, and the Master Jesus and the Master Christian Rosenkreutz belong to this Lodge.[64]

The vast majority of the Dutch anthroposophists were extraordinarily connected with Henry Steele Olcott, but also with Annie Besant. These included Elisabeth Vreede's parents and, in a certain respect, Elisabeth Vreede herself. Soon, however, she experienced the concrete problematic nature (of the Eastern School)—with increasing clarity over the years—and understood that Rudolf Steiner's path made sense and was logical and consistent. Later she spoke in retrospect of a time of the most difficult soul trials, but also of a deep inner experience. ("It was a time of the strongest experience that one can go through."[65]) It was necessary to attain the "courage for the insight," that the highly regarded Annie Besant was on a false path; and the Christian-Rosicrucian development stream was really more connected with Rudolf Steiner and led into the future. Elisabeth Vreede—as also her parents—decided absolutely for Rudolf Steiner's path and even moved in the beginning of 1910 to Berlin, "in order to connect myself completely with Rudolf Steiner's movement," as she recorded in the manuscript from the last years of her life.[66]

Elisabeth Vreede did not care much for Berlin, it being much different from Munich and Stuttgart. She wrote in letters about the monotonous sea of houses and of her feeling of "oppressiveness in Berlin." Yet it was clear to her that Rudolf Steiner's place of residence here was the center of his work, and this was all that mattered. Everything originated from Berlin and from the quarters in the house in the back of 17 Motz Street. That included the internal and the public lectures, the esoteric lessons, lecture tours, lecture cycles, and books. Nowhere were more public lectures held by Rudolf Steiner than in the capital city of Germany. Elisabeth Vreede wanted not only to have maximum participation in this work, but also wanted to help as much as possible and as much as her forces allowed. For this reason she decided to move to the unloved city and into the same house where Rudolf Steiner and Marie von Sivers lived, as well as many other anthroposophists who worked in the organization of the lectures and the anthroposophical publishing. On February 15, 1910, Vreede wrote to her friend, Li Content, whom she knew from her student days in Leyden:

> It is perhaps childish, but it is such a pleasant feeling to live in the same house with the Doctor. And when I see from the light in his room that he has returned from his trip, it gives me such a feeling of safety. A few times I came home in the evening at the same time as he, and he let me in. It is then still a long way across the dark courtyard and is totally dark up the stairway of our garden house. The Doctor always lets the women go in front of him, which always gave me a feeling of a world that's turned around.[67]

Whenever possible, Elisabeth Vreede accompanied Rudolf Steiner, as an independent and open listener, on his lecture tours to German cities and surrounding countries. In September 1910 in the old Court House in Bern she heard his lecture cycle on the Gospel of Matthew (*According to Matthew*, CW 123), in which he spoke in detail about the Essene, Jesus ben Pandira, and the Bodhisattva Question. Christian Morgenstern was present also.

In Berlin Rudolf Steiner asked Elisabeth Vreede to hold natural science lectures in the branch, in order to help with the

Elisabeth Vreede: Passage from letter to Li Content, February 15, 1910

understanding of Spiritual Science—its historical consciousness prerequisites and task—among the members. He encouraged her to speak about higher mathematics, but also about the origin of the natural sciences: their views, concepts, and hypotheses. He wanted her to write a book about the justification or non-justification of the hypotheses in the natural sciences. Elisabeth Vreede did not feel up to this task, however. Instead, she helped type his transcribed lectures and helped with the mystery dramas in Munich, which were performed annually from the summer of 1910 onward. She performed; sewed costumes; worked on the scenery; and typed the texts for the actors once Rudolf Steiner had read the continuation of the manuscript to the actors in the morning and then gave it to her afterward. She stressed in a letter to Li Content,[68] "It is very interesting to see the Doctor's handwriting with all the changes and drafts, and so on." When possible, she also wrote down meticulously his directorial indications, addresses and lectures in Munich.

Berlin, however, remained difficult for Elisabeth Vreede, and she never felt at home there. In February 1912 (two years after moving there) she again said in a letter that the city was a nightmare, "this endless noise—and a recreational city with its complete lack of outer beauty." Then, however, she added:

> Today I had the great privilege to speak privately with the Doctor—a privilege that many would wish for and that I—lucky one that I am—had, and asked for on an average of every three months. And as he said, "You will still remain with us longer, won't you?" (He always worried that the money would run out.), I felt that I could not be brought to leave, even if I were beaten. Thus, one can see my peculiar mood concerning Berlin—most wonderful and most terrible of all cities.[69]

Generally, Elisabeth Vreede could speak personally with Rudolf Steiner every three months, although she saw him much more often in the stairway and in his apartment with the daily work. He was friendly, polite, and full of humor. "Then one has to do with him as a human being. Incidentally, my relationship to him was never other than as student to teacher, a teacher with whom one feels that suprahuman forces hold sway in him."[70]

Elisabeth Vreede accompanied Rudolf Steiner to Helsinki (then called Helsingfors), Finland, a few months later, in April 1912. Three years after the presentation in Düsseldorf, Rudolf Steiner again announced a large course on cosmology, to which many Russian friends came. This course is titled, *Spiritual Beings in Heavenly Bodies and in Kingdoms of Nature* (CW 136). On board the ship Elisabeth Vreede sat right beside him, which was painfully uncomfortable for her, as she wrote later to Li Content: "It was very uncomfortable."[71] About the lectures themselves she commented, "There is no better or more complete introduction to anthroposophical astronomy." With Marie von Sivers's permission, Elisabeth Vreede sent her notes of the lectures directly to her parents in The Hague.

Elisabeth Vreede also attended the Easter Festival in a Russian Orthodox Garrison Church in Helsingfors from April 6 to 7, Still Saturday to Easter Sunday. The emotion of the faithful and the Easter Brother kiss moved her, and also the sight of Rudolf Steiner among the faithful. ("I will not easily forget having seen him in the crowd with a small lighted candle in his hand."[72]) Elisabeth Vreede was dissatisfied with the ritual ("The service was somewhat long-winded and monotonous. The priests were not very appealing."[73]) Also Rudolf Steiner gained little from the church service that he followed standing up for hours. Later he spoke clearly about it: "Among the saddest memories of my life is what comedy the priests-comedians, the terrible inner liars, made of the eternal truth."[74] Yet the Easter night experience together made a deep impression on Elisabeth Vreede. Margareta Woloschin wrote about the further course of the night with the Russian friends:

> We did not arrive at the hotel till around 3:00 a.m. There the good Cleopatra Christoforova, the hotel owner, had ordered the Easter meal for us. We arrived in the joyful mood that animates

Inträdeskort
till
D:r Rudolf Steiners
Föredragscykel
i
Helsingfors 1912

Namn: *Fräulein J. E. Vreede*

Entrance ticket Helsinki (then called Helsingfors), 1912

every Russian on Easter night, especially glad to have Rudolf Steiner celebrate with us. He stood at the door of the dining hall and shook hands with each of us. The rapturous enthusiasm with which we were filled encountered his very earnest, stringent, questioning look. When we had taken our seats at the table, he cut the Easter bread into a hexagram, shared it among us, stood up and held an address, the meaning of which was as follows: "The whole history of humankind is the entombment of the Godhead. We, with our consciousness, are only capable of celebrating the entombment on Good Friday. We do not have the ability to comprehend Easter with our intellect. We can only celebrate Easter in vowing to follow the path to the spirit. I now understood the else dear, questioning look that had met our enthusiastic joy."[75]

A few days later, after his address to the Russian friends on April 11, Rudolf Steiner showed them the *Kalendar 1912/13* (CW 40), which he had just received in a package in Helsinki. On the inside of the book cover were the words "In 1879, after the birth of the 'I.'" The calendar contains historical commemorative indications for each day that Rudolf Steiner had put together himself; zodiac images from Imme von Eckardtstein; and in the back is the "Soul Calendar," meditations by Rudolf Steiner for every week of the year. In the foreword to the verses (which Rudolf Steiner gave particularly to the Russian anthroposophists) one can read:

> As human beings, we feel united with the world and its temporal changes. We find the likeness of the world's archetypical image in our own being. This likeness is no sensory or pedantic imitation of the archetype. What the great world reveals in its temporal flow corresponds to a pendulum swing in our being that does not move in the element of time. Our sensory and perceptual being, we feel, corresponds much more to the nature of summer, woven through with light and warmth. During winter's existence, we feel ourselves much more grounded in ourselves and living in our own thought and will worlds. Thus, the rhythm of inner and outer becomes for us what nature in its temporal alternation represents as summer and winter. A great mystery of existence can arise if we bring our

Rudolf Steiner, foreword to Soul Calendar, *1912 (page 1)*

"All of Heaven seemed to be called down" (1879–1913)

das eigene Seelenweben im Bilde an den Eindrücken des Jahreslaufes erfühlen kann. Es ist an ein fühlendes Selbsterkennen gedacht. Dieses fühlende Selbsterkennen kann an den angegebenen charakteristischen Wochensätzen den Kreislauf des Seelenlebens als zeitloses an der Zeit erleben. Ausdrücklich sei gesagt, es ist damit eine Möglichkeit eines Selbsterkenntnisweges gedacht. Nicht „Vorschriften" nach dem Muster theosophischer Pedanten sollen gegeben werden, sondern vielmehr auf das lebendige Weben der Seele, wie es einmal sein kann, wird hingewiesen. Alles, was für Seelen bestimmt ist, nimmt eine individuelle Färbung an. Gerade deshalb aber wird auch jede Seele ihren Weg im Verhältnis zu einer individuell gezeichneten finden. Es wäre ein leichtes zu sagen: so, wie hier angeführt, soll die Seele meditieren, wenn sie ein Stück Selbsterkenntnis pflegen will. Es wird nicht gesagt, weil der eigne Weg des Menschen sich Anregung holen soll an einem gegebenen, nicht sich pedantisch einem „Erkenntnispfade" fügen soll.

Rudolf Steiner, foreword to Soul Calendar, *1912 (page 2)*

timeless rhythms of perception and thought into correspondence with nature's temporal rhythms. If we do so, the year becomes the archetype of the human soul activity and thus becomes a fruitful source of true self-knowledge.

In the following annual *Soul Calendar,* we place the human spirit in the changing moods of the year from week to week. Here we can feel our soul's weaving in the image of the impression of the course of the year. The aim is a "feeling self-knowledge." This feeling self-knowledge can be experienced through these typical weekly verses expressive of the soul-life's circular course as timeless in relation to time. However, let it be clearly stated: our intention is to create the possibility of a path of self-knowledge. "Rules" are not given on the model of theosophical pendants. Rather, indications are given for what could be a living weaving of the soul. Whatever is appropriate for souls always takes on an individual coloring. Precisely for this reason each soul must find its way in relation to its own individually honed path. It would be easy to say: If it wishes to culminate a bit of self-knowledge, the soul would meditate exactly as it is laid down here. But this is not said, because each person's own path should get its direction on its own, and not just pedantically follow "a path of knowledge."[76]

For Elisabeth Vreede, publishing this Calendar was an important stage of the path of her biography. The theme that Rudolf Steiner gave it belonged to the kernel of her life. Very likely Steiner showed her the *Calendar* immediately. Years later he gave her the original manuscript, possibly after the founding of the Section for Mathematics–Astronomy at the Goetheanum.

Then concerning the *Soul Calendar,* Rudolf Steiner spoke in a Berlin lecture to the members of the Anthroposophical Society soon after his return from Helsinki:

> These meditation formulations...contain what can be enlivened in the soul and that then really correspond to a living relationship of the soul forces to the forces of the macrocosm. What we can call the course of time is directed and led by spiritual beings; these spiritual beings, through their mutual connections, their

living mutual relationships, actually determine and make the time. Meditation of the verses evoke an imagination of the relationship of the beings that determine the course of time.[77]

The *Calendar* began with the Easter Festival and stressed the year-number 1879 instead of 1912. Per Rudolf Steiner, the Mystery of Golgotha, not the birth of the Jesus child, founded a new calendar that should find its way into culture. "We wanted to draw attention to the fact that it is extremely important to take the year of the Mystery of Golgotha as the beginning of our calendar, and not the year of the birth of Jesus. The Mystery of Golgotha took place on a Friday, April 3 in the year 33 at 3:00 p.m."[78] With the Golgotha event, the actual birth of the "I" of the human being occurred in a historical deed of consciousness. Rudolf Steiner repeatedly stressed its significance, independent of any denomination, in his lectures about the *Soul Calendar*.

> It does not matter where on Earth the human being lives or to which religious denomination he or she belongs; what came into the world through the Mystery of Golgotha holds good for all human beings. Just as it is true for the whole world that Caesar died on a specific day, and not on a different day for the Chinese or yet another for those in India, it is just as much a simple fact of esoteric life that the Mystery of Golgotha occurred on this particular day and that it has to do with the Birth of the "I." It is a fact of an international nature.[79]

Rudolf Steiner wanted the *Calendar* to be published annually from 1912 (or "1879") on. This did not happen. He pointed repeatedly to the cultural task, the life task, of the anthroposophic movement in the Rosicrucian intention that is connected to the Calendar. To this task belongs also standing up for and supporting the continuation of Easter as a movable feast; it's spiritual significance; earthly–cosmic orientation; and the temporal determining of the date according to what is read from the course of the year. The date for Easter Sunday was, and is, the first Sunday after the full Moon following the spring solstice. Already in 1912 many forces worked against this out of economical and administrative grounds.

> The attempt today to set Easter on a specific date instead of reading its date from the heavens belongs naturally to the signature of our time that plunges outer relationships ever further into materialism and forgets what is connected with the spiritual. It will perhaps be necessary that in the anthroposophical stream the memory of the concrete dates through the cosmic relationships, and not through money, be protected in the face of industrialism, commercialism, and materialism. It will be the first great sign that the outer and inner cultures (the materialistic and the spiritual) must go their separate paths, side-by-side, if the outer culture manages to break the Easter date away from being determined from the starry world.[80]

In light of this background on the whole, Rudolf Steiner welcomed the anthroposophist Imme von Eckardstein's inquiry about the Calendar and set to work on the development of the Calendar. He wrote the Introduction, the information for each day, and finally the fifty-two weekly meditations. (*"Long, detailed spiritual experience and research is condensed in these fifty-two formulations that can be time formulas for an inner soul experience that can be connected to the processes of the divine-spiritual experience."*[81])

Elisabeth Vreede was very impressed with the Calendar that was introduced in Helsingfors and the indications given in the lectures that followed—in a spiritual respect, but also in view of the whole manner of Rudolf Steiner's actions. The Calendar was practical and helpful, which she liked. "Thus, something is thereby given that has grown from our way of thinking and is useful for everyone, through the use of which one can, in turn, come a step nearer onto the path of the spiritual than through other means" (Rudolf Steiner).[82]

~

"Our theosophical movement, the Doctor said, actually no longer fits in the framework of the Theosophical Society. Therefore, one sees that

Frühling.

A. Osterstimmung (7.–13. April).

1. Wenn aus den Weltenweiten
   Die Sonne spricht zum Menschensinn,
   Und Freude aus Seelentiefen
   Dem Licht sich eint im Schauen,
   Dann ziehen aus der Selbstheit Hülle
   Gedanken in die Raumesfernen
   Und binden dumpf
   Des Menschen Wesen an des Geistes Sein.

B. Zweite Woche (14.–20. April).

2. Ins Äussre des Sinnesalls
   Verliert Gedankenmacht ihr Eigensein;
   Es finden Geisteswelten
   Den Menschensprossen wieder
   Der seinen Keim in ihnen
   Doch seine Seelenfrucht
   In sich muß finden.

C. Dritte Woche (21.–27. April).

3. Es spricht zum Weltenall
   Sich selbst vergessend
   Und seines Urstands eingedenk
   Des Menschen wachsend Ich:
   In dir befreiend mich
   Aus meiner Eigenheiten Fessel
   Ergründe ich mein echtes Wesen.

D. Vierte Woche (28. April – 4. Mai).

4. Ich fühle Wesen meines Wesens
   So spricht Empfindung
   Die in der sonnerhellten Welt
   Mit Lichtesfluten sich vereint;
   Sie will dem Denken
   Zur Klarheit Wärme schenken
   Und Mensch und Welt
   In Einheit fest verbinden.

Rudolf Steiner: Soul Calendar

in the future something different will have to be created, in order to offset this anomaly, but it is all still very provisional at the moment."[83] Elisabeth Vreede wrote this to her friend Li Content four months prior to Helsinki, at the end of 1911. One year later the Anthroposophical Society was founded in Cologne. Elisabeth Vreede was present at this founding. She was also at the first General Meeting in Berlin at the beginning of 1913, and heard Rudolf Steiner's autobiographical lecture that he had to give because of accusations and misrepresentations from the theosophical side.[84] She also traveled with Steiner to Holland for the Easter Festival that brought a special constellation (Good Friday fell on the spring solstice and the Easter full Moon on Still Saturday.). Rudolf Steiner spoke impressively about this on Easter Sunday (March 23) in her hometown of The Hague,[85] with a view to Elisabeth Vreede and surrounded by a great course of lectures on the spiritual evolution of the human being.[86] In the summer of 1913 the last mystery dramas were performed. Then came the laying of the Foundation Stone for the Johannes building in Dornach and the trip to Oslo (then called Kristiania) for his lectures on *The Fifth Gospel*. "It was amazingly wonderful!"[87]

Elisabeth Vreede had no Christian upbringing and no religious instruction in school. "Uneducated" but also unencumbered, she learned about the events of The Turning Point of Time from Rudolf Steiner's research.[88] She went from astronomy and cosmology to Theosophy to Rudolf Steiner and to Christology—from the mysteries of the stars to the mysteries of Christ's three years on Earth. In his earlier lectures on the Gospels Rudolf Steiner had always handled the events in Palestine as symbols for initiation processes; and as pictorial forms of expression of a spiritual cosmic doctrine and a teaching concerning the human being that, due to the conditions of today, must be worked out and formulated anew. In the last years he went ever again into the concrete, real processes of Christ's incarnation and the circle of Apostles.[89] These descriptions culminate in the beginning of 1913 in Norway; and Elisabeth Vreede was happy and fortunate to be there. Much in light of her receptivity and knowledge of the work

Elisabeth Vreede: Notes of an Esoteric Lesson by Rudolf Steiner
Oslo (then called Kristiania), October 5, 1913

shows that she was one of the few people who understood the context of these special lectures; their historical working and spiritual worth within Anthroposophy.[90]

In a certain way, Rudolf Steiner continued his Christmas lectures at the turn of the year 1913/14 by speaking first of all about *The Building Stones to the Mystery of Golgotha* and the destiny of humanity of the Nathan soul in a lecture course titled *Christ and the Spiritual World: On the Search for the Holy Grail*. These were the last lectures Christian Morgenstern attended. Rudolf Steiner held a moving address in Leipzig in honor of his dying friend. This address was accompanied by recitations of the as yet unpublished poetry, *We Found a Path*. In Steiner's lecture cycle shone renewed a special, macrocosmic knowledge deeply connected with the Grail mysteries and a new Christology in the light of Michael. Morgenstern wrote this verse that Elisabeth Vreede loved: "He spoke, and as he spoke, there appeared in him the zodiac, Cherubim and Seraphim, the solar star, the planets wandering from place to place. All this sprang forth from his sound lightning fast, a cosmic dream, newly found, all of heaven seemed to be called down through his own Word."[92]

After the course in Leipzig, Elisabeth Vreede's days in Berlin were numbered. She lived in the "most wonderful and most terrible of all cities" for four years. Now she went to Dornach near Basel in Switzerland to help with the building of the Goetheanum, and to help with the Independent School for Spiritual Science that should arise there. Elisabeth Vreede was in her thirty-fifth year of life. Many anthroposophists moved at this time to Dornach where the New should attain form. Among those anthroposophists was a sculptor from England with whom Vreede had become friends at Motzstrasse 17—Edith Maryon.[93]

Rudolf Steiner himself proved to be decisive for Vreede's moving, however. Vreede wanted to continue being where the center of his work was and to help with this work. She wanted also, in the coming years, to take in the totality of his teaching and schooling and to collaborate in representing them—also in her specialized area of knowledge, for which Rudolf Steiner asked her repeatedly. The center of the anthroposophic movement moved to Dornach with him, although Motzstrasse 17 and The Philosophical-Anthroposophical Publishing Company in Berlin were maintained for the time being.

2

"Dr. Steiner was very pleased with my lectures" (1914–1923)

Dornach

"Elisabeth Vreede brings together thorough anthroposophical insight with an excellent clarity about how Anthroposophy should be introduced into the individual sciences."
—RUDOLF STEINER[94]

Elisabeth and children at the entrance of House Vreede (Arlesheim, undated)

On May 3, 1914, Elisabeth Vreede wrote from Dornach to her parents:

> Saturday as I...came into the cupola after having eaten, I saw a pair of new legs. I studied them eagerly: black pants and immaculate black shoes, whereas we were all covered up to our ankles with mud because it had rained that day.
>
> Suddenly I knew; it was, of course, the Doctor. He was considering, together with Lille, who was already in the cupola, how the wood should be fitted together. Afterward, he crept out; better said, he did not creep at all. Ordinary people creep out, but with the Doctor I had the feeling that he didn't even have to stoop down. He greeted me in a friendly manner and asked immediately how I was. I hope to see him soon again!

Shortly after this meeting in a cupola of the "Johannes building" Elisabeth Vreede met Rudolf Steiner again. This time they met in the house of the dentist, Emil Grosheintz, who had donated a large portion of the land for the building.

> He [Rudolf Steiner] was sitting there. He had two new sketches with him. He had apparently made the sketches for the window of the main entrance, and he showed them with almost childlike joy, which he often has when something good is achieved. They were quite remarkable. Beside the one was written, "And the Light of the Spirits was the Light of Human Beings." This seemed to me to have something to do with Lucifer. The other was much more expressive and easier to recognize. It was Ahriman as a world-serpent, passing over the seven planets, which looked exactly like seven hinges or pivots in his body. Beside it there stood on top of a quite high mountain peak—the Doctor says it's the highest mountain on Earth—the human being penetrated by lightning bolts.

Beside this is written, "And the Spirit of the Heaviness gathers the Resistance." The Doctor seemed to have great joy in this sketch. I took advantage of this occasion and asked for a conversation. He found that to be good immediately.[96]

The conversation with Rudolf Steiner had to do with an acquaintance of Elisabeth Vreede, and not with herself. Thus began her time in Dornach.

~

Elisabeth Vreede helped in the building office and with the engraving of the glass windows. She took part in doing the mathematical calculations for the cupolas; she carved the pillars and worked wherever she was needed. In the beginning she lived with Edith Maryon, and then with her parents who moved to Switzerland from Holland and spent the autumn of their life helping with the building. Elisabeth Vreede also inspired other friends from Holland for Dornach in an active and people-friendly manner. They either came or they donated money.

She recorded very little about her first years in Dornach. Like the other coworkers, she worked from early till late, inspired by the building community, the results of the work becoming visible, and the powerful lectures Rudolf Steiner gave from early summer 1914 onward about the building idea that provided the impulse for the artistic work. Vreede will have experienced directly more than others Edith Maryon's sculptural work together with Rudolf Steiner on the Christ group. This was because of her personal friendship with Maryon and the degree of their mutual closeness. This work was done for the most part away from other people in Rudolf Steiner's workshop (as of 1916 also in the upper atelier or carpentry workshop), which remained closed to the general population.

On the other hand, Elisabeth Vreede also experienced the first difficult crisis of the Dornach community. This involved the emotional-hysterical outbursts of many members after Rudolf Steiner married Marie von Sivers at the end of 1914, and various further psychopathological phenomena,[97] that resulted in difficult, out-of-control crowds of anthroposophists[98] and the extremely tense soul conditions of many individuals in a highly charged mood of the time. On January 23, 1914, Rudolf Steiner spoke in Berlin at a meeting of the Johannes Building Association about the intended "ideal of the whole" of the Dornach site and social space. He spoke about building forms and inner developments.

> What in the construction style will allow the whole colony to appear as an ideal unity will be an outer impression of a harmony that will be an inner harmony. I say what I am now saying partially as wish; partially as hypothesis; partially as something for which I myself do not know what word I should choose for it. It should be an impression of the inner harmony of those individuals living in this colony!
>
> In the sense of the Anthroposophical Society it will be impossible that in this colony there will ever be the slightest discord, or mutual incompatibility; or that a mean word should pass between the members of this colony; or even an unfriendly look or grimace should be made to another. And it will be superb if that pours itself over all the outer forms like a personified peace, so to speak. Even then, however, if it could really come to an unfriendly word or look through some small thing in the *Gemüt*, the eye will be drawn to the forms, and because forms stimulate thoughts, a peaceful smile will pass over the distorted countenance.
>
> When we consider all of this, we then really have the foundation or reason for the impulse to create something unified there.[99]

Like Vreede, Rudolf Steiner had a lot of humor—which he also used.

It is not known whether Elisabeth Vreede stayed in Dornach the whole time in the first months after the outbreak of World War I in August 1914, or whether she traveled sporadically to Holland or Berlin. Rudolf Steiner spent half of each year during the war in Germany, during which he gave lectures, wrote books, and tried to work internally but also publicly in those difficult times. It is also possible that Elisabeth Vreede was in Berlin at least part of the time in 1914 and 1915, before moving back there completely in 1916 to work in

The "Johannes building," June 1914

Elisabeth Rotten organization for the welfare of the prisoners of war. What moved her to take this step in her second Moon Node (thirty-seven years old) is not known.

Rotten was three years younger than Vreede and grew up in Berlin, the child of Swiss parents. She studied philosophy and German studies and met in Marburg, among others, Hermann Lietz and Gustav Wyneken, whose reform-pedagogical approaches impressed her deeply. In 1913 she completed a doctorate in "Goethe's Primordial Phenomena and the Platonic Idea" in Marburg and then went to teach German Literature at the University of Cambridge, before returning to Berlin in 1914. In The Hague in 1915 she was part of the founding of the "Internationalen Frauenliga für Frieden und Freiheit" (International women's league for peace and freedom). Whether Elisabeth Rotten made a passing connection with Anthroposophy or became acquainted with Vreede in The Hague is not known at all.

Elisabeth Vreede's social and spiritual horizon was broad; she knew and was interested in many people, also outside of Anthroposophy. Her resolve to want to do social work, and to work with it for peace during the war years found little possibility for development in Dornach. She wanted to be active but was not an artist; so she worked in Berlin caring for English prisoners of war. Being Dutch, she could move around freely, and she took in two German children. As far as is known, Elisabeth Vreede never entered into a partnership or had a family. Yet she had an absolute love for children, for whom she often took a stand and supported unconditionally. It was not reported how long both children stayed with her or what their destinies were, also whether or not Vreede maintained contact with them and their families later.

Elisabeth Vreede heard Rudolf Steiner's Berlin lectures as she had done in the past. A great deal indicates that she took in the idea of the physiological and social threefolding and its Rosicrucian background, soon after it was formulated; also Steiner's presentations about the driving forces and working powers of the events of the war. Elisabeth Vreede most likely found to be quite exemplary that Rudolf Steiner was prepared in the beginning of 1918 to insert The *Soul Calendar* meditations (with a shorter foreword) into the packs of Waldorf-Astoria cigarettes for the soldiers at the front. Steiner's meditations, thanks to Emil Molt's mediation, were included a few months later in Hermann Hesse's publication *Bücherei für deutsche Kriegsgefangene* (Library for German prisoners of the war). At the end of the last year of the war Steiner wrote for Elisabeth Vreede herself on Christmas Eve of the year in 1918:

> Erkennt der Mench sich selbst:
> Wird ihm das Selbst zur Welt;
> *Erkennt der Mensch die Welt;*
> *Wird ihm die Welt zum Selbst.*
>
> If one truly knows oneself:
> The self becomes the world;
> If one truly knows the world,
> The world becomes the self.[100]

~

Following the end of the war, Elisabeth Vreede dedicated herself decisively to making the Threefold-idea known publicly and to its actualization. She was the first anthroposophist to give lectures on this topic in England and helped to distribute Steiner's "*Anruf an das deutsche Volk and die Kulturwelt*" (Appeal on the German people and the culture), in Dutch in Holland together with a small group of friends. She also worked actively for the Threefold Social Organism in Switzerland. Nothing was below Vreede, who had absolved a profound college study and a doctorate in natural science. She took on administrative, as well as practical, tasks that had little to do with her specific education. Already during the war Rudolf Steiner had asked her to hold introductory lectures on Anthroposophy and Goethean natural science in Basel. Vreede was willing to do this and continued to hold such lectures, even though with an emphasis on the social aspect. At the same time she did many other things that were necessary. She did not stand in the spotlight but worked in the background; she was not on any payroll but worked as a volunteer. Because of her family's wealth she did not need to be paid and thus worked in the sense of the "Social Law."

In Dornach, Elisabeth Vreede wanted to see, among other things, that Rudolf Steiner's written works and lectures were collected and represented there as the center of the intended Independent School for Spiritual Science. Already during the war years she engaged in the development of the Library at the Goetheanum. In the first summer after the war (1919), she took on—together with her friends, Sanne Bruinier and Isi Mackenzie—a large private anthroposophical library from an estate and began to build an archive of Rudolf Steiner's lectures. As of January 1910, Vreede had lived quite near to Marie von Sivers and learned to know and value her as the publisher of Rudolf Steiner's written works and lectures. Yet she saw the necessity to set up an independent archive of Rudolf Steiner's lectures that went far beyond the work being done by the Philosophical-Anthroposophical Press. This archive should be chronological, complete and be, in its social organization, not as the basis for a book and lecture cycle edition, but be available to anyone who is interested in Rudolf Steiner's work and to those who send written inquiries.

Elisabeth Vreede had more scientific and social orientation than Marie von Sivers; besides that, she had a comprehensive memory of Steiner's lecture activity. This memory was unique in the anthroposophic movement; no one had her corresponding capabilities that she was willing to place selflessly in the service of an "Archive." She received permission from Rudolf Steiner for her beginning activity of collecting earlier lecture notes and buying all existing copies with her own money. A certain tension in her relationship with Marie Steiner-von Sivers became evident from the first. Although Vreede wanted nothing for herself, Marie Steiner felt this initiative to be an invasion into her own realm as the responsible publisher of Rudolf Steiner's writings and lectures, and as testamentary heir and protector of his works. In spite of this, Vreede began her work on the archive soon after receiving permission through a brief conversation with Marie

Elisabeth Vreede, 1919

Steiner and Rudolf Steiner in Stuttgart. Already in October 1919 an announcement went out to all members of the Anthroposophical Society with the request for them to give or to sell copies of lectures from the first years of Anthroposophy. Every evening in a room in the carpentry studio that served by day as a place to sell anthroposophical books, Vreede began her systematic work with the collection: the proofreading and correcting errors in the copies, and much else that is implied with this work. "In the evenings, when the women (the booksellers) were gone, I could sit there and organize the archive."[101] In the winter of 1919, together with Sanne Bruinier and Isi Mackenzie—both of whom soon left the work[102]—she spoke again with Rudolf Steiner. "He told us that we could collect a copy of all the lectures; from Frau Dr. Steiner we could get a copy of the Dornach lectures. When we asked him what to call the archive, he answered promptly, 'It must be called *Rudolf Steiner Archive at the Goetheanum*.'"[103]

Even during the first years of war, Elisabeth Vreede took part in setting up a small reading room in the carpentry complex, in creating a place where Rudolf Steiner's books and lectures could be read and possibly be lent. Much in the future would depend on whether the coworkers at the Goetheanum were actually intimately familiar with Rudolf Steiner's work and intentions and if they knew what they were working for; and also whether inquiring people could find a concrete access to anthroposophic Spiritual Science at a place that strove to become an "Independent School for Spiritual Science" and, with it, a center of knowledge. As was Marie Steiner-von Sivers, Elisabeth Vreede was aware of how priceless every presentation by Rudolf Steiner was, but also how difficult and demanding the access to a work was, the individual aspects of which were scattered through thousands of lectures. Rudolf Steiner had encouraged the various professional groups to collect all the different aspects of a field and the question-and-answer sessions and to penetrate their various perspectives as prerequisite for the further work.[104] Such an effort in the individual areas of life had scarcely begun, but yet it belonged to the necessities or the development of the intended School and its research

ANTONIA EBERSOLD

Allmendingen b. Bern
10. Juli 1933

Sehr verehrtes Fräulein Dr. Vreede,

hier sende ich Ihnen für das Archiv Spruch und Worte Dr. Steiners, die ich Ostern 1923 von Dr. Steiner erhielt, als ich um Rat für meine damaligen Schülerinnen fragte.

Seien Sie von Herzen gegrüsst.

Ihre Antonia Ebersold.

Diesen Spruch gab Dr. Steiner Ostern 1923 in Stuttgart. Er gab ihn für ein siebenjähriges Mädchen, für das ich um Rat gefragt habe, weil seine Phantasie im Spielen etwas abgeirrt war.

Die Wortgruppen schrieb Dr. Steiner für ein 10 jähriges, phlegmatisches Mädchen auf, das diese Worte täglich eurythmisch mit mir üben sollte.

A. E.

"Dr. Steiner was very pleased with my lectures" (1914–1923)

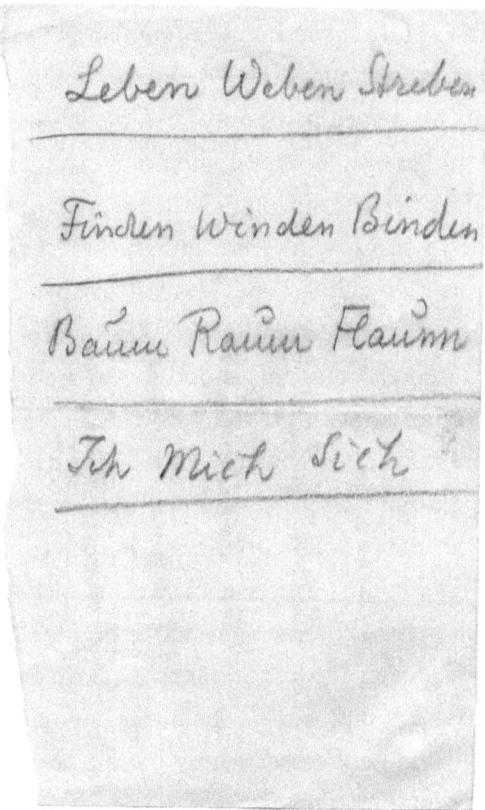

Wo ich stehe
Wo ich gehe
Sieht Gottes Auge
Auf mein Gehen
Auf mein Stehen.

Leben Weben Streben

Finden Winden Binden

Baum Raum Flaum

Ich Mich Sich

Rudolf Steiner's exercises given over by Antonia Ebersold (1933)

Institute. Here Elisabeth Vreede's initiative began with a far-sighted vision. The Rudolf Steiner Archive at the Goetheanum founded by her would exist, in the end, until 1935 (over sixteen years) and would be used with gratitude by many hundreds of people. Vreede was the center point of this archive; she created not only a complete chronological index of Rudolf Steiner's lectures, but also drew up thematic overviews and offered tours through the lecture cycles and the individual lectures for visitors. Charlotte Fiechter[105] wrote of her, "Her memory at that time held the lectures so exactly that she could repeat even the most vague or incomprehensible elements correctly. Dora Krück von Poturzyn described Elisabeth Vreede as a 'living subject index.'"[106]

According to George Adams, Vreede felt reverence toward Rudolf Steiner's work and had, at the same time, a practical sense. She had a unique overview: "Often she knew immediately (without having to look it up) where, when and how Dr. Steiner spoke from the most varied viewpoints on a specific theme."[107] Vreede's earnestness, developed power of judgment, colossal memory, and alert intelligence helped the inquirers further, as long as they were truly interested. She showed the door to those who were merely inquisitive or nosy and was not willing to deal with them. Instead of spending her time in frustrating discussions, she would rather lay out for them a subject index of Rudolf Steiner's natural scientific lecture cycles. For everyone else, on the other hand, the Archive was open and, as Elisabeth Vreede said, it remained "dust-free through active use." "That seemed to me to be the sign of an anthroposophical Archive."[108] In the following years many anthroposophical friends bestowed upon Elisabeth Vreede valuable documents, and after 1925 she also received meditative exercises that Rudolf Steiner gave to individuals. Vreede had a tremendous knowledge of Rudolf Steiner's esoteric teachings and had at her disposal many copies of (his) Esoteric Lessons, which she had produced herself or had collected. Many people had absolute trust in her and gave her valuable notes.

The problem with Marie Steiner that had existed from the beginning did not resolve itself in all the coming years. Later, long after

Rudolf Steiner's death and the loss (or withdrawal) of her Archive, Elisabeth Vreede wrote upon reflecting about the difference of opinion with Marie Steiner:

> This opposition was not openly expressed, because such a thing was not done in Dornach. Rather, it erupted below the surface repeatedly. Frau Dr. Steiner had the idea that the Archive consisted of our collecting copies of the lectures and thereby alleviating her of this effort. And all the copies would be there and be at her disposal when she needed them. The Archive existed only for her when she wanted to print them.
>
> I had the idea, however, that this should be a social matter, being accessible to all members. These views split wide apart from each other. I acted as much as possible in the sense of Marie Steiner's view and have for this reason left much undone that I would have liked to do with the Archive otherwise....
>
> Thus through the years whenever Frau Dr. Steiner needed lectures, for instance to print them, a little piece of paper would come in. On it was written approximately: "To the archive, send lecture such and such." Some people felt it to be insulting, but I will not complain, as it just corresponded to the other view that Frau Dr. Steiner had of the Archive.[109]

Elisabeth Vreede said that she wanted to avoid drawing Rudolf Steiner into this conflict; she did not want to burden him or put him into a position of having to vote against Marie Steiner-von Sivers. Marie Steiner, on the other hand, stressed that Rudolf Steiner had not wanted the Archive from the beginning; he was "forced" into it.[110] At another occasion, she said in reflection, "The Dornach Archive came about through Fräulein Vreede's collector's enthusiasm, without the agreement of, and against the wish of, Dr. Steiner."[111] Lili Kolisko wrote a commentary, saying that Dr. Vreede was not a person "who would do something *against* Dr. Steiner's will."[112]

The activity for the Rudolf Steiner Archive at the Goetheanum was only one aspect of Vreede's social working in Dornach. She was a founding member and Secretary of the branch of the Anthroposophical Society at the Goetheanum; was on the Executive Council of the Anthroposophical Society in Switzerland and worked in the organizing of conferences at the Goetheanum, "which, owing to the fairly confused circumstances prevailing at that time, was neither an easy nor an appreciated task."[113] Also Vreede's friend, Edith Maryon, worked in this selfless way and took care of much else besides her own artistic work.[114]

Elisabeth Vreede also continued to give specialized scientific lectures herself. At the invitation of the medical student Madeline van Deventer (whom she knew since 1915), Vreede spoke with great success to Dutch students in Utrecht on Anthroposophy. ("She agreed to do this and found the proper tone in the... world of students."[115]) Rudolf Steiner himself requested her lecture with the title, "The Justification of Mathematics in Astronomy and Its Limits," (which among other things examined Albert Einstein's Theory of Relativity) for the opening of the Goetheanum in the fall of 1920, and was more than pleased with it. "Dr. Steiner was very pleased with my lecture (in any case, more so than I myself) and wish to see it printed immediately."[116]

In this evaluation Vreede's contributions differed significantly from many lectures given during the three-week course at the Goetheanum, concerning which Steiner later stated firmly that they (the other lectures) did not do justice to the building. Steiner was, however, happy about Elisabeth Vreede's presentation on a high level. Vreede was an exceptional phenomenon and was, besides Lili Kolisko, the only woman who represented and spoke for a genuine field of natural science. Rudolf Steiner wanted her to be present in all the School courses that followed and, according to Vreede, was surprised, "that I was so often crossed off the program for some reason by the organizers of these (courses)."[117] This puzzling action was not surprising to Elisabeth Vreede. She had often experienced similar things; the act of being overlooked and the crossing out; being ignored; and annulment. Yet, when Rudolf Steiner was involved and was asked, he insisted on Elisabeth Vreede's collaboration. Her representative mathematical-astronomical discipline was absolutely important to him; but also important to Vreede herself. The number of invitations for her (to speak) was limited, so she did the detailed daily tasks. Among these was the extensive correspondence around registrations for conferences and time-intensive work of invoicing in the office.

Elisabeth Vreede was also quite involved in the preparations for Rudolf Steiner's Dutch lecture tour in February and March 1921. In Holland Rudolf Steiner spoke in various cities and stressed quite honestly the necessity of a "world school association" for the facilitation and support of institutions for an independent spiritual and educational life.[118] "Such a world school association must include all of those people who are interested in having ascending forces enter into the forces of humanity's development to offset the terrible declining forces that we have in humanity today. For such a world school association would not be a kind of alliance from the impulses that already exist; it would not attempt to fashion the world according to the old diplomatic or other such methods. Such an alliance, such a world school association, would attempt to build a world alliance from the deepest human forces, from the human soul impulses."[119]

Elisabeth Vreede grasped the motive for founding this "world school association," its urgency and its broad horizon (that reached beyond the Waldorf school) as few others (including Edith Maryon) were able to do, and she took it up in her will. Vreede had a good eye for posing of historical tasks—also for the political situation of the present time—and, in turn, she was one of the few who understood Steiner. In an evening discussion on April 8, 1921, during the second Dornach college course and in connection with a social-science lecture, she said (soon after his return from Holland):

> One must do what is right. As Rudolf Steiner explained in Holland, it is not a matter first and foremost to found individual schools, which could exist in addition and only slowly and carefully achieve the right to exist. It is a matter of something much greater; it is

Edith Maryon (undated)

truly to actualize the free spiritual life! We have a spiritual life today that needs, above all, fresh air and without this fresh air, it will succumb. Among the public, a demand must arise from this mood that the spiritual life must be freed!

Naturally, all of this does not mean that single schools should not be established, such as the Waldorf school; but one should not just bring in a school or Institute here and there because all of them have a miserable existence in the legal connection. Actually, they always have a sword hanging over their heads as to whether they are allowed now or not. Schools that can exist only by the grace of the state should not be founded. Our Goetheanum is also a school—an independent college. First and foremost, the possibility must be created that a world school association would exist that feels the need powerfully enough to support and preserve the existence of such institutions as Waldorf schools and the Goetheanum. It is necessary that something concrete already exist for this. There are indeed teachers' organizations and artists' associations; for them it would be a positive goal to work toward a free spiritual life. The goal to be ventured must be greater than merely setting up single schools; everything must be thought and grasped in a greater manner, so that one also sees the greater (comprehensive) connection.[120]

Rudolf Steiner was pleased about the statement and stressed the following in the further course of the discussion: "The other thing I want to point out, and that Fräulein Vreede also said, is that from the first what should be striven for with the world school association should be put on an broad basis and be taken up with a creative courage and a comprehensive view.

~

Half a year later, on October 27, 1921, Rudolf Steiner laid belatedly the "Foundation Stone" for a house that Elisabeth Vreede and her parents had been residing in for some time. This was "Haus Vreede" at Auf der Höhe 1, in Arlesheim. More than seven years earlier in Berlin, Rudolf Steiner said that it was very much hoped that a settlement of Anthroposophists would arise around the Goetheanum. It would also be wished that the houses would have an ideal connection with the College in both (architectural) form and purpose. Edith Maryon had designed such a house for her friend Elisabeth Vreede upon her request, but then Rudolf Steiner had made a model for it himself.

Elisabeth Vreede was able to acquire the property for the construction of the house from Ita Wegman, who opened her clinic in Arlesheim in June 1921. How long Vreede and Wegman had already known each other is not documented. Very possibly they had met during the early time of the theosophical–anthroposophic movement; at the latest it would have been since 1907 at the Munich Congress and the decision for (joining) Rudolf Steiner's esoteric school.[122] Vreede and Wegman were about the same age and lived independently and self-determined. There is much indicating that they became aware of one another early on. Both were natives of Holland, even though Wegman spent most of her childhood and youth in Dutch-India (as the daughter of Dutch colonists, as was Elisabeth Vreede's mother). Both decided, unlike the majority of the Dutch theosophists, to go with Rudolf Steiner and not with Annie Besant. Whether Wegman and Vreede were friends at that time is not known, as a correspondence from the early time was not preserved. Ita Wegman had, with foresight, attained the land on "Auf der Höhe" from Arlesheim to the boundary of the area of Dornach—the *"Schwinbächli"*—with the intention to build homes for her coworkers. She did not, however, deny Elisabeth Vreede's and her parents' wish, and thus the first house at "Auf der Höhe 1" was built according to Rudolf Steiner's model. His foundation stone verse is as follows:

> May soul live in this house
> May it be permeated with spirit
> Seeking firm will
> In the depths
> So that devout consciousness
> May develop
> In every room of the building
> And so that from above

> The blessings of the spirit
> And the grace of God
> May be able to unite
> In all who live within.[123]

Rudolf Steiner's verse was buried under the pillars of the entrance. The house consisted of nine modest rooms; the walls were painted dark red, dark blue, and dark violet; the house was furnished with black and ultramarine varnished furniture. Elisabeth Vreede planted a yew, a copper beech, and an oak. She followed Rudolf Steiner's advice to paint the large stairwell in an orange-red color (to make the climb easier) and not to put a fence around the garden, but rather to plant *roses*. She resided in two small, simple rooms on the attic floor, from where the observation of the night sky was possible. Elisabeth Vreede, just as Charlotte Fiechter, lived "just as much with the stars as with human beings," and this was essential to her. By day the house looked out directly on the Goetheanum to the south; nothing stood between the two buildings to separate them.

Elisabeth Vreede and her parents were extremely hospitable; Haus Vreede was often called *"Villa Taubenschlag"* (*Taubenschlag* refers to being crowded or mobbed). Many anthroposophical friends could come and find open, spiritually quite stimulating accommodations. Among these were many Waldorf school teachers from Stuttgart (like Caroline von Heydebrand and Karl Schubert); later also the pedagogues of The Hague School that Elisabeth Vreede would take an energetic part in opening in 1923. Her parents, Hendrik and Jacoba Elisabeth Vreede, were still present a very long time in the house and in the anthroposophical conversations in the dining room. Vreede's mother died in September 1925, her father eight years later. Colonel Olcott and Helena Petrova Blavatsky were held in great honor as always; not, however, Annie Besant and Leadbeater. It was reported that an "earnest tone" prevailed in the house; the beginning of the 1920s and the years that followed were in no way easy. Even though the "personified peace" (Steiner) in Dornach never became a reality, Haus Vreede was one of the few completely successful construction

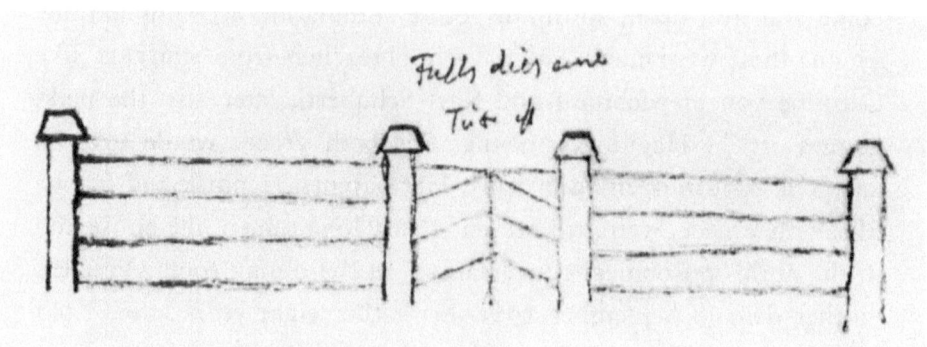

*Rudolf Steiner: model for the "Vreede House" (above);
sketch of the Garden gate (below)*

projects in the surroundings of the Goetheanum, in the sense of what Rudolf Steiner planned in architectural and social respects.

⁓

Rudolf Steiner emphasized anew Elisabeth Vreede's contribution to The Hague College Course in the spring of 1922, and wrote in the Dornach weekly news that she united "thorough anthroposophical insight with an excellent clarity about how Anthroposophy should be introduced into the individual sciences":

> Fräulein Dr. Elisabeth Vreede is tireless in actively introducing Anthroposophy into the mathematic natural sciences. Her lecture in The Hague handled astronomy. The task is difficult. For with anything Dr. Vreede undertakes in this direction, one must point to a necessary, methodical change of thinking. She succeeds in this with all who want to be aware of only what is essential.[125]

Elisabeth Vreede strove energetically for almost twenty years to penetrate her special field with Anthroposophy. Now Rudolf Steiner attested in her hometown that she had successfully fulfilled this path.

In The Hague, Elisabeth Vreede participated in the founding of an Independent Waldorf School and after the College Course, she traveled further with Rudolf Steiner to England. While still in Holland, on Maundy Thursday, she heard his (Steiner's) moving Christological lecture on the "Teachings of the Resurrected One."[126] Rudolf Steiner then expanded on this Christ-motif in London.

Edith Maryon also joined this tour. Along with Vreede, she followed Steiner's lectures in her English homeland. These lectures also spoke of the dangerous situation of Anthroposophy in the present day, of the examination of those forces at work, not the least of which were a determining factor in the "Sculptural Group" in Dornach.[127]

> Anthroposophy's testimony has very powerful opponents inspired by ahrimanic powers, and they are growing stronger and stronger. I am telling you this today so that you will not be surprised to learn that the budding anthroposophic movement increasingly has to battle terrible adversarial forces. Insight into the intentions

behind anthroposophical endeavors must alert us to terrible aspersions and other types of attacks by enemies who do not want this movement to survive. But no matter how strong these enemies may be, our own positive energy must be equally strong.[128]

The political climate in Germany had radicalized dangerously in 1922, and Rudolf Steiner's Anthroposophy and Steiner himself were vehemently attacked. The initiative connected with him for threefolding the social organism and the opening of the Stuttgart Waldorf School and the construction of the Goetheanum, with the claim of an "Independent School for Spiritual Science," called the enemies into the open. Steiner let there be no doubt that this was not a matter of personal aversions, but rather a world historic fight that had to do with the future of the Christ impulse. Thus understood, it was a question in all oppositional writings, articles, polemic attacks and educational lectures whether the spiritualization of the sciences intended by the Goetheanum—it's concrete penetration with Anthroposophy and, with it, it's imbuing with the Christ impulse under the premises of the twentieth century—could succeed or not. Elisabeth Vreede had to return to Dornach before Rudolf Steiner and wrote to him on April 22, 1922: "It is a difficult, troublesome time. I am all the more grateful for the strength and courage the Easter days in London gave me."[129]

Elisabeth Vreede and her friends needed this "strength" and this "courage" to withstand what was to come. At the end of 1922 the Goetheanum was completely destroyed by fire. Four weeks later in Steiner's studio, Edith Maryon suffered a hemorrhage of the lungs, an aggravated recurrence of an old illness that she could no longer overcome. Her difficult illness lasted a brief six months, which Elisabeth accompanied with deep compassion. Edith Maryon's quiet work on behalf of Rudolf Steiner was exemplary; it was without any sensation and without all personal ambition, selfless and on a high technical level. This work centered on the Christ figure;[130] the wooden group survived the fire. The building—for which it was intended as the culmination—was destroyed. Edith Maryon looked out of the windows

Edith Maryon: Ahriman study

of her room in the lower eurythmy house upon the ruins; for years the view had been of the double cupolas of the building in all their unique beauty. Rudolf Steiner spoke of the destruction of the Goetheanum as the death of a living being. In his memory of the building, the Dutch Willem Zeylmans van Emmichoven, a close friend of Vreede's, and who had been at the Goetheanum in December 1920 and April 1921, wrote:

> As I returned to Dornach at Easter 1921, the Goetheanum, in its surroundings of blossoms, revealed to me more clearly than three months ago that it was formed according to the law of the plant, of the living. I sensed it to be a living being to which I felt connected from then on. I tried to understand how such a huge building can come across as organically living. When I saw it for the first time in the deep snow, I felt only that something special was working here but could not understand what. Now it became experience. The forms and their metamorphoses opened up to me; I understood why columns that no longer play a role in modern architecture stood here, and I sensed them to be the "I"-nature of these metamorphosing forms. The colored light of the windows fit so wonderfully into the spring nature. When one entered the Goetheanum and did not judge it aesthetically the way one usually does in other buildings, but surrendered oneself and waited to see how this being accepted one, then one could achieve a new kind of spatial experience. Whereas architectural spaces generally have the nature of closing something off, it was quite the opposite here. The soul was not held back by the walls; it did not bump against the walls; there arose instead the feeling that the forms made visible here led further into the world of the spirit. The wall was, in its forms, living and took the forces of the soul into itself, so that they could expand and unite with the universe. Such living forms could arise because they were discovered from the etheric laws according to which the plants grow. Through this, the forms became organs through which the spiritual can express itself directly.[131]

All of this was now destroyed; everything connected with the forms and colors and what they made possible. Elisabeth Vreede did not record how she experienced the night of the fire. There were also no notes remaining in Edith Maryon's hand. After January 1, 1923, one no longer saw the Goetheanum from Haus Vreede. The view to the south passed over an empty hill that still smoldered for a long time. Destruction and death processes had made their entry into Dornach.

In the first three months of 1923 a young married woman who expected a child—a very poor student from a good family—helped Elisabeth Vreede with the Rudolf Steiner Archive at the Goetheanum in the carpentry shop, which had been preserved from the fire. Theodora Kunert, later Krück von Poturzyn, came from Leipzig in order to earn a little money in Switzerland in the difficult time and circumstances of 1923, a year of progressing inflation, unemployment, and poverty in Germany. At the end of March she returned to her husband, the musical scholar Ernst Kunert. Her child was born on August 8. He was given the name Willfried Immanuel by Rudolf Steiner. Elisabeth Vreede became his godmother and wrote a letter to him.

> Now you shall be baptized so that you can become a real Willfried Immanuel! I want to give you a small saying that your angels should whisper in your year, but only for the baptism!
>
> *Born into the light,*
> *You are now a Sun Being.*
> *Bring love to the Earth*
> *That it can again become whole.*[132]

Willfried Immanuel was a child with a special destiny. At the beginning of 1924, four months after his baptism, his mother was to bring him to Arlesheim and Dornach on the advice of Elisabeth Vreede. The circumference of his head kept expanding. Vreede picked up the mother and child at the Basel train station and found lodging for both in her house and admission in the Clinical-Therapeutical Institute with Ita Wegman. Thus began a complicated treatment in a difficult, life-threatening situation.[133] Elisabeth Vreede supported Theodora and Willfried Immanuel Kunert where she could; it was

Und getauft sollst Du
nun auch werden, damit
Du ein wirklicher Willfried
Immanuel werden kannst!
Da möchte ich Dir einen
schönen kleinen Spruch
sagen; den soll Dir Dein
Englein ins Ohr flüstern,
aber nur für die Taufe!

„In das Licht hineingeboren
Bist Du nun ein Sonnenwesen.
Liebe bringe Du der Erde
Dass sie wieder kann genesen."

Elisabeth's baptism letter for Willfried Immanuel Kunert (October 6, 1923)

"Dr. Steiner was very pleased with my lectures" (1914–1923)

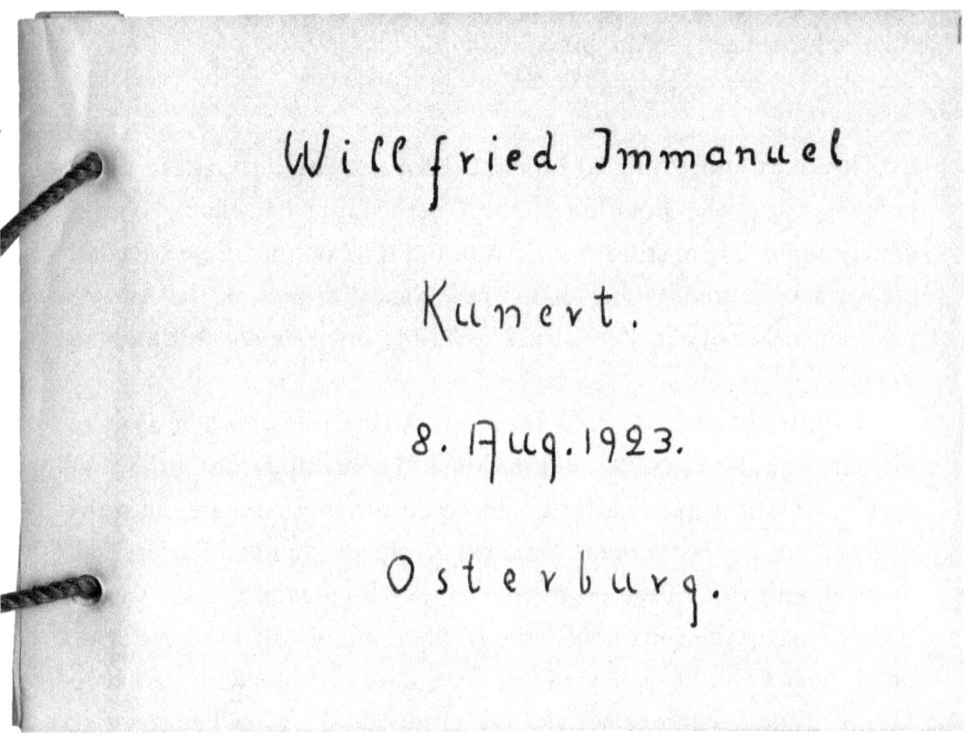

From a book of children's names bought by Elisabeth Vreede,
which was given by Rudolf Steiner

unsentimental, engaged, practical and direct. Haus Vreede and Elisabeth Vreede, as godmother and companion of the child, held their own in great need—*"May soul live in this house."*

~

As Theodora and Willfried Immanuel Kunert came to Arlesheim in January 1924, the situation at the Goetheanum had changed completely again. There still stood no new building on the hill; yet Rudolf Steiner set the foundation for the new social forming of the Anthroposophical Society for Christmas, with the involvement of Elisabeth Vreede.

Rudolf Steiner had exerted himself during the whole of 1923 to give the impulse for self-examination and contemplation in the community of Anthroposophists as a prerequisite of a next step into the future.[134] In the last several years the Anthroposophical Society had failed drastically, in the protection of the Goetheanum and its effective defense in the spiritual battles of the time, but also in the setting up of the School. Very little of this School was visible, with the exception of Rudolf Steiner's activity (and individual efforts like those of Lili Kolisko). Most of the anthroposophists were occupied with other things—the difficult business initiatives and the Stuttgart school, the difficulties of living with one another, and the dilemmas of the time. Even the completion of the construction of the Goetheanum had finally stagnated because of a lack of money and a decreasing number of workers for the initiative. The incentives that Steiner gave were also taken up only conditionally in 1923.

Efforts to reorganize the Society, as a prerequisite for the new building, progressed very slowly. Elisabeth Vreede who worked intensively on raising money for the rebuilding (of the Goetheanum),[135] heard and understood much in Dornach, Stuttgart, and The Hague, where Rudolf Steiner spoke drastic words at the founding of the Dutch National Society.[136] She also experienced in all clarity the inner moments of this whole complicated event. She participated in two Esoteric Lessons that took place in Rudolf Steiner's house in

May and November. The Lessons were given for a small circle, with the participation of Ita Wegman and various friends who had asked Steiner how Dornach was to be protected.[137] The answer was given in the Lessons: through inner, esoteric work.[138]

Rudolf Steiner also gave the answer to the question about the spiritual protection and the future of the Goetheanum in the lecture course he gave in November 1923 in The Hague, parallel to the founding of the Dutch National Society. This was *Der übersinnliche Mensch—anthroposophisch erfasst* (published in English as *Supersensible Man* and *At Home in the Universe*, neither of which includes the following passage). It was a mystery course, which Elisabeth Vreede took deeply into her heart, on the real being of Anthroposophy and the hierarchical cosmic connection of the human being. In his last lecture (of the course), Steiner said the following:

> When we are able to take in anthroposophical knowledge not merely by reading or hearing, but when we come, through living anthroposophical examination, ever more and more to experience the content of Anthroposophy with our hearts and minds and souls, then it will be really as if not merely the meaning of the ideas penetrate into our souls when we are together in the anthroposophical branches and study Anthroposophy with others, or when we remain alone in our room; rather it will then be as if living cosmic beings entered into our souls. Then Anthroposophy appears to us ever more and more as something living, as having being. And we will then indeed become aware of how something knocks at the portal of our heart and says: *Let me in, for I am you yourself; I am the true being of your human being!*[139]

While still in The Hague, shortly before her return to Dornach, Rudolf Steiner asked Elisabeth Vreede unexpectedly to do a special task. She was to travel by train to Berlin with Marie Steiner-von Sivers, in order to close the apartment in Motzstraße and the publishing house, or to prepare for the transfer of its inventory to Dornach. A few weeks earlier Adolf Hitler's first attempt at a coup (Putschversuch) had occurred in Munich, whereupon Rudolf Steiner decided to

Elisabeth Vreede (undated)

give up the apartment as the Berlin work center and move everything to Dornach. He could not continue to work openly in Germany due to the political conditions. However, many personal papers, notebooks, correspondence, and manuscripts were still in Berlin; in addition, the entire inventory of the publishing house that Marie Steiner and Johanna Mücke had built up was still there. Of course, Elisabeth Vreede did what Rudolf Steiner asked, although the relationship with Marie Steiner and the task were in no way easy. In questions about the Archive Elisabeth Vreede had experienced that Marie Steiner demanded vigorously for herself the rights to Rudolf Steiner's written works. Rudolf Steiner stayed out of it because of gratitude for her life commitment and because he knew that people must reach a solution themselves, both within themselves and among one another. Now, however, he asked Elisabeth Vreede, whose discretion and reliability he knew—and also her earnestness and carefulness—to help Marie Steiner with the complicated task of closing the Berlin properties, a matter that directly affected his lectures and written works. Marie Steiner and Elisabeth Vreede accepted. It is possible that Rudolf Steiner hoped this would change the strange circumstances of the Archive and, thereby, of their whole relationship. Vreede wrote in retrospect concerning the course of activity in Berlin:

> Fräulein Mücke and I performed the quite strenuous business; we spent ten hours a day sorting papers, etc. I will not indulge in further descriptions of this peculiar action, but will say only that I felt instinctively that I would have to show the greatest consideration toward Frau Dr. Steiner in this delicate business. I complied totally with her wishes and, as I noticed on the third day that she'd had enough of my help, I declared immediately that I wanted to leave. She still gave me an errand to run in Stuttgart, which I took care of there. When I arrived in Dornach on November 24, I noticed that the doctor had already received a good report about me. He was extremely pleased, friendly, and grateful.[140]

Marie Steiner had to remain longer in Berlin to settle old business difficulties there. In Dornach, however, Steiner held powerful

[1924]

Mr Francis Jozeph Cossens
geb: 21 nov 1894
zwischen 11-12 Uhr Nachts.

Liebe Lili,
Dr Steiner möchte gerne von mr Cossens eine Himmelkarte haben.
Es sind wegen seiner Krankheit einige dringende Fragen zu lösen die nur gelöst werden können, wenn man weiss wo der Mond stand bei seiner Geburt u. s. w
Hast du Zeit dazu?
Herzl. Gruss
dein Ita

Seine Krankheit ist ein Muskelschwund der Heredität ist. Beginn der Krankheit mit 19J. in 1913.

Ita Wegman's hairsplitting question to Elisabeth Vreede (undated)

"Dr. Steiner was very pleased with my lectures" (1914–1923)

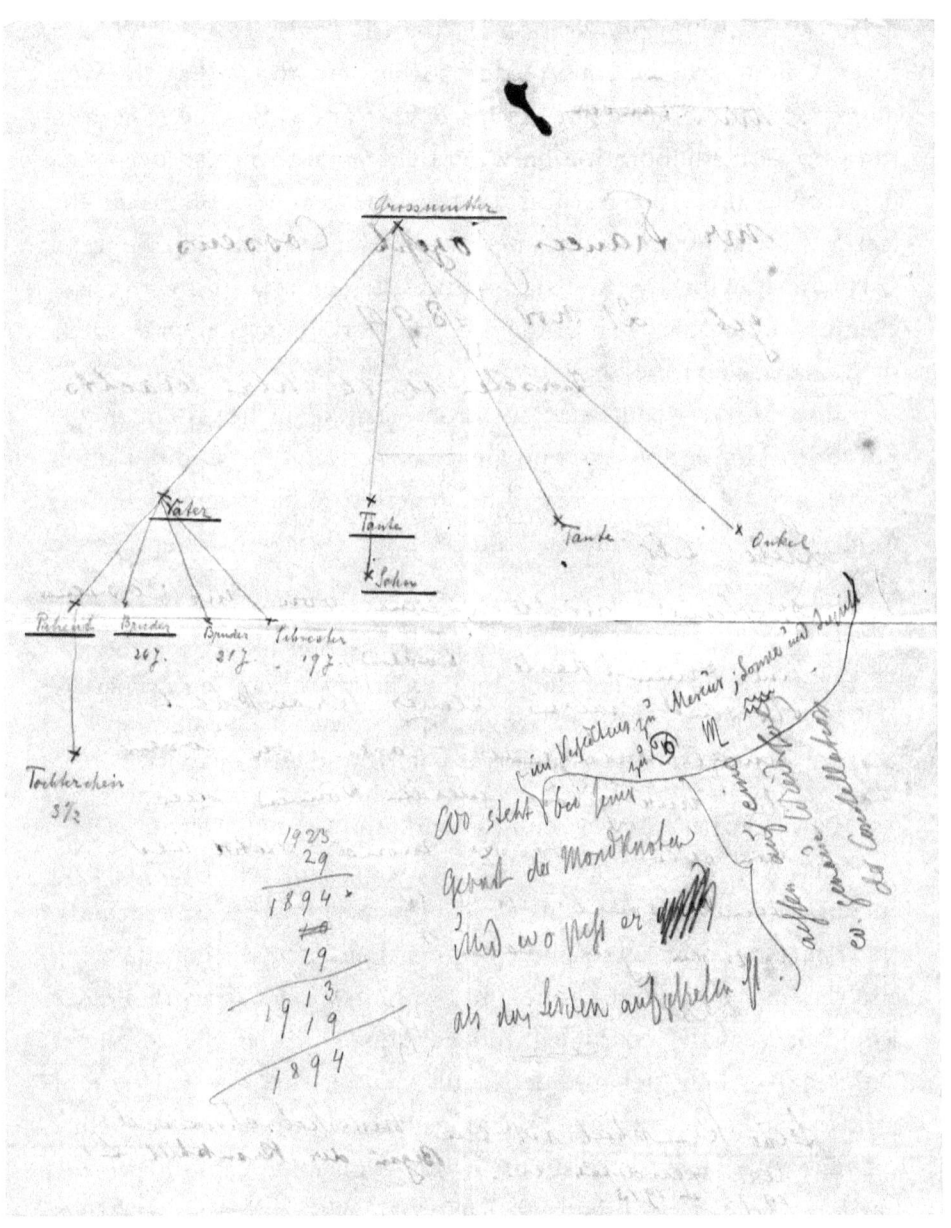

Back of the letter, with Rudolf Steiner's questions

mystery lectures in preparation for the Christmas Conference. For several months Elisabeth Vreede had become aware that Ita Wegman stood at Steiner's side, as his doctor and colleague. The relationship and collaboration between the two of them had deepened perceptibly since the burning of the Goetheanum. In his public lectures on anthroposophic medicine Steiner mentioned Wegman particularly with all enthusiasm since the summer of 1923. Every evening in October both of them began working in Steiner's studio on a medical textbook.

Edith Maryon continued to lie seriously ill in her room in the Eurythmy House; she could no longer be active in the studio. Rudolf Steiner and Ita Wegman treated her together. With Wegman, Steiner went quite obviously into the future. Later Elisabeth Vreede wrote about this time:

> He had without a doubt made the preparation mostly together with her, if not with her alone, for the Christmas Conference. Frau Dr. Wegman acted pretty arrogant toward me at that time; she treated me on various occasions as a fairly negligible quantity.[141]

Apart from her extensive clinical work, Ita Wegman was completely taken up with the closeness to Rudolf Steiner—by the schooling and encouragement he gave, which took place with concentrated mantric effect and in an atmosphere of great familiarity.[142] For anything else she had only limited time and awareness left. Elisabeth Vreede would have gladly continued and developed further the encounter with Ita Wegman, not just personally, but also in view of the new mystery-medical-cosmological arrangement of which Rudolf Steiner spoke. Single medical questions in this connection came to Vreede, but most went back directly to Rudolf Steiner. Thus she would get the requests for the horoscope of the children in need of special care or individual causality aspects for which Steiner asked astronomical indications. Ita Wegman, however, turned seldom or never to Vreede. This is not surprising if one comprehends Wegman's day and has an idea of what her inner life was like in the second half of 1923. "Pretty arrogant"—that's how Elisabeth Vreede experienced Wegman at this time. In other circumstances she was lively and totally engaged.[143]

Elisabeth Vreede was not close to Ita Wegman at the end of 1923; she kept to herself and was often alone. Shortly before Christmas she found out that Rudolf Steiner had her, together with Marie Steiner and Ita Wegman (as well as two young men, the Swiss author Albert Steffen and Steiner's secretary, the social scientist Guenther Wachsmuth), in mind for positions on the Executive Council of the Anthroposophical Society that would be newly founded. This constellation promised to become complicated. Yet, it belong to what the Christmas Conference brought with it, and it changed Elisabeth Vreede's life decisively.

3

"Tested to the ultimate degree"
(1924–1925)

The Christmas Conference and the Esoteric Executive Council

"Naturally, it is necessary, since I am taking on the work myself, that those who will stand at my side will be those people who, through preparing themselves for the conditions of the work, will be able to work with me at the center."
—RUDOLF STEINER [144]

Middle row from the left: Ita Wegman, Rudolf Steiner, Marie Steiner, Elisabeth Vreede (Arnheim, July 1924)

With the Christmas Conference of 1923/24, Rudolf Steiner undertook a last attempt to turn the destiny of the Anthroposophical Society once again into the future. He took over the chairmanship personally and founded it—and the Dornach School—totally anew, in a decisive effort to preserve the working conditions of Anthroposophy or to create it newly again. Steiner installed an *Esoteric Executive Council* of the General Anthroposophical Society. This Executive Council was to imbue the Society with Anthroposophy; it was to be an *initiative Executive Council,* not an *administrative Council.* "*It must be an Initiative-Council. It must take on the tasks that are given to it by the spiritual world; it must take up these tasks and lead them into the world; it must not be merely an administrative Council.*"[146] In addition, School departments (faculties or Sections) for individual areas of life were formed and instituted. After many failed developments of the previous few years, they should attempt to complete the construction of Dornach and allow the Independent School for Spiritual Science to become a reality in its specific spiritual task for civilization. "[The Christmas Conference] should, above all, introduce or bring into being an epoch of the anthroposophic movement in which the concrete facts of the spiritual world should be spoken about without hesitation or inhibitions.... A stronger impulse than was used before is necessary if the spirit that humanity needs is to enter."[147]

Concerning the members of the "closest working Executive Council,"[148] Rudolf Steiner said that he wanted to work together with them in the greatest manner possible and that their selection was made accordingly. "Naturally, it is... necessary, since I am taking on the work myself, that those who will stand at my side will be those people who, through preparing themselves for the conditions of the work, will be able to work with me at the center."¹⁴⁹ These are the people "who have dedicated their life completely to the anthroposophic cause, outwardly and inwardly."¹⁵⁰ All of the members of the "closest Executive Council" were, at the same time, leaders of the Sections of the School (for Spiritual Science).

The appointment of Elisabeth Vreede to the Executive Council was a surprise for many people. In explanation Rudolf Steiner said simply, "Another member I have to suggest is one who has been tried and tested to the utmost degree for the work in Dornach, both in general and down to the very last detail, one who has proved herself ever again to be a faithful member."¹⁵¹ Indeed Elisabeth Vreede had worked selflessly and with great skill for nine years in Dornach (and before that in Berlin and Munich). She undertook both major tasks and all the detailed tasks in affairs within her field of specialty, but also in many other fields that affect the Anthroposophical Society as such. Steiner's unusual formulation of "ultimate degree" Vreede herself connected with the successful mission in Berlin; that is, to Marie Steiner's acceptance of their work together in a complicated situation. She wrote many years later in retrospect: "For me, there is no doubt that this episode led to all the 'fuss' about 'to the ultimate degree a loyal coworker,' with which the Doctor introduced me as a member of the Executive Council on December 24 [1925]."¹⁵²

Elisabeth Vreede was aware from the beginning of the explosive nature of the constellation with Ita Wegman and Marie Steiner in the Executive Council. In comparison to later speculations by people who wanted to interpret the whole composition karmically, Elisabeth Vreede saw the criteria for the selection as practical, without personal elevation. With regard to her own person and her selection, Vreede maintained objectively, psychologically clever and modestly that, "The Doctor still needed someone he could place *behind* Frau Dr. Steiner on the Executive Council whom both he and she (difficult question!) could accept to a certain extent. ("To a certain extent" refers to Frau Dr. Steiner!) The time in Berlin had proved to him that I could get along with her. Thus, he took me."¹⁵³ For Elisabeth Vreede, there was no doubt that the spiritual center of the work of the Executive Council was situated between Rudolf Steiner and Ita Wegman. In any case, Vreede had experienced the close collaboration of both from the beginning, even though she knew the background and circumstances only in their initial stages. Even the Christmas Conference, per Elisabeth Vreede, was "prepared" by Rudolf Steiner together with Ita Wegman; not administratively, but in the spiritual-social aspects.[154] In London eight months after the Christmas Conference, Rudolf Steiner spoke with unmistakable clarity about his "dear friend and colleague in the medical and other areas of spiritual research, in the whole realm of spiritual research."[155] Vreede wrote in her retrospective of December 1934 concerning the personnel constellation of the Executive Council around Rudolf Steiner that, per Steiner, *"in its totality, had an esoteric task"*[156]: "It seems to be that the doctor wanted to balance Steffen and Wachsmuth, on the one hand, who were completely without traditions and showed no continuity, and Frau Dr. [Steiner] and me, on the other hand—whereas he himself, with Frau Dr. Wegman, represented the working spiritual principle."[157]

Elisabeth Vreede did not stand in an especially positive relationship to Ita Wegman in December 1923. She felt herself to be overlooked by Wegman as a *"quantité négligeable"* (negligible quantity) and virtually forgotten, even though she had known her a long time and valued her. Vreede wrote later that at that time, Ita Wegman was "truly not inspired by a wish to collaborate."[158] Independently of that, however, Vreede saw clearly how important Wegman became for Steiner: "the directly working spiritual principle...." People such as Guenther Wachsmuth and Albert Steffen, who were also appointed to the Executive Council, had little or no awareness of this fact. Marie Steiner, on the other hand, did indeed, but for her the situation was definitely difficult.

*Rudolf Steiner: The Foundation Stone Meditation
of the Christmas Conference; Elisabeth Vreede's handwriting (page 1)*

*Rudolf Steiner: The Foundation Stone Meditation
of the Christmas Conference; Elisabeth Vreede's handwriting (page 2)*

*Rudolf Steiner: The Foundation Stone Meditation
of the Christmas Conference; Elisabeth Vreede's handwriting (page 3)*

"Tested to the ultimate degree" (1924–1925)

Weihnachtsspruch

In der Zeitenwende
trat das Weltengeisteslicht
in den irdischen Wesensstrom.
Nachtdunkel hatte ausgewaltet;
Taghelles Licht erstrahlte in Menschenseelen;
Licht, das erwärmet die armen Hirtenherzen;
Licht, das erleuchtet die weisen Königshäupter.
Göttliches Licht, Christussonne,
Erwärme unsre Herzen,
Erleuchte unsre Häupter,
Dass gut werde, was wir aus Herzen gründen,
Was wir aus Häuptern zielvoll führen wollen.

Rudolf Steiner: The Foundation Stone Meditation
of the Christmas Conference; Elisabeth Vreede's handwriting (page 4)

When introducing the Section leaders, Rudolf Steiner said in connection with naming the ailing Edith Maryon who was to take on the Section for the Visual Arts:

> And there is another person who has marked out her territory in the world so clearly that whenever advice or help is needed in the realm of mathematics and astronomy it comes from her. You, and especially those resident in Dornach, can see from the content of my most recent lectures, including those given here before the last cycle, how unnecessary it is, especially in the field of astronomy, to go back to the more ancient conceptions. If you consider a small note in my memoirs, which are now appearing in *Das Goetheanum*—at the very beginning of the article coming out this evening—you will see how very profound the reasons are for the motto over Plato's Academy: "God geometrizes." And, indeed, it is possible to penetrate platonic instruction only by means of mathematics—I am speaking of platonic instruction, not spiritual-scientific instruction. Everything that needs to be put straight in this field must be put straight, and I believe you will be as enthusiastic as you were in the other cases when I tell you that, in the future, I shall let this area be tended through *Fräulein Dr. Vreede* as the Section leader.[159]

It was important to Rudolf Steiner to have a "Section for Mathematics and Astronomy"[160] in Dornach; "the astronomical science has the greatest possibility to be led back into spirituality."[161] It was possible for Rudolf Steiner to found this School Section because Elisabeth Vreede lived and was present in Dornach. His mystery lectures directly before the beginning of the Christmas Conference, but also the evening lectures during the Conference, were permeated with macrocosmic contemplations. Knowledge of the cosmos is part of Anthroposophy's core; conscious reunion of human beings with their greater surroundings, which have been almost completely lost in the past few centuries. Soon after the Christmas Conference Rudolf Steiner wrote, "Anthroposophy is a path of knowledge that wishes to lead the spiritual in the being of the human to the spiritual in the cosmos."[162] With Ita Wegman, he could establish a new art of healing, and with Marie Steiner the stage and speech arts and eurythmy. Steiner had hoped to work closely with Guenther Wachsmuth, Albert Steffen, and Edith Maryon to further the fields of natural science and the arts. Elisabeth Vreede, however, represented the knowledge of the stars—astronomy, cosmology, and cosmosophy, with which she belonged to the core of what Rudolf Steiner intended with the School in Dornach.

Unlike with the other Section leaders, with the introduction of Elisabeth Vreede, Rudolf Steiner accentuated not only her competence in her field but also her *social* capabilities. Precisely she, per Steiner, gave "advice and help" everywhere, "whenever one needed to know something in the mathematics–astronomy field." Indeed Elisabeth Vreede had special talents in relating to and understanding others. In spite of her high intelligence and her specialized knowledge that enabled her to work independently, she participated in a practical manner in many studies, research activities, and in the requests and wishes of other people. "She accepted the other people and let them stand beside her as equals. Never did she show a sense of superiority over others (Fiechter).[163] Vreede possessed organizing clarity, overview, objectivity, warmth, and a great sense of humor that she once described as "what frees a person in the spiritual life."[164] Indeed she was of a choleric temperament and could therefore be morally irascible. Yet, she had a great deal of patience with people, could recognize significant works already in their first beginnings and was always ready to support them with a secure feeling for individual freedom and responsibility. It was out of this fundamental inner nature that she built up and led the "Rudolf Steiner Archive at the Goetheanum" and other initiatives. This was not lost on Rudolf Steiner. As a rule, she got over human disappointments quickly; she was a mature soul and was filled with positivity and goodwill toward others. Mathematician Ernst Bindel wrote:

> She kept to the primary colors, the primary nature, of human beings and accepted their little cracks and the light. When she sensed the primary nature as being real, she then gave her whole love. Yet

this love was, in turn, totally unsentimental; she expressed herself much more in a loving interest for everything that moved the other person, whether the greatest or the smallest thing. Without much fuss she was helpful to the other person and maintained unwavering loyalty to that one, as long as the person remained loyal to him- or herself.[165]

In this way Elisabeth Vreede was an ideal Section leader, and her appointment was fully justified. Vreede was just as lacking in prominence and popularity as Edith Maryon; she did not like being in the spotlight and worked selflessly in the background. At the same time, she was capable of speaking impressively and convincingly before a large audience about mathematical and astronomical principles. She was able to rethink much and to change what needed to be corrected scientifically. Elisabeth Vreede was an unusual woman, an exception in Dornach, as was Ita Wegman. The anthroposophical social milieu during these years was made up of men who led the initiatives and gave the significant presentations. Women worked mostly at home or with the costumes and veils for the stage, in the arts. This division of the roles does not belong to the central nature of Anthroposophy, but was a constituent element of the time. An experienced business woman and dominant, successful director of the clinic such as Ita Wegman was quite unusual; but also a woman educated in mathematics and astronomy, a woman in a masculine field of science, caused a commotion and was a bone of contention. The corresponding judgments and half-consciousness emotions, however, were of little interest to Rudolf Steiner. He appointed those to the Executive Council and to the leadership of the School faculty who were capable of accomplishments and were competent; those who had distinguished themselves in their field and promised a future; people with whom he could work closely together and whose path of destiny he was aware of.

~

Little was known later about the work of the "esoteric Executive Council" during Rudolf Steiner's life in 1924. The exact minutes of the meetings do not exist, but Elisabeth Vreede indicated that this activity was surrounded by difficulties. "Positive work," per Vreede, could have hardly taken place. "Dr. Steiner had too much old rubble to clear away."[166] The difficulties of the old Anthroposophical Society had in no way disappeared through the Christmas Conference. Old dignitaries and functionaries continued to work; also old traditions and hindrances; also old practices and misuses. In the Executive Council meetings Rudolf Steiner said repeatedly in very clear language what he thought of individual "prominent figures" of the Anthroposophical Society and their manner of behaving; about ways of diplomacy and half-finished deeds; about personal vanities; about lack of transparency in office; misuse of power, and more. Hedwig Zaiser, who was close to Elisabeth Vreede and later lived a longer time in her house, wrote, "What was said and the judgments about people in the Executive Council meetings with Dr. Steiner in the course of 1924 were her (Elisabeth Vreede's) guideline. They were extremely strict in some cases, as she revealed to me in private conversations."[167]

In the beginning of June 1924 Rudolf Steiner authorized a list of "Goetheanum-speakers"; only these people should, and were, allowed to speak as representatives for the General Anthroposophical Society (under the name of the Goetheanum). A new impulse should begin from the core of Anthroposophy, its esoteric center. At the Christmas Conference Rudolf Steiner said:

> Whatever the realm, we must stand in the world under the sign of the full truth as representatives of the essence of Anthroposophy. We must be aware that if we are incapable of doing so, we cannot actually further the aims of the anthroposophic movement. Any veiled representation of the anthroposophic movement leads in the end to no good.
>
> If we ask ourselves over and over again what we must do to make ourselves better liked by this circle or by that circle in the world, by any circle that does not like us today; if we keep asking ourselves how we should behave in this field or in that field so as to be taken seriously here or there; if we do this, we shall most

certainly not be taken seriously. We shall only be taken seriously, if at every moment in whatever we do, we feel responsible toward the spiritual world. We must know that the spiritual world wants to achieve a certain thing with humankind at this particular moment in historical evolution; it wants to achieve this in the most varied realms of life, and it is up to us clearly and truly to follow the impulses that come from the spiritual world. Though this might give offense initially, in the long run it is the only beneficial way. Therefore, we shall also only come to terms among ourselves if at every opportunity we steep ourselves in whatever impulses can come from the spiritual world.

Many compromises were made in the last number of years by prominent representatives of the Anthroposophical Society. Rudolf Steiner spoke of "falseness" and wanted a clear, new beginning—*"and it is our responsibility to follow in clarity and truthfulness the impulses from the spiritual world."*

Among the difficulties of the Executive Council work in 1924 from the beginning, as Elisabeth Vreede continued to maintain, was not only the problems of the "old" Anthroposophical Society, but also the tension between individual members of the newly created group. Especially for Marie Steiner the situation was more than unfamiliar. She had actually led the Anthroposophical Society for twenty-one years at the side of Rudolf Steiner; now she saw herself confronted with people like Ita Wegman and Elisabeth Vreede in a circle of responsibility that she herself, as a "colleague," did not want and would not have created.[170] As with all of Rudolf Steiner's decisions and intentions, Marie Steiner respected also this; yet the situation was complicated. At the beginning of 1935 Elisabeth Vreede wrote in a retrospective, "It is true...that, from the first moment, there were differences in this Executive Council that then led to the unhealthy development that did come about. Through these conflicts (which later arose with increasing frequency), the brief time of Rudolf Steiner's work in the Executive Council was basically painful and sad, despite the wonderful lectures and so on."[171]

> Anthroposophische Gesellschaft.
>
> Sekretariat: Dornach b/Basel (Schweiz). Telephon: Dornach 133. Postcheck V 5827.
>
> Haus Friedwart 1.Stock. den 6. Juni 1924
>
> Sehr geehrter Herr Dr. Schubert,
>
> Mit Bezug auf unsere Ausführungen im Mitteilungsblatt Nr. 20 vom 25. Mai 1924 gestatten wir uns, Ihnen mitzuteilen, dass wir als Vorstand der Anthroposophischen Gesellschaft am Goetheanum Sie als einen von uns autorisierten und im Namen dieser Anthroposophischen Gesellschaft sprechenden Redner in Zweig- und öffentlichen Vorträgen anerkennen.
>
> Mit freundlichem Gruss
>
> Dr. Rudolf Steiner, Vorsitzender   Dr. I. Wegman

Karl Schubert's recognition as "Goetheanum speaker"

The year 1924 was a "painful and sad time," per Vreede, with regard to the esoteric Executive Council in Dornach. Rudolf Steiner said to Oskar Schmiedel already in December 1923, "If the agitation and propaganda against Ita Wegman continues, it will lead to the shattering of the Society."[172] On the other hand, the time after the Christmas Conference had a special fullness such as Dornach and the Anthroposophical Society had never seen before. Although the School and Society had to be newly formed and instituted and many tasks connected with them had to be taken care of, Rudolf Steiner moved forward with a tremendous tempo with (spiritual) content. Immediately after the Christmas Conference he continued his general anthroposophical lectures on a high level, and parallel to this, he gave instruction for medical students and doctors; instruction that, first of all, showed how they should begin to penetrate esoterically a specialized field and that spirit should ensoul the new School.[173] He began the Class Lessons and the karma lectures in mid-February; at Easter he held a large members' conference that connected with much from the Christmas Conference. Then the Class Lessons and lectures followed in Paris—the agriculture course, the curative education course, and all the rest—in a breathless, forward-pressing dynamic. *"It was a powerful stream of real spiritual life that went through the [anthroposophic] movement at that time"* (Vreede).[174]

Elisabeth Vreede was in Paris in May 1924 and traveled with Steiner and Wachsmuth during the beginning of June to Koberwitz by Breslau, where the course on agriculture took place at the castle of Count Keyserlink. Steiner included Vreede fully and decisively and pointed out in different ways the significance that her astronomical work would have for working with the new agriculture; she would work as a knowledgeable colleague in directing the agricultural tests of the newly established research organization from the Goetheanum.[175]

As in the old mystery centers and olden times, so in the future there should be made possible from Dornach an agriculture on a scientific level that takes into account the cosmic forces, influences and the times.[176] This was to take place with the support of Elisabeth Vreede

"Tested to the ultimate degree" (1924–1925)

Das Archiv wird für diejenigen, die ein bestimmtes Fachstudium betreiben geöffnet sein :

Täglich (ausser Sonntag)

von 10 - 12

Anfragen zu richten an Frl. Dr Vreede.

RUDOLF STEINER-ARCHIV
AM GOETHEANUM
DORNACH, Schweiz

Open hours for the Rudolf Steiner Archive at the Goetheanum (Easter 1924)

and Guenther Wachsmuth, who was the leader of the Section for Natural Science, but also of Lili Kolisko and her "Biological Institute at the Goetheanum," in which the pioneering research in the nature of substance was already done. Elisabeth Vreede had great respect for Lili Kolisko; respect for the particular quality of her specialized work and her inner composure. On the way back from Koberwitz, Elisabeth Vreede was with Rudolf Steiner and Guenther Wachsmuth in Jena and at "Lauenstein," where young anthroposophists, with Steiner's support, had founded a home for curative education shortly before.

On June 18, 1924, Rudolf Steiner gave indications for the education and treatment there for each individual child. A few weeks later, those working with curative education were to come to Dornach for a special course (in Curative Education). In the late afternoon of the day before traveling to Stuttgart Rudolf Steiner wanted surprisingly to go yet to Weimar, where years earlier he had lived and worked for seven years.[30] ("Evening was gradually approaching, even though the Sun still stood high in the summer sky. Dr. Steiner had to think about traveling further. He said he would gladly stop briefly in Weimar."[177]) The trip to Weimar was by car. Guenther Wachsmuth, Steiner's secretary, later described the evening spent together in the city. Wachsmuth's report that was published in 1941 in his book *Die Geburt der Geisteswissenschaft* (The birth of Spiritual Science), which mentioned Rudolf Steiner's anecdotes, the humorous search for his former residence, and the happy mood. ("On this day in Weimar, Rudolf Steiner's mood was one of fulfillment, carried by the work of the previous days, and reminiscing, brought forth magically by Weimar's atmosphere."[178])

Wachsmuth recalled attending the theater and seeing a play by Schiller, but not which play—it was (just a "play by Schiller"). Later it was recorded in a chronicle that it was "The Maid of Orleans."[179] Wachsmuth did not mention that Elisabeth Vreede was with them at Lauenstein or in Weimar. It was either forgotten or consciously ignored—six years after she had been removed from the Executive Council and the Society. ("He showed *me* the house where he had lived.... He took *me* to that café" [Wachsmuth].[180]) However, Elisabeth Vreede wrote her memories of the time with Rudolf Steiner in Weimar already on June 21, 1924, immediately after her return to Arlesheim. She had totally different, more exact and finer emphases than Wachsmuth. She recorded the experiences immediately, which was three months before the beginning of Rudolf Steiner's final illness:

> The Schiller House and the Goethe House were already closed. Dr. Steiner tried to find Professsor Wahle, the current director of the Goethe–Schiller Archive, hoping he would let him in despite the late hour. The director was not at home. Also, we did not meet anyone he knew in the park where we went for a walk. In the evening we went to a performance of *Wallensteins Tod* [Wallenstein's death] presented "in honor of the Members of the Schiller Association." There were also no representatives from the old days to be seen in the Weimar Theater; it appeared to be more of a student presentation, and the audience was made up mostly of young girls who were boarders and the corresponding young boys.
>
> Because our train left for Stuttgart at 11:00 p.m., we had to leave the theater before the performance was over.
>
> This visit in Weimar after many years' absence (It was exactly twenty-seven years since Dr. Steiner's move from Weimar to Berlin and about twenty years since his last lecture there) had a somewhat tragic character. As wonderful as it was for us, his companions, to travel to Weimar with Dr. Steiner and to talk with him about his time there, it was clear that Dr. Steiner had hoped somehow to find a connection to the time of his work there—a resonance for the account of this time that he had just begun in his *Autobiography*. Yet as it turned out, nothing and no one, not one person, knew him in spite of the fact that many gazed at him in astonishment when they passed by. He noticed the desolation and emptiness of the city already in the early evening. On the way to the train station he said, "The city has become completely foreign to me." Only then did it occur to us that we could have contacted one of the anthroposophists there, perhaps to gain access in this way to the people desired. Apparently, Dr. Steiner had fully intended to allow his work there to be re-enlivened. It was, however, completely over; it was history.

Am 18. Juni 1924 war Herr Dr. Steiner in Jena, unmittelbar vor Breslau kommend und besichte die Heilanstalt für pathologische Kinder Lauenstein, die von einigen jüngeren Anthroposophen gegründet war. Herr Dr Günther Wachsmuth und ich waren mit ihm. Gegen 5 Uhr verliessen wir Jena per Auto und fuhren nach Weimar. Nachdem wir bei Chemmi Hürs den Kaffee genossen, wanderten wir durch Weimar. Das Schillerhaus, das Goethehaus waren schon geschlossen. Herr Dr Steiner versuchte den jetzigen Direktor des Goethe- und Schiller- Archivs, Prof Wahle, zu finden in der Hoffnung durch die Protektion der späten Stunde in das Archiv zugelassen zu werden, doch er traf ihn nicht zu Hause. Auch im Park, wo wir spazierten, traf wir der keine Bekannten angetroffen. Abends gingen wir in eine Aufführung von "Wallensteins Tod" veranstaltet zu Ehren der Mitglieder des Schillerbundes. Auch im Theater waren keine repräsentativen Weimarer der alten Zeit zu treffen, es schien sich nur um eine Schülervorstellung zu handeln und das Publikum bestand ganz über

Elisabeth Vreede: Memories of a stay in Weimar on June 18, 1924 (page 1)

Elisabeth Vreede: Memories of a stay in Weimar (page 2)

Elisabeth Vreede: Memories of a stay in Weimar (page 3)

Festspiele des Deutschen Nationaltheaters
zu Ehren
der Mitglieder des Deutschen Schillerbundes

Mittwoch, den 18. Juni 1924 / Außer Platzmiete

Wallensteins Tod

Trauerspiel in fünf Akten von Friedrich v. Schiller
Einrichtung und Spielleitung: Ernst Hardt

Wallenstein, Herzog von Friedland, Generalissimus im dreißigjährigen Kriege	Carl Schreiner
Oktavio Piccolomini, Generalleutnant	Hans Illiger
Max Piccolomini, sein Sohn, Oberst bei einem Küraffier-Regiment	Rudolf Rieth
Graf Terzky, Wallensteins Schwager, Chef mehrerer Regimenter	Eduard Heß, a. G.
Illo, Feldmarschall, Wallensteins Vertrauter	Max Bevck
Isolani, General der Kroaten	Wilhelm Holz
Buttler, Chef eines Dragoner-Regiments	Wilhelm Werth
Hauptmann Deverour / v. Buttl. Hauptm. Macdonald / lero Regt.	Hugo Brandes / Bruno Ferrand
Gordon, Kommandant von Eger	Richard Salzmann
Major Geraldin	Paul Glitsch
Ein Adjutant	Josef Salten
Oberst Wrangel, von den Schweden gesendet	Rudolf Bach
Baptista Senî, Astrolog	Peter Großmann
Schwedischer Hauptmann	Peter Großmann
Herzogin von Friedland	Martha Kaibel-Schiffel
Thekla, ihre Tochter	Kaete Nadel
Gräfin Terzky	Erika Kristen
Fräulein Neubrunn, Hofdame der Prinzessin	Elisabeth Schulz
von Rosenberg, Stallmeister der Prinzessin	Hennig Nolte
Kammerdiener des Herzogs	August Nehkopf
Erster Küraffier	Rudolf Bach
Zweiter Küraffier	Hennig Nolte
Dritter	Max Darmünzel
Page des Wallenstein	Käthe Hopf
Bürgermeister von Eger	Hans Antony
Ein Bedienter	Ernst Rosé, a. B.

Pappenheimische Küraffiere. Buttlerliche Dragoner. Pagen. Bediente. Kammerfrauen

Die Szene ist in den vier ersten Akten zu Pilsen, im letzten zu Eger vom 23. bis 25. Februar 1634

Spielwart: Otto Schnelting

Nach dem 3. und 4. Bilde je 10 Minuten Pause

Preise der Plätze
(einschl. Gebühr für Kleiderablage und Theaterzettel sowie Abgabe für den Altersunterstützungsschatz)

Fremdenlauben, 1. u. 2. R. 6,— G.-M.	I. Rang, hintere Reihen 5,— G.-M.	II. Rang, Mitte 3,50 M.-G.	
Fremdenlaube, hint. Reihen 5,70	I. Saalplatz 5,—	II. Seite 3,—	
I. Rang, Lauben 5,50	II. 4,50	III. Mitte 2,50	
I. „ 1. Reihe 5,20	III.	III. 1,50	

(Über sämtliche Plätze im Saal und II. Rang Mitte ist bereits verfügt)
Bestellte Karten müssen spätestens 30 Minuten vor Beginn der Vorstellung abgeholt werden

Kassenöffnung 6 Uhr   **Anfang 7 Uhr**   **Ende 10¾ Uhr**

Freikarten I, II und III haben keine Gültigkeit

Krank: Marlies Homann, Claus Clausen, Bernhard Vollmer

Wochenspielplan:

Donnerstag, den 19. Außer Platzmiete **Tannhäuser**, große romantische Oper in drei Akten von R. Wagner Anfang 4½, Ende 8¼ Uhr

Freitag, den 20. Außer Platzmiete **Egmont**, Trauerspiel in fünf Akten von Goethe Musik von Beethoven Anfang 6, Ende 10¼ Uhr (Über sämtliche Plätze im Saal und II. Rang Mitte ist bereits verfügt)

Sonnabend, den 21. Für die Jenaer Freie Volksbühne: **Peer Gynt**, ein dramatisches Gedicht von Henrik Ibsen Musik von Edvard Grieg Anfang 7, Ende 11½ Uhr (Verkäufliche Eintrittskarten: Fremdenlauben)

Sonntag, den 22. Außer Platzmiete **Figaros Hochzeit**, komische Oper in vier Akten von Mozart Anfang 5, Ende 8½ Uhr

durch sie davon gehört. Es ist in diesen Fällen nicht verlangt worden, dass etwas von der Sternkonstellationen gewusst wird, sie schienen für die Erkenntnis des Krankheitsbildes zunächst nicht notwendig. Selbstverständlich wären sehr viele Aufschlüsse daraus zu gewinnen, aber gerade diese Wissenschaft, nicht okkultisch, sondern rein geisteswiss. betrieben, ist erst ganz an ihrem Anfang. Ist es doch die letzte und höchste der geistigen Wissenschaften. Ich glaube nicht, dass wir durch Betrachtung des gewöhnlichen Horoskopes viel gewinnen. Was hier vorliegt, ist offensichtlich eine abnorme Verbindung zwischen Geistig-Seelischen und Physisch-Leiblichen, die jetzt aber wieder „normal" gemacht werden muss und die Ursachen dazu liegen selbstverständlich ganz in „karmischen" Regionen. Dieses auch aus den Sternkonstellationen abzulesen zu können wird doch nur mit tiefster Esoterik möglich sein.

Ich glaube nicht, dass Herr v. Klöckner viel weiter kommen würde, wenn er bloss einzelne Vorträge lesen könnte. Es handelt sich tatsächlich um ein gründliches Sicharbeiten in das Wesen der Anthroposophie, wie Sie ja auch sagen. Allmählig, hoffe ich, werden wir eine wirklich geisteswissenschaftl. Astrologie herausarbeiten

Herrn Schaefer werde ich bald schreiben;
Mit besten Grüssen Ihre E. Vreede.

Elisabeth Vreede: letter to Ernst Kunert, February 17, 1924

At 11:02 p.m. we departed from Weimar for Stuttgart.[181]

Elisabeth Vreede even took the theater handbill with her and saved it. The stages along the way with Rudolf Steiner were significant in every detail. Elisabeth Vreede had no obsessive desire to collect things as was insinuated. The task was given to her to write a history of Rudolf Steiner's work and life based on a complete existing archive and estate. Much could have been presented in greater detail and more deeply than has been possible to this day, or ever will be.

~

Only four days after Vreede wrote her notes on Weimar, the Curative Education Course began in the carpentry shop; she was present. Elisabeth Vreede followed with great love the development of the Stuttgart Waldorf School from the beginning onward. She also supported The Hague Waldorf School with all her strength and energy. In the meetings of the Executive Council she experienced how closely and concretely Rudolf Steiner wanted to form the relationship of the Goetheanum to the Stuttgart School after the Christmas Conference.

In April 1924 a large education conference took place for the first time; it was organized by the Executive Council of the General Anthroposophical Society together with the college of teachers. Vreede had diverse connections to the Waldorf school, both human and objective. Together with Eugen Kolisko, among others, she was active in arranging vacation accommodations for children of the school who were in need of rest and recovery,[182] and she let youth from The Hague School camp out in the garden at her house at "Auf der Höhe 1." Now, at the end of June 1924, she was present at the Curative Education Course in the carpentry shop of the Goetheanum and carried her godchild, Willfried Immanuel Kunert, in a small basket with her to the course. The treatment of this severely ill child had become very difficult in the last months. The attempt to conquer the progressive hydrocephalus was not successful; but Ita Wegman's and Rudolf Steiner's faith in the therapy was unshaken. Steiner asked Elisabeth Vreede to do a birth

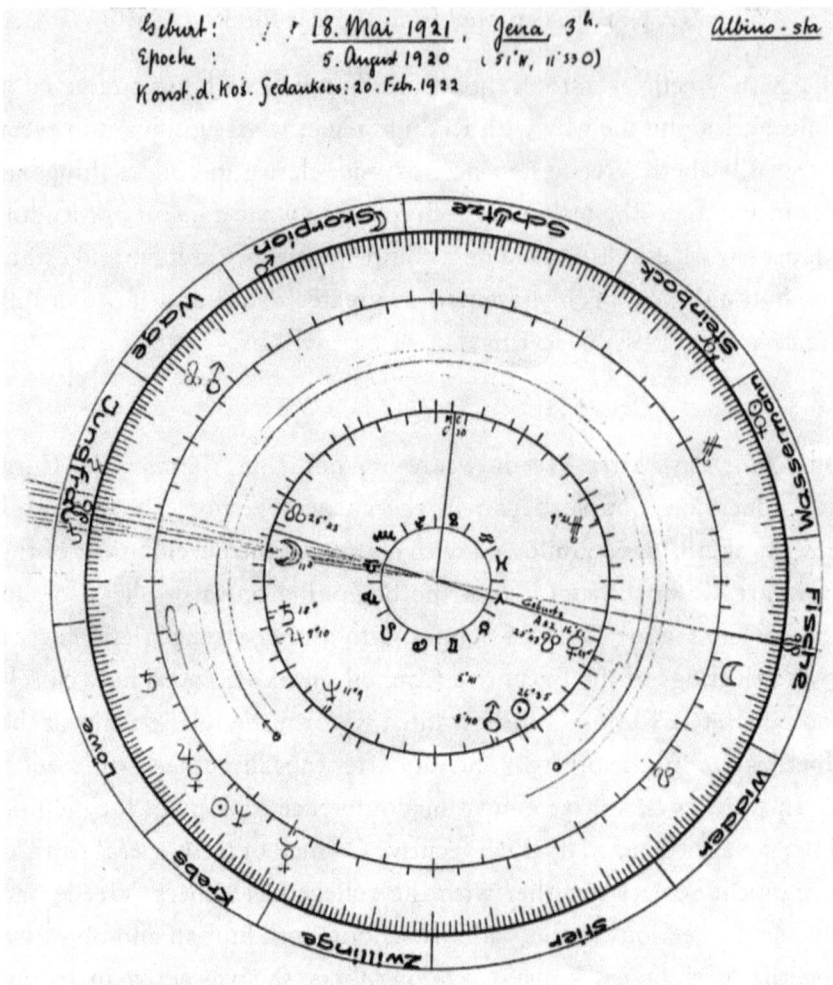

Elisabeth Vreede: Horoscope for a child in need of special care; from the "Curative Education Course"

star chart for several children in the Curative Education Course, also for Willfried Immanuel. Already in February Ernst Kunert, the child's father, had asked about this. Vreede had answered at that time:

> In this case, it is not required to know something from the star constellations; for the time being it appears not to be necessary for knowledge of the picture of the illness. Of course, quite a few insights could be attained from it, but *this* science, done in a manner that is not amateurish but as a pure Spiritual Science, is totally in its beginning. It is, nevertheless, the last and highest of the Spiritual Sciences. I don't think that we achieve much by considering the ordinary horoscope. What we have here is apparently an abnormal connection between the soul-spiritual and the physical, bodily aspects that must now be normalized again. The causes for this condition naturally lie totally in karmic spheres. To be able to read this also from the stars will be possible only with the deepest esotericism.[183]

Yet, later Rudolf Steiner asked Elisabeth Vreede to work out not only the birth horoscope of the child but also of the parents.[184] The constellations of the prenatal existence were significant; the "constellation of the cosmic thought."

In July 1924, Elisabeth Vreede was at the lectures in Arnheim (Rudolf Steiner's last lectures in Holland); in August she was in Torquai; then came the large September courses in the beginning of his being bedridden in the days of Michaelmas. Rudolf Steiner was completely exhausted from his absolute devotion to the future in wrestling with adversarial powers and an Anthroposophical Society remaining behind and failing in much.

~

During his illness, Elisabeth Vreede saw her teacher seldom—or not at all. In contrast to Ita Wegman who was with him daily, as well as to Guenther Wachsmuth and Albert Steffen who had regular meetings for affairs of the Anthroposophical Society. Elisabeth Vreede stood on the outside of the studio. Marie Steiner-von Sivers had been traveling a long time. When she returned to Dornach for three months, she spoke with Rudolf Steiner for one hour daily. Such a necessity did not exist for Vreede, so she remained in the background, as was often the case in her life.

For months Elisabeth Vreede would have liked to discuss much about the setting up of her Section with the teacher. Owing to a heavy schedule of appointments and duties in Steiner's life, there was no possibility of this. In September alone, he had received hundreds of members with questions—not Elisabeth Vreede, however, who was aware of the precious nature of Rudolf Steiner's time and fragile condition; thus, she pressed him in no way. Wilhelm Kaiser, a young astronomer and colleague of Vreede, had prepared a publication for the "Astronomy Course" in January 1921. It was a paper on Steiner's lectures with a discussion of their content and was waiting for his permission to issue it. Elisabeth Vreede would have liked to move forward with this, because the course would deal with the spiritual core of her Section.

On January 1, 1925, she wrote to Rudolf Steiner in his studio about this. However, she received only a short answer: "in my condition now, it is really completely impossible for me to deal with this. I do not have the strength to do it, and I risk something bad if I were to destroy my strength with such a matter."[185] Rudolf Steiner's condition was painful at that time, yet a few weeks later he looked at Kaiser's treatise and gave permission for its publication. Thus, the course was published in the year of Rudolf Steiner's death, with the title *Astronomy in the Light of Spiritual Science*.

Also Elisabeth Vreede's contact with Ita Wegman for conversation was probably very marginal. Wegman seldom left the studio; yet, they saw and spoke with each other in passing. Elisabeth Vreede sent regularly from the library in the carpentry shop the books Rudolf Steiner needed for writing his *Autobiography* (*Mein Lebensgang*) to Ita Wegman in the studio. "She (Wegman) always said in return that he was always grateful; he was very caring toward the Archive."[186] A few days before his death, Elisabeth Vreede inadvertently drew

"Tested to the ultimate degree" (1924–1925)

Rudolf Steiner into difficulties that had to do with the Archive and her own person. Guenther Wachsmuth had decided to merge the Rudolf Steiner Archive with the library in the carpentry and to put Günther Schubert in charge of both. He had already had a conversation with Schubert about this (who declined due to an overload of work). Vreede was more than disconcerted over Wachsmuth's high-handedness. Wachsmuth, thirty-one years old, went energetically and goal-oriented to work at the Goetheanum. His attitude was that of organizer and "man of action," without much consideration for others and with limited knowledge of important connections. He barely saw Elisabeth Vreede's work—or not at all. She had built the Archive herself, through her own commitment, capabilities, and years of effort. Later Elisabeth Vreede wrote about this occurrence and its consequence.

> That such a thing was possible at all, that someone could go behind the back of another and take the authority to decide about that person's work without giving a thought to the human being who had done the work and who was connected to it with her whole soul—that was what crushed me. I could not sleep at all that night. The next day I saw Dr. Wegman, who was taking care of Dr. Steiner. She asked me what was wrong, because I looked so bad. I told her what had happened; and without my asking her to, she told Dr. Steiner about it. Dr. Wegman...told me afterward that Dr. Steiner then told Dr. Wachsmuth off. The Doctor said to him, "Wachsmuth, you may not do such a thing. The Archive is Fräulein Vreede's work. You may not take it away from her![187]

Then Rudolf Steiner died late in the morning of March 30, 1925, a Tuesday. Marie Steiner was on her way from Stuttgart; Albert Steffen and Guenther Wachsmuth (whom Wegman let be called) and Ita Wegman was with the teacher in the hour of his death. Not, however, Elisabeth Vreede who sat in the anteroom of the studio along with Margarete Kirchner-Bockholt and a few other friends. She was not asked in, not even by Ita Wegman. Again, she was forgotten or overlooked, as so often in her life.

Rudolf Steiner's sculpture of the head of the Christ figure

"Tested to the ultimate degree" (1924–1925)

Yet, Vreede's thoughts in this situation were not about her own personal condition, the special circumstances of her biography; nor with Wegman, or Wachsmuth, or the Archive. Her thoughts were with Rudolf Steiner—the spiritual teacher whose life work she had accompanied closely for over twenty-one years and who died beside his Christ sculpture.

"*In Christo morimur*—In Christ death becomes life."

4

"Executive Council's Idylls" (1925–1935)

The Decade after Rudolf Steiner's Death

"I will determine my stance totally out of myself."
—Elisabeth Vreede
(General Meeting, 1934)[188]

"I declare herewith that I strove throughout more than ten years to perform my activity on the Executive Council—under infinitely difficult circumstances—with the deepest feeling of responsibility."
—Elisabeth Vreede
("Document of Justification" 1935)[189]

Elisabeth Vreede (undated)

The shared sorrow over Rudolf Steiner's death was great. Yet, already on March 30, 1925, the paths of the members of the esoteric Executive Council went in different directions after the poor cohesion during the preceding year. "The fight over the continuation of the Society broke out immediately in the first moment" (Vreede).[190]

Guenther Wachsmuth organized the funeral service "in a glowing manner," right after the announcement of Rudolf Steiner's death. "One had the feeling that he really blossomed out in this task" (Vreede).[191] In comparison, the tense and adverse mood with regard to Ita Wegman could be felt in the first hours after Marie Steiner's arrival in Dornach. It did not surprise Vreede, but was of a disconcerting and disturbing nature.[192] According to Marie Steiner's intentions three days later, Elisabeth Vreede was at first not supposed to ride with the others in the Executive Council's car to the cremation in Basel; rather it was to be Miete Pyle Waller and her husband. On the way back home to Dornach the confrontation continued.

> Frau Dr. Wegman said that she hoped we would often come together for meetings in Dr. Steiner's studio. Frau Dr. Steiner said that she had the intention to ask the Executive Council to let her have the studio, in order to organize Dr. Steiner's estate.... Upon Dr. Wegman's objection, saying that we want, however, to keep the studio in commemoration together, she said that the studio held no good memories for her anyway. She said that Dr. Steiner was always together with Fräulein Maryon in there, and quite pathetically she yelled out, "I have put up with what no other woman would have!"—I shuddered at this outburst of petty jealousy in precisely *this* moment.[193]

Marie Steiner's outburst hit Elisabeth Vreede hard, in view of Rudolf Steiner and her departed friend, Edith Maryon. Only later did she realize that it was also (or, first and foremost) meant for Ita Wegman. So it continued, with an extreme strain on the soul forces and bewilderment over the death of the teacher, all in great chaos. On the same day, in the Executive Council's car, the fight over the urn occurred between Marie Steiner and Ita Wegman, after a second trip back from the Basel cemetery. It was an almost absurd situation.

> I saw in an image the whole Anthroposophical Society collapse; like a flash of lightning I became aware that the possibility that we should lead the Anthroposophical Society together was definitely over, before we had even begun to approach our tasks.... Never in my life have I had such a clear imagination as in this moment. (Vreede)[194]

One day later Albert Steffen brought a letter from Marie Steiner into the Executive Council meeting. She announced her withdrawal from the Executive Council and made recommendations for alternative personnel. Afterward Ita Wegman, Elisabeth Vreede, Albert Steffen and Guenther Wachsmuth persuaded Marie Steiner to remain on the Council instituted by Rudolf Steiner and given such high power—this Council that she considered "a nothing" after March 30, 1925. The mood of the meetings, per Elisabeth Vreede, continued to be "terrible."

> Frau Dr. Steiner acted like the queen who was to be satisfied under all circumstances. She scolded Dr. Wegman at every opportunity and often made her cry in the meetings. Herr Steffen accepted Frau Doctor, mostly in an outwardly polite, gentlemanly manner. I remain silent as much as possible. Dr. Wachsmuth brought the newest practical matters that had to be handled, since Dr. Wegman had not gotten involved at all with the office of secretary in a concrete way (which would otherwise have led to endless difficulties with the others). And since the death of Dr. Steiner, Dr. Wachsmuth had managed all the business that came in a reliable and independent manner. The only point that Dr. Wegman brought forward was the leadership of the Class.[196]

There was little understanding within the esoteric Executive Council for Ita Wegman's relationship to the Class, although

Rudolf Steiner had expressed her special responsibility repeatedly in word and deeds.[197] Only Elisabeth Vreede was willing to recognize "that great responsibility in the matter of the Class had been conferred upon her by Rudolf Steiner,"[198] although also her Knowledge about the circumstances of this time was quite limited. Ita Wegman strove for continuing to hold Rudolf Steiner's Class Lessons. Marie Steiner, however, wanted to wait. Wegman knew what significance Rudolf Steiner placed on these Lessons for the further progress of the General Anthroposophical Society and the Dornach School, and she felt that she had the authority to repeat the Esoteric Lessons by reading Rudolf Steiner's original wording aloud to others.[199] Rudolf Steiner had admitted her into the leadership of the First Class. The Lessons were, per Vreede, the "only point" that Ita Wegman addressed in the weeks following Rudolf Steiner's death; they were essential to her.

After the successful declaration of permission, Ita Wegman finally held a First Class Lesson at the Anthroposophical Conference in Paris on May 23, 1925. It was two months after Rudolf Steiner's death and in the presence of Elisabeth Vreede who lectured in Paris on astronomy. "Dr. Wegman told me herself before this Class Lesson that she wished to begin in Paris where she could prepare in a smaller, closed group for the difficult task of holding the Class in Dornach. That seemed insightful and justified."[200] The Lesson in Paris was not a matter of internal politics in the Dornach leadership Council, although at least Marie Steiner was against it. As Ita Wegman then held her first (Class) Lesson in Dornach, Albert Steffen introduced her as the "secretary" whom the Executive Council asked to do this, in spite of an agreement beforehand that Ita Wegman's special responsibility for the First Class was to be expressed. Rudolf Steiner had spoken *expressis verbis* about the fact that Ita Wegman is in the leadership of the Class; and as of September 1924, new Class members were admitted in a ritual that included a handshake with him and Ita Wegman.[201] Ita Wegman herself was admitted by Rudolf Steiner into the joint responsibility or shared leadership of the Class after a cultic-ritual act. In connection with this procedure, Steiner gave her his Rose Cross.[202] With the exception of Elisabeth Vreede, no one in the circle of the Executive Council colleagues wanted to know anything of this, also not when Ita Wegman—whether they wanted it or not—began to speak about it. In no way did she enter into the position of responsibility for the Class as secretary, but rather on the basis of her spiritual working jointly with Rudolf Steiner. She tried repeatedly in the next years to awaken an understanding among her colleagues, but did not succeed. She held the Dornach Class Lesson in spite of the introductory words of Albert Steffen. Elisabeth Vreede, however, wrote:

> It was like a slap in the face, because this formulation [invited as secretary by the Executive Council] completely covered up the fact of Frau Dr. Wegman's special connection with the Class and introduced her as being somehow asked by the Executive Council, without it becoming noticeable why one would select precisely the secretary to do this. I have always felt this announcement by Herr Steffen to be a betrayal....[203]

At the end of the Class Lesson followed, per Vreede, the next irritation from the circle of the colleagues. "Just as the reading ended and Frau Dr. Wegman said she would now write the mantras on the blackboard so the members could copy them, and she began with the first mantra with which Dr. Steiner began every Lesson, Frau Dr. Steiner called out loudly to Frau Kolisko who sat near her, 'Did Dr. Steiner ever *write this* mantra?' Then she stood up energetically and left the hall in an ostentatious way."[204]

So it went on, in a "decline by degrees" (Lili Kolisko),[205] emotional and hurtful, far beneath the necessary spiritual level and in a real lack of knowledge and consciousness.[206] Rudolf Steiner had Edith Maryon in mind for the Executive Council, which did not come about due to her illness and early death on May 1, 1924. Maryon's presence might have had a balancing effect as an advanced, quiet esotericist with whom Steiner also had an intensive working relationship. The burning of the Goetheanum, however, had destroyed everything, even the

Meine lieben Freunde,
Bevor ich zur Klassenstunde übergehe
d. h. bevor ich dasjenige vorlese, was
Dr Steiner uns gegeben hat in der ersten Klassenstunde
~~die er~~ in Dornach am 15ten Februar 1924
~~gegeben~~ gehalten hat, möchte ich noch einiges
sagen. nach der Weihnachtstagung
Dr Steiner gründete in der Hochschule für
Geisteswissenschaft eine esoterische Schule,
die er die Michael Schule nannte und
die aus 3 Klassen bestehen sollte.
Die Michael Schule ist also identisch mit
der Hochschule für Geisteswissenschaft,
Michael Schule ist der esoterische Name
für die Hochschule für Geisteswissenschaft.
Es wurde eben in Dornach mit dieser
Schule ein Anfang gemacht, und zwar
mit der ersten Klasse.
Leider musste es bei der 1sten Klasse
bleiben.
Dasjenige was vorgelesen wird, und es
kan nur vorgelesen werden, meine
lieben Freunde, weil dadurch Michael
Worte unverändert, so wie Dr Steiner
sie gesprochen hat Ihnen wiedergegeben
wird; dasjenige was vorgelesen wird

Ita Wegman: Introductory words before a Class Lesson, 1925

life of the English artist who had come to Dornach with Vreede and was very connected with her.

Ita Wegman was "constantly attacked" in the Executive Council meetings during the first months after Rudolf Steiner's death.[207] Yet, in no way did Vreede stand by Wegman without reservations. She supported her in the Class issue and in moral elements. Vreede was, however, in no way in agreement with the first article that Wegman published unexpectedly at the end of April 1925 in the *News Sheet*, where she appeared to be speaking for the whole Executive Council about plans. It seemed to her to be a non-collaborative declaration of a principle and completely one-sided. ("The essay by Frau Dr. Wegman—the content was completely unknown to me, otherwise, I would have fought against it with all my might—was biased to a much stronger degree, or one-sided, than I had expected."[208]) Ita Wegman knew well that her position in this article in no way represented a consensus in the Executive Council. Yet, she wrote:

> It was clear to us, whom Rudolf Steiner selected to be the Executive Council, that we may not abandon positions arranged by him. It was clear to us that it is a sacred duty—if we want to take seriously what the Master gave us from the spiritual world—to remain as a group around him; so that, although he is not with us physically, he can still work among us and in us. This attitude prevailed in us. Thus, we still consider Rudolf Steiner as the first president within our Executive Council and all Executive Council members as in the functions in which Rudolf Steiner installed them.[209]

Elisabeth Vreede shared Ita Wegman's view of the esoteric Executive Council, at least in principle, yet not Wegman's high-handed, socially independent action.

Thus, Vreede took an independent stance in Steiner's instituted leadership Council soon after Rudolf Steiner's death. She stood, as always in her life, independent and free in her own power of discernment. The developments of the next years should have brought her close to Ita Wegman; also others shoved her strategically into this closeness. Elisabeth Vreede, however, did not see herself there (in this closeness) and wrote in the beginning of 1935 in retrospect:

> I have had to fight throughout the years against the other Executive Council members' attempt—especially that of Herr Steffen—to throw me into one "party" with Frau Dr. Wegman. Through the years, they have wanted constantly to turn my actions for the "whole Executive Council" into the opposite. If Frau Dr. Wegman has not held it against me that I constantly pull away from her for the good of the whole Executive Council, it is because she, too, wanted to remain loyal to the "whole Executive Council.[210]

Despite all of the Executive Council difficulties and in spite of heavy personal strokes of destiny—among them the death of her mother in May 1925 and of her godchild Willfried Immanuel Kunert in November of the same year—Elisabeth Vreede took up her work with her Section. The School Section "for Mathematic and Astronomic Views" had to be organized and further developed, even if the General Anthroposophical Society had no leadership Council capable of functioning. In 1937, fourteen (two times seven) years after the Christmas Conference, Elisabeth Vreede wrote in a retrospective:

> It was necessary to build this Section completely from the primordial beginning. With this work I have always attempted to look around wherever possible to see where seeds of a spiritualized mathematics or astronomy could be found. I have tried to bring all those striving in this field into a relationship with the Goetheanum and the Section for Mathematics and Astronomy. In 1926 I published the course *Das Verhältnis der Astronomie zu den verschiedenen naturwissenschaftlichen Gebiete* [The relationship of astronomy to the various natural scientific fields]. In 1929 I began to distribute basic astronomical concepts through circulars. In five years I worked through the field of astronomy and also did an overview of astrology in the light of Spiritual Science, as far as was possible for me to do. These circulars met with great approval. In spite of the fact that I advertised it only once in the *News Sheet* and the fact that it was hushed up in every General Meeting and

Was in der Anthroposophischen Gesellschaft vorgeht

Nachrichten für deren Mitglieder

2. Jahrgang, No. 17 — 26. April 1925

Das Abonnement des „*Goetheanum*" wird durch das Mitteilungsblatt erhöht auf jährl. 19 Fr., halbjährl. 10.50 Fr., vierteljährl. 5.75 Fr. Die gleiche Betragserhöhung kommt zu dem Abonnements-Preis für das Ausland hinzu. Das Abonnement für „*Was in der Anthroposophischen Gesellschaft vorgeht*" ohne „*Das Goetheanum*" beträgt jährlich 11 Fr., halbjährl. 6 Fr., vierteljährl. 3.25 Fr., wobei für das Ausland entsprechend der Postgebühr eine Erhöhung eintritt.

In Erinnerung an die Weihnachtstagung
Dr. I. Wegman

In vollem Bewusstsein, aber ohne ein Wort über die Zukunft gesprochen, ohne Anweisungen oder Botschaften für diese oder jene Persönlichkeit hinterlassen zu haben, ist der Meister von uns weggegangen. Und eine direkte Frage diesbezüglich wurde bewusst mit nein beantwortet. Warum war das?

Klar vor unserem Geiste steht die Weihnachtstagung, die ein einschneidendes Ereignis für die Anthroposophische Gesellschaft bedeutet. Kein Mitglied, das diese Tagung mitgemacht hat, ist nicht voll davon überzeugt, dass die Anthroposophische Gesellschaft mit dieser Tagung eine Vertiefung und eine Richtung bekam, die gegenüber dem Bisherigen einen neuen selbständigen Ausgang schuf. Sie war von jetzt an nicht nur die Anthroposophische Gesellschaft allein, sondern in ihr war nun auch die Anthroposophische Bewegung darinnen, weil Rudolf Steiner als Führer dieser Anthroposophischen Bewegung mit unerhörtem Elan, mit neuer Arbeitskraft, mit neuen Impulsen beseelt, diese mit der Anthroposophischen Gesellschaft verschmolz, die vorher getrennt von der Bewegung eine eigene Verwaltung mit eigenem Vorstand hatte. Von diesem Moment an, es war am 25. Dezember 1924, entstand ein neues Karma für die Anthroposophische Gesellschaft; zu dem alten, was sie hatte, kam neues hinzu, Rudolf Steiner identifizierte sich nun ab mit der Gesellschaft!

Ob jedes Mitglied es damals recht begriffen hatte, ob es begriffen, dass es von jetzt an neue und schwerwiegende Verantwortlichkeiten zu tragen hatte? Hat es begriffen, welch eine Opfertat geschehen war? Rudolf Steiner nahm das Karma der Anthroposophischen Gesellschaft in sein Karma auf. Es war ein unerhörtes Wagnis, eine Tat, bei der man, als sie geschah, fast die Erschütterung des ganzen Kosmos empfinden und fühlen konnte. Von diesem historischen Momente hing es jetzt ab, ob die geistigen Mächte, die mit solch grossem Wohlwollen und Freigebigkeit die anthroposophische Bewegung, welche Rudolf Steiner selber war, mit Geisteswissen begnadete, so begnadete, dass von diesem Wissen auch gesprochen werden durfte und zwar so gesprochen, wie es gesprochen wurde, jetzt mit dem gleichen Wohlwollen sich auch der Anthroposophischen Gesellschaft gegenüber sich verhalten würden. Die Führung der Anthroposophischen Gesellschaft fordert Verwaltung, in der Gesellschaft äussern sich die Wünsche, die Gedanken und das Wollen der Mitglieder. Ist es möglich, dass durch diese hindurch das Licht aus der geistigen Welt mit derselben Kraft und Intensität strömt? Das war die bange Frage, und man musste warten, wie sich die Dinge weiter entwickeln würden.

Inzwischen ging die Tagung weiter glänzend vor sich. Rudolf Steiner setzte für die Gesellschaft den Vorstand ein. Dieser Vorstand war von ihm mit Michaelsimpuls gewählt und so eingeteilt, wie die Arbeit mit diesem Vorstand mit ihm möglich war. Nicht die Gesellschaft setzte den Vorstand ein, sondern er, Rudolf Steiner, mit der Begründung, dass dieser Vorstand mit ihm im Zusammenhang stünde, er nannte ihn deshalb esoterisch.

Klar wurde dies ausgesprochen, und die Anthroposophische Gesellschaft, die ihre Mitglieder in grosser Anzahl geschickt hatte zur Tagung, erfasste mit Sicherheit die Tragweite der Situation, begeisterte und erwärmte sich und stimmte zu, und viele, ja die meisten versprachen sich heilig, in diese neue Situation sich einzufinden und dem Meister mit erneuten Kräften, mit neuem Fühlen und Wollen zu dienen.

Eine Welle der Begeisterung entzündete sich, etwas Grosses war geschehen, das fühlte jeder bewusst oder unbewusst, das Gefühl war da. Aber die bange Frage stand noch immer vor uns, wie wird das Geistige weiter verlaufen? Nun, auch auf diese Frage kam eines Tages die Antwort. Erschütternd war es, diese Antwort aus Rudolf Steiners eigenem Mund zu hören.

Es war dies in Paris, als er zum erstenmal zu den dort anwesenden Mitgliedern, die nur in kleiner Anzahl sich dort versammelt hatten, diese so wichtige Botschaft mitteilen konnte, die Botschaft, dass der Strom der geistigen Offenbarungen nicht aufgehört hat zu fliessen, und dass die geistigen Mächte mit noch grösserem Wohlwollen als vorher die Anthroposophische Gesellschaft begnadet haben mit geistigem Gut. Wie war mit einem Male die Spannung gelöst, wie jubilierte man innerlich vor Glückseligkeit. Die geistigen Mächte sind uns gut gesinnt, weil die Weihnachtstagung in der richtigen Gesinnung von den Mitgliedern aufgenommen war. Wie strahlte das Gesicht unseres Meisters, wie beglückt war er selber, wie dankbar sassen seine getreuen Schüler um ihn versammelt in dem kleinen, hübschen Saal in Paris. Und nun flossen die Wahrheiten mächtig aus seinem Mund. Immer mehr und mehr gab er. Die frohe Botschaft, die zum erstenmal in Paris ausgesprochen wurde, wiederholte er in Dornach, Torquay, London, in Holland, und wichtige Wahrheiten aus der geistigen Welt wurden gegeben. Man erlebte es, wie noch immer neue Schleusen aus der geistigen Welt geöffnet würden, um das geistige Gut hindurch zu lassen. Unvergessliche Zeit, jeder fühlte sich gehoben, jeder fühlte sich täglich in festlicher Stimmung, es war auch, als ob Götter Feste feierten!

Kurz war die Zeit, aber intensiv in ihren Wirkungen. Jeder, der in der richtigen Art die Weihnachtstagung, die Michaelstagung mitgemacht hatte, konnte es an sich selbst erleben, wie er umgewandelt, wie er ein anderer Mensch wurde, wie die geistige Welt ganz nah herangerückt war, ja man befand sich in ihr.

Dann wurde der Meister krank. Erst war es nur eine körperliche Erschöpfung, dann zeigte es sich, dass die Krankheit tiefere Ursachen hatte, Karma wirkte sich aus. Vom Januar 1925 an sprach er nicht mehr von Erschöpfung, sondern von Karmawirkungen. O, mögen die Mitglieder nicht an solchen Äusserungen vorbeigehen, sie sind tief ernst zu nehmen.

Nun verliess er den physischen Plan und hinterliess uns zu dem, was vorher war, das Neue, was in der Weihnachtstagung ausgesprochen wurde, das neue Situationen hervorgerufen hatte, das neue Gruppierungen notwendig machte.

65

"Executive Council's Idylls" (1925-1935)

Alles dasjenige, was er vorhatte, zu regeln und was er nach der Weihnachtstagung in den verschiedenen Konferenzen ausgesprochen hatte, konnte noch in den letzten zwei Monaten seines Lebens erledigt werden, sodass durch eine Fügung des Schicksals noch die Erledigung alles Geschäftlichen möglich war, kurz vor seinem Tode. Und so konnte er seinen physischen Körper verlassen, ohne es für nötig zu halten, noch weitere Anweisungen zur Führung der Anthroposophischen Gesellschaft zu hinterlassen.

Uns, die er als Vorstand gewählt hatte, war es klar, dass wir unseren durch ihn bestimmten Posten nicht verlassen durften; uns war es klar, dass es heilige Pflicht ist, wollen wir ernst nehmen dasjenige, was der Meister aus der geistigen Welt uns übermittelt hatte, um ihn gruppiert zu bleiben, damit er, obgleich nicht mehr physisch unter uns, doch unter uns und in uns wirken kann. Diese Stimmung waltete in uns. Und so betrachten wir Rudolf Steiner noch als ersten Vorsitzenden inmitten unseres Vorstandes und alle Vorstandsmitglieder in den Funktionen, in welche Rudolf Steiner sie eingesetzt hat.

Möchten die Mitglieder uns entgegentreten mit den gleichen Gefühlen, die wir hegen für die Gesellschaft, um nach den Intentionen unseres Führers, Rudolf Steiner, weiterzuwirken und weiter zu arbeiten, um das Vermächtnis, die Weihnachtstagung, zur Wirkung zu bringen.

Erinnerung an Rudolf Steiner
Ludwig Graf Polzer-Hoditz

„Das Wesen des Menschen als Schlüssel zu den Geheimnissen der Welt." So lautete das Thema seines öffentlichen Vortrages, als ich Rudolf Steiner das erste Mal hörte. Es war im November des Jahres 1908 in Wien. Mein Vater hatte mich auf ihn aufmerksam gemacht, weil er wusste, dass ich mich für solche Probleme interessiere. Wir sassen nebeneinander im Saale des Ingenieur- und Architektenvereins. Das gemeinsame Erlebnis dieses Vortrages liess uns einander näher fühlen als gewöhnlich. Seit diesem Tage sprachen wir immer von Rudolf Steiner, wenn wir uns trafen. — Mein Vater war damals schon 74 Jahre alt, versäumte es nachher nie, Rudolf Steiner zu hören, wenn dieser nach Wien kam. — Für mich war dieser Vortrag das bedeutsamste, tiefgreifendste Erlebnis meines Lebens; ich suchte fortab jede mögliche Gelegenheit, Rudolf Steiner zu hören und wurde dann auch bald sein Schüler. Mein Vater starb 1912, bald nachher begann Rudolf Steiner, mit mir über ihn zu sprechen. In den vielen persönlichen Besprechungen, die er mir so oft und ich darf sagen, so gerne gewährte, sprach er mir dann immer von ihm. Auch anderen gegenüber erwähnte er oft, wie der liebe alte Herr, mit dem feinen, schmalen Gesicht, den er immer in seinen Vorträgen sah, einen besonderen Eindruck auf ihn machte.

Mit der Erzählung dessen, weiss ich, dass ich im Sinne unseres unsterblichen, ehrwürdigen, grossen Menschheitsführers handle.

Rudolf Steiner stellte in dem erwähnten Vortrage einleitend vor die Seelen seiner Hörer, gleichsam als Hintergrund dem Vortrage dienend, um die Welt- und Menschenrätsel handeln sollte, das Bild Rafaels, die Sixtinische Madonna. Er wies darauf hin, wie das Bild Anknüpfungspunkte zeigt an das Welten- und Menschenrätsel. Die Engel in den Wolken erscheinen wie die Genossen des Kindes in den Armen der Mutter, sie weisen hin auf das Weltenrätsel. Das Kind selbst, das der Mutter beigegeben ist, spricht vom Menschenrätsel, wie der Mensch in sich die Möglichkeit hat, aus sich heraus zu schaffen, eine Verbindungsbrücke zu sein zwischen der geistigen und physischen Welt. Er entwarf in grosszügigen Linien eine Skizze von der Weltentwicklung, wie diese mit dem Werden der menschlichen Wesensglieder zusammenhängt, wie der Mikrokosmos aus dem Makrokosmos gestaltet wird. Der Mensch, der aus dem Weltenschosse herausgeboren ist, fühlt sich dann selbst als Gebärer neuer Welten, wenn das hellscherische Bewusstsein erwacht, und die Welt bevölkert sich dann für ihn mit geistigen Wesenheiten, die an einer Zukunfts-Umwelt arbeiten. Zum Schlusse zeigte er, wie dieser Künstler zum Teile auch aus der Tradition heraus in sein geheimnisvolles Bild das Welt- und Menschenrätsel hineinmalte, es künstlerisch lösend.

Mein Vater und ich jubelten innerlich, wir waren beide Suchende, gaben uns nie zufrieden mit den Verlegenheitsantworten der Wissenschaft und Kirche, auf die vielen Fragen, die jede gesunde Seele wegen ihrer Nichtbeantwortung beunruhigen müssen. Diese Ketzereigentümlichkeit hatten wir gemeinsam, nur war er skeptischer als ich veranlagt. Ich war sicher, dass es vernünftige Antworten auf solche Fragen geben müsse wie: „Was hat es für einen Sinn, dass der Mensch aus den Erdenstoffen und -Kräften seinen Leib aufbaut, sich nährt und arbeitet, um dann wieder, wenn er die Stoffe nicht mehr aufnehmen kann, die Erde zu verlassen; oder: in welchem sinnvollen Zusammenhange stehen die körperlichen Vorgänge und Handlungen des Menschen mit dem Ganzen der Welt, wie sind die ungleichen Menschenschicksale, die oft scheinbare Ungerechtigkeit zu verstehen? Ich war überzeugt, dass es wenigstens einen Menschen auf Erden geben müsse, der damit beginnen wird, diese Fragen geistgemäss zu beantworten. Seit dem November 1908 wusste ich, dass ich ihn gefunden hatte. Bald stellte sich bei mir ein Gefühl ein, das ich so empfand, wie ich aus einem düsteren Labyrinth ins Licht, ins Freie geführt worden wäre. Es hörte für mich seither das trostlose Suchen auf; ich war schon gleich damals ganz sicher, ihn gefunden zu haben, denjenigen, der die Menschheit wieder zum Geiste führen wird. Die vielen Aufforderungen noch anderswo zu suchen, empfand ich immer als Einladung, wieder in das düstere Labyrinth zurückzukehren, dem ich glücklich entronnen war.

Und dann kam eine Reihe der schönsten Lebenserinnerungen in der Umgebung Rudolf Steiners, so viel ich konnte, mitteilnehmend an seinem heiligen Lebenswerke.

Das grosse unerschöpfliche Thema, das er von den verschiedensten Gesichtspunkten behandelte, formulierte er mir persönlich einmal so:

„Im Weltengeheimnis schaut sich der Mensch.
Im Menschengeheimnis offenbart sich die Welt."

Diesem Thema, das immer wieder neue Fragen aufwarf, galt immer sein Wort, es ertönte immer wieder in neuer Kraft und Weisheit, ihm opferte dieser herrlichste aller Menschen das Leben.

Alle seine Eröffnungen waren immer eine weitere Ausarbeitung des damals im November 1908 empfangenen grosszügigen Entwurfes einer Welt- und Menschheitsbetrachtung.

Seine Anthroposophie oder Geisteswissenschaft ist mir wie ein leuchtendes, lebendiges Sonnengewebe, gewoben aus Tausenden herrlicher, von ihm aus der geistigen Welt gesponnenen Geistesstrahlen, jeder einzelne Strahl auch wieder ein Ganzes für sich.

Von Rafael sprach Rudolf Steiner, als ich ihn das erste Mal hörte. Seine letzte Ansprache an uns Anthroposophen in Dornach am 28. September 1924 handelte wieder von Rafael. Das hat auf mich einen ganz besonders tiefen Eindruck gemacht und die vielen Erinnerungsbilder der schönen Erlebnisse mit ihm, aus der Zeit des Lernens und Werdens unter seiner lieben Führung, die in den letzten Tagen an meiner Seele vorbeigezogen, standen alle im Glanze dieser im Sternenkleide leuchtenden Seele.

66

News Sheet, *April 26, 1925 (page 66)*

other such occasions, the circular reached more than a thousand subscriptions through word-of-mouth by the original subscribers. In addition, there were approximately two hundred more subscriptions for the English translation. I published letters on astrology together with Willi Sucher in 1934/35. And thus, also more.[211]

Vreede held many lectures on astronomy and encouraged the work of young mathematicians and astronomers such as Ernst Bindel, Hermann von Baravall, Ernst Müller, Willi Sucher, and George Adams. Quite often, out of respect for the achievements of the others, she wrote the reviews of the publications herself.

As always before, Elisabeth Vreede was active in various ways with giving advice and support. She also made it possible, through her seminars and courses, for the members of the General Anthroposophical Society to find an understanding of, and entryway into, a field that was closed for most of them. She also brought an understanding of the significance of this field for the penetration of Anthroposophy as the Christ-imbued cosmosophy that Rudolf Steiner had always referred to. With her presentations Vreede strove, as Section leader at the Goetheanum, to create "a new feeling and willing in the connection of the human being with the cosmos."[212] She lectured as an objective scientist, and yet found ever again words and pictures "through which the sublime beauty of the Sophia shone."[213] She could speak so wonderfully about shooting stars.

About Elisabeth Vreede's lectures and also her Class Lessons, a listener later wrote:

> Her power of thinking had something Jupiter-like—multifaceted. When she lectured or read the Class (Lesson), her brow shone like a star. Her way of thinking made it possible for her to grasp immediately what Rudolf Steiner brought and in spite of great respect for him, to form her own independent judgment, just as he hoped members would do.[214]

Vreede published from 1927 on—not only her "astronomy circulars," but also, mathematic mailings in which she brought out,

Vorwort.

Mit diesem Werke gelangt der umfangreichste und wohl auch umfassendste der naturwissenschaftlichen Kurse, die *Rudolf Steiner* vor den Lehrern der Waldorfschule gehalten hat, zur Veröffentlichung im Wortlaut. In keinem andern Kurse hat der grosse Lehrer soviel grundlegendes Methodisches und soviel die einzelnen Wissenschaften Verbindendes gegeben wie gerade in diesem „astronomischen Kurs", dem er ja gleich mit den ersten Worten ausdrücklich den Titel gab: „Das Verhältnis der verschiedenen naturwissenschaftlichen Gebiete zur Astronomie". Naturforschern, Ärzten, Mathematikern und Astronomen werden die Wege gewiesen, um die Sonderung ihrer Gebiete zu überwinden; es werden zu gleicher Zeit dem Fachmann, jedem auf seinem Gebiet, die bedeutendsten Hinweise gegeben, sein Spezialfach umzugestalten im Sinne einer geistgetragenen Wissenschaft. Unermessliches Verantwortungs- und Pflichtgefühl wird daraus erwachsen. Um so mehr jetzt, da der Schöpfer dieser Weisheitsgabe nicht mehr physisch unter uns weilt. Konnte er noch kurze Zeit vor seinem Hingange die Bearbeitung dieses Kurses durch W. Kaiser („Astronomie in geisteswissenschaftlicher Beleuchtung", Der Kommende Tag-Verlag) entgegennehmen, diese seine Arbeit selber können wir nur seinem ewigen Geiste widmen, der mit seinem Werke verbunden bleibt, wenn dieses in seinem Sinne fortgeführt wird.

Vor der Drucklegung wurde der Text, der in einer stenographischen Nachschrift vorhanden war, sorgfältig durchgesehen. Bei dieser verantwortungsvollen Arbeit habe ich Herrn *E. A. K. Stockmeyer* von der Waldorfschule in Stuttgart für seine bereitwillige Hilfe herzlich zu danken.

Für die mathematisch-astronomische Sektion
E. Vreede.

Dornach, am Goetheanum, Mai 1926.

*Elisabeth Vreede: Foreword to the first edition
of the "Astronomy Course," Dornach, 1926*

among other things, important excerpts of Rudolf Steiner's lectures and answers to questions (as the first and only Section, and on the basis of her comprehensive work knowledge); she also took on the initiative to build a star observatory near the Goetheanum. In early summer 1927 she accomplished it, again out of her own financial means.[215] On June 28 she invited Albert Stefan to observe an eclipse of the Sun, sending him the following letter:

> Dear Honorable Herr Steffen,
>
> Because you are known to be an early morning riser, I dare to invite you to the observatory to see the eclipse of the Sun. It is, of course, not all set up, but instead of ladders, we now have thrones (table and chair). Herr Pfeiffer will perform crystallization experiments through a telescope at the same time, which should be quite interesting. Please do come, too! The eclipse begins at 5:15 a.m.; will be at its peak at 6:12 and ends at 7:10 a.m. It should be at its best at around 6:10 a.m.[216]

Despite all the conflicts in the Executive Council, Elisabeth Vreede attempted to maintain friendly, human contact and to open a door for Albert Steffen to her work. She valued him as an author. She always read his newly published works and congratulated him for them.

~

Around the observatory there were many activities that were closely coordinated with Lili Kolisko, and at the same time were run together with her. Among these were plant experiments, using water irradiated by the Moon and planets; Elisabeth Vreede wanted to publish this work in a book. When possible, Vreede would try to carry out the research work announced by Rudolf Steiner in Koberwitz. From 1929 until her death, she published the *Star Calendar*, which was originally supposed to be titled "*Bauern-Kalendar*" (Farmers' calendar) and was intended especially for farmers. At the end of her introduction to the first edition she wrote:

Those who have studied Rudolf Steiner's spiritual-scientific cosmology, such as is presented in his *Outline of Esoteric Science*, will know how the Earth and everything on it originated from the "heavens"—how the stars and planets are not the faraway worlds that people feel they are, but rather they are close to us and are connected to the other kingdoms of nature. It is not only warmth and light that the Sun sends to the Earth, but from the whole surroundings right up to the stars, those forces streamed to the Earth that bring about the growing and developing; the forming and blossoming; the sprouting and budding. Etheric formative forces and astral movement-rhythms, as well as spiritual impulses stream down to the Earth from the universe. When the Moon shines upon quiet fields, when Venus gleams as the evening star, or when Saturn lets its pale red light radiate they point to the effects that prevail between Heaven and Earth, which must be recognized and experienced again by human beings.

Precisely those farmers who walk the paths shown by Rudolf Steiner can develop a sense for these effects. For the greatest teacher of humanity has pointed out the cosmic spring that pours it itself in a fructifying way onto the Earth, without which not one seed could sprout; not one blade (of grass) could grow. And he brought this spring into connection with the Being of Christ: From heaven Christ descended to Earth; into the Earth he poured his being in the days of Holy Week. And since that Easter, the Earth is his body from which green sprouts forth, the grain that becomes the bread of the human being.[217]

Vreede's *Star Calendar* went from Easter to Easter each year and connected the resurrection of nature in the course of the year of the northern hemisphere with the spiritual fact of Christ's resurrection, just as did Rudolf Steiner's calendar and the *Soul Calendar* of 1912. In her "Foreword" to the *Star Calendar* of 1930/31, Elisabeth Vreede wrote, "Easter should be the true festival of the resurrection for us. From that, the new forces are sent into the old world; it has an impact on the course of the year that can be compared only with the Christmas Festival."[218] Vreede's *Star Calendar* came out with a beautiful colored book cover; she also published a rotating star chart. She had the

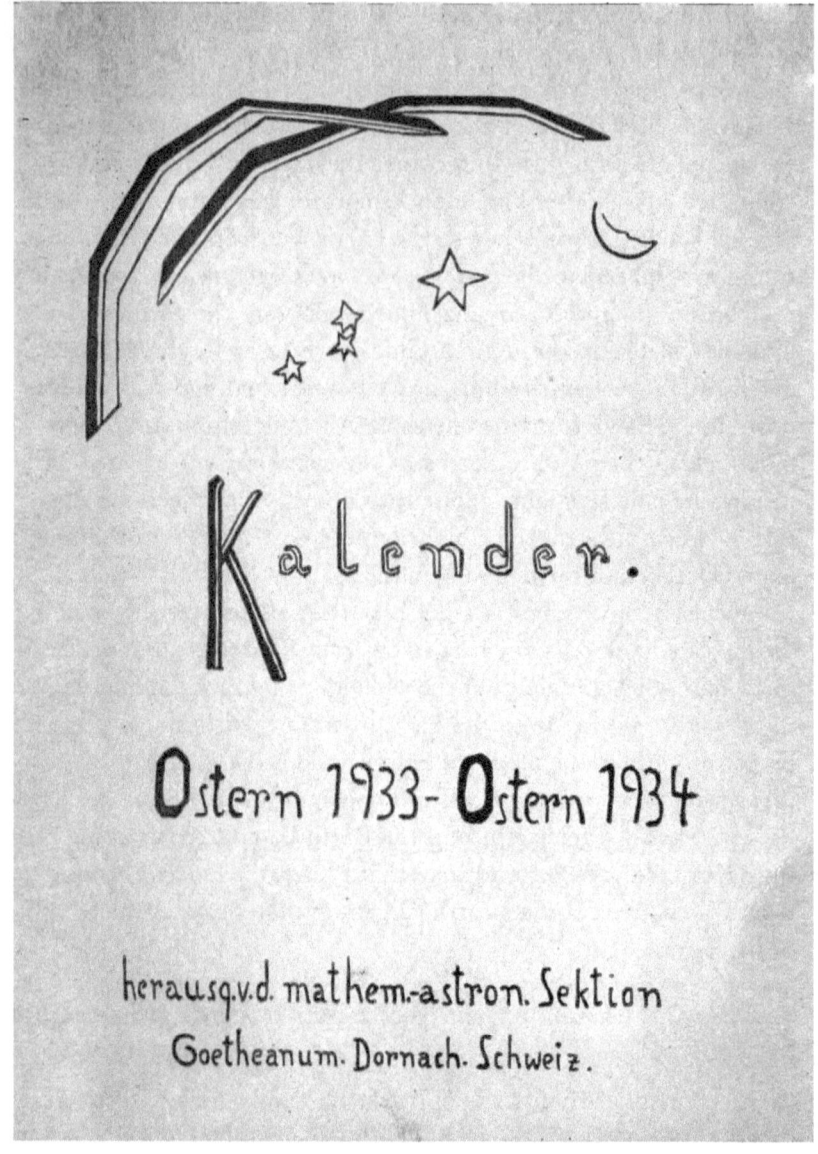

Star Calendar, *Easter 1933–Easter 1934*

Section room in the Goetheanum (that she moved into at the beginning of 1928 and opened officially on Easter) painted in etheric-rose color, which created quite a stir.

—

Elisabeth Vreede traveled a great deal, though she was not absent from the Goetheanum as frequently as Ita Wegman and Marie Steiner were. She took part in the opening of Willem Zeylmans van Emmichoven's clinic in The Hague (she had asked her to allow her to use the Foundation Stone mantra of her house for the founding of his therapeutic institution[219]). Vreede spoke a few months later in the summer of 1928 on "Spiritual Aspects of Astronomy" at the London World Conference. This conference was on the "periphery" shortly before the opening of the second Goetheanum and was, however, controversial in Dornach, the "center." Like Ita Wegman, Willem Zeylmans, Daniel Nicol Dunlop, and other cosmopolitan-oriented anthroposophists, Vreede worked for the international spreading of Spiritual Science, especially in Western English-speaking countries.

As early as autumn 1924 Rudolf Steiner intended that there should be a large open conference in the capital cities of Europe in the next years. These were to be in addition to the events at the Goetheanum.[220] The Dornach School (College) should not be an end in itself but should serve the world; it should be prepared to deal with others' concerns, problems, and tasks. With the Christmas Conference Rudolf Steiner had clearly included these along with the movement connected with the "World School Association." He said on December 27, 1923, that the national general secretaries are to be considered equal in relation to the central Council and as extended Executive Council by their presence in the Council meetings in Dornach.[221] Vreede worked closely with the General Secretaries preferred by Rudolf Steiner—among them were Zeylmans and Dunlop—and rejected consequently a hierarchical leadership model that she saw embodied especially through Albert Steffen.

Wednesday, July 25

Art

10.15 A.M. LARGE HALL. **Anthroposophy and the Artist.** BARON A. ROSENKRANTZ.

12 NOON. ART GALLERY. Exhibitions of Goetheanum Paintings, by various Artists.

2.30 P.M. LARGE HALL. **The Artistic Use of Concrete.** M. WHEELER, M.A., F.R.I.B.A.

4 P.M. Exhibition of Paintings. MISS HILMA AF KLINT (Upsala). With an address.

5 P.M. LARGE HALL. **Music in the East and West.** MR. ZAGWYN. Illustrated on the piano by MR. JAN VAN DEN BERGH.

8.15 P.M. LARGE HALL. **The Evolution of Music in the light of Anthroposophy** (with musical examples). MISS JEANNE DE MARE.

8.15 P.M. RUDOLF STEINER HALL. Demonstration of Eurhythmy by Artistes of the Goetheanum School of Eurhythmy, Dornach.

Thursday, July 26

Natural Science

10.15 A.M. LARGE HALL. **The Earth as an Organism.** DR. GÜNTHER WACHSMUTH, Secretary of the General Anthroposophical Society, Leader of the Science Section of the Goetheanum, Dornach.

12 NOON. LARGE HALL. **Spiritual Aspects of Astronomy.** FRL. DR. E. VREEDE, Leader of the Astronomical and Mathematical Section of the Goetheanum, Dornach.

3 P.M. LARGE HALL. **Experimental Researches into the Formative Forces of Nature** (illustrated by lantern slides). EHRENFRIED PFEIFFER. (In German. English translation by G. Kaufmann, M.A.).

5.30 P.M. RUDOLF STEINER HALL. Demonstration by the English students of the Rudolf Steiner School of Eurhythmy, London.

8.15 P.M. LARGE HALL. **Influences of the Stars on Earthly Substances** (Scientific experiments at the Biological Institute of the Goetheanum). Illustrated by Lantern Slides. L. KOLISKO.

From the program of the World Conference in London

Steffen, who was president of the General Anthroposophical Society as of the end of 1926, acted with the rank of president in a controlling, domineering leadership style. Vreede held the right to this claim—in spite of her respect for his literary work—to be false and not corresponding to the positions of social responsibility of the Christmas Conference. At the time of the London World Conference in the summer of 1928, she had not played a role in the Executive Council's decisions for a long time. The management of the business of the Goetheanum passed over, since 1925, more and more to Steffen and Wachsmuth, with the involvement of Marie Steiner. Executive Council meetings took place seldom, although Vreede attempted repeatedly to demand them. Marie Steiner and Ita Wegman were often away from Dornach, and there were many other reasons for the meetings not taking place. To Wachsmuth, Vreede was an old-fashioned, outmoded anthroposophist and notorious for continually complaining and who disturbed the management at the Goetheanum. He thought it might be best not to involve her and to inform her afterward. He considered her to be incidental, of little significance, and without a specific task on the Executive Council.

Vreede wrote at the beginning of 1935 in a retrospective on many years, "There has been no activity on the Executive Council to speak of for a long time."[222] *"One could almost say that Fräulein Dr. of Philosophy Elisabeth Vreede was a member of the Executive Council whose opinion was considered to be of very little value"* (Lili Kolisko).

A few weeks before the London World Conference Vreede documented for herself impressions of the situation of the Executive Council at the Goetheanum in a humorous way in *"Vorstandsidyllen"* (Executive Council's Idylls]. She reported various smaller and larger events in a prosaic form. Among these was how in the fall of 1926 she read in the Arlesheim newspaper about the visit by the Swiss President of the Federal Council and his reception by the Executive Council at the Goetheanum, at which she, as well as the other readers of the newspaper, were not involved. On another occasion, she read in the "Weekly" about a Vacation Conference at the Goetheanum, and that the Executive Council had to give up on the preparation and organization of content for it because of too much work. "The Executive Council has handed the organization of the Vacation Conference over to the branch at the Goetheanum, due to the fact that the preparations for the opening of the Goetheanum this summer have placed great demands (on the Executive Council)." She wrote:

> Strange! That they see themselves as so extremely weighed down by things that one knows nothing about! So overtaxed with unknown preparations for a program no one ever knew about that they must give up their work and responsibility! That sounds suspicious. Have I perhaps become a little crazy, that I can no longer make sense of the facts?[223]

Vreede also reported on a course for French-speaking participants in which Emil Grosheintz had sent her tickets for admission that she should distribute further.

> I think that I am not crazy. I have just forgotten that I am actually a traveling salesperson for underwear—Baumberg underpants or the like—that's how I feel. In the other envelope there were many splendid tickets for entry with a picture of the Goetheanum on the back. One appears to know what is appropriate. It is indeed nice of him—the way he values me! What trust in my sphere of work! Who could find fault![224]

Vreede counted this as her "Executive Council Idylls"—the seventh one was titled "Politics":

Idyll of "Politics"

> The carpentry building was to be planted with greenery. This appeared to have been decided by I don't know how many heads in the Executive Council (one to three people come into consideration there). For M. E. the question of *what* should be planted at the carpentry building is absolutely a matter of spiritual life; that means, it should be decided by the whole Executive Council, which is obliged to manage the spiritual life at the Goetheanum. I think it makes a big difference whether the carpentry building is

intertwined, for instance, with roses or ivy. Be that as it may, one day the carpentry was richly adorned with Ivy. The already fairly rotten wood wall was covered with moist soil and ivy planted into it. It was to happen also with the neighboring buildings. Only the wall on Frau Dr. Steiner's side was spared and was planted with a hedge of roses. Now, there is the reading room of the Archive and Library and my small archive room that was added or enlarged later respectively. (I paid for the whole building of the addition and for half of the expansion; the other half was probably taken care of by the Library.) Already the year before, friendly hands from the Archive and Library staff had planted a small flower bed by this annex as far as was possible; it could not be done yet on the north side under my window because the lumber for the Goetheanum construction still lay there. On the west side rose bushes and flowers enjoyed a friendly luxurious growth.

One day a gardener appeared and begins to pull out the roses and flowers to plant Ivy in their place. Protest from the volunteer gardeners: we will not let our plants be pulled out! Yes, I must do it; the head gardener ordered it. The head gardener is called to come. Yes, I must do this so that everywhere it looks uniform; the architect ordered it. The architect is called. Yes this must happen thus; Dr. Wachsmuth ordered it. Dr. Wachsmuth is away on a trip.

At this stage, I become aware of the situation. *I, too,* now order: ivy out, roses back in. In front (where, because of the powers that be, a bed was arranged) we will plant cuttings of hedge roses from my garden so that it won't cost anything. And thus it happens. The next day already there is growing all of the old roses and the new rose cuttings. The men from the state took the ivy with them and probably used it elsewhere.

At the end then came an invoice from the Building Administration for 1.50 (Swiss) Franks for the removal of the ivy. To this day we have not paid this invoice, of course—as obedient as we otherwise are. One night I even dreamed about the ivy—just as can happen in a dream that the same words continue persistently to pass through one's soul, and so it was with this one too. The words were:

Ivy, the growth of the louse,
the mouse and the grave's house.

Our roses bloom quite beautifully for the third summer and are the joy of many passersby.[225]

～

Yet, Elisabeth Vreede was in no way ready to give in. Rudolf Steiner had created the Executive Council as an "Initiative Council" and had transferred to them collectively the responsibility for the leadership at the Goetheanum and for the General Anthroposophical Society. Vreede held steadfastly to this position of the task ("that the responsibility for the leadership of the Anthroposophical Society as such should come to the Executive Council"[226]). When she read in the *News Sheet* on July 14, 1928, the "Invitation" by Albert Steffen to the opening of the second Goetheanum,[227] she wrote him the following:

> I see from the "Invitation" that you continue ever further to take the path that leads to creating a completely new situation from that of the Christmas Conference. Otherwise, it would not be possible,
>
> 1. that such an invitation would come from you personally;
> 2. that members are required to pre-register for lectures at the opening;
> 3. that the program should be put together on the basis of the brief summary of the content that was sent.
>
> I see item 1 as a further removal of the Executive Council; item 2 as a denial of the intentions of the Christmas Conference; and item 3 as the beginning of the abolishing of free spiritual life at the Goetheanum.[28]

Elisabeth Vreede wanted the Executive Council (as Initiative Council in the sense of the Christmas Conference) to organize the opening together. She wanted to see, as a priority, consideration of those whom Rudolf Steiner had authorized as "Goetheanum speakers." She wrote later, "Because I trust Rudolf Steiner's faith in these people...."[229] "Rudolf Steiner did not leave us in the dark concerning some others as to how far he valued them, or valued them less. All of that could have served the Executive Council as guidelines after Rudolf Steiner's

Carpentry shop (Schreinerei), *Goetheanum, Dornach*

death."²³⁰ Instead, more and more, "followers" were preferred at the Goetheanum—those people who gathered around Albert Steffen or Marie Steiner. Among those named by Rudolf Steiner as "Goetheanum-speakers" were such people as Eugen Kolisko, Walter Johannes Stein, Caroline von Heydebrand, Karl Schubert, Daniel Nicol Dunlop and George Adams-Kaufmann. They accomplished outstanding, internationally recognized anthroposophical work, but because of their connection with Ita Wegman, they had not come under consideration for a long time. They were "taboo" and were held actually to be enemies of the Goetheanum. Elisabeth Vreede wanted "that the conferences at the Goetheanum would again be an expression of what lives in the whole movement that would be followed with interest—what lives in the whole movement and that comes to expression also here in the Goetheanum."²³¹ In no way could she achieve this.

Albert Steffen reacted indignantly to Vreede's letter of July 14, 1928, and repeatedly threatened, as a result, to withdraw (from the Executive Council). With the conference for the opening and the course of events little or nothing changed. Six months later Steffen criticized the quality of Vreede's professional work and wrote her about the text of the Section Circular on July 1, 1929:

> Although I no longer have responsibility for the activity of the Section leaders, I consider it yet to be my duty to let you know that I do not agree with the manner in which you treat your theme "Life between Death and Rebirth in the Light of Astrosophy." I must say this all the more because I have just now read lecture cycle number [CW] 37, on which you base your work. Yes, I am very concerned about the spiritual-scientific reputation of the Independent School when these issues are handled so superficially as has happened in this circular.²³²

~

"Superficial" treatment of complex topics was not Vreede's way of doing things, even when Albert Steffen's "correct methods" were not the same as hers. One year later, in 1930, she spoke up when Adolf

Arenson, an old, close friend of Marie Steiner's and member of the Anthroposophical Society, presented a publication on Rudolf Steiner and the "Bodhisattva" (*"Rudolf Steiner und der Bodhisattva des 20. Jahrhundert"* [Rudolf Steiner and the Bodhisattva of the twentieth century]). This was from a lecture that Arenson gave in Stuttgart and repeated at the Annual General Meeting of the General Anthroposophical Society in spring 1930, after Albert Steffen emphasized his "special importance." Vreede, who knew the exact details of Rudolf Steiner's lectures on the subject and the context of his presentations, held Arenson's description of Steiner as the bearer of the Bodhisattva as absolutely false and dangerous.

On April 7, 1930, Elisabeth Vreede wrote to her colleagues on the Executive Council and asked—to no avail—for a meeting about this issue and warned of the danger of a sect. Finally, she held two lectures on this topic in Holland that she repeated in Stuttgart the second week of July, at the request and invitation of Eugen Kolisko. Vreede's extraordinarily expressive presentations showed the depth and variety of her insight in the topic and her understanding for the spiritual scientist Rudolf Steiner. She spoke from the living memory (Deventer) and corrected the picture of Rudolf Steiner in his work for the anthroposophic movement—in the context of a thorough, objectively profound and living description of the development of the anthroposophic Christology; in the examination of that Eastern esotericism in which the Theosophical Society and movement—but also Arenson's Bodhisattva-interpretation—had remained.

Vreede's lectures brought new thinking, a new way forward. They took place in the middle of her time on the Executive Council, five years after Rudolf Steiner's death. These lectures were a clear-cut witness of the activity of her teacher and were delivered powerfully, without any gesture of authoritativeness and without attacking Arenson. They were given in a gesture of freedom toward the power of judgment of the listeners. In an irregular General Meeting in December of the same year, Elisabeth Vreede was reproached for her presentation as being directed "against the spirit of Dr. Steiner."[223] In fact, her lectures must be deemed as very probably the best that had been spoken or written since March 30, 1925 about the history of Rudolf Steiner's work. "Accused of being a heretic" (Vreede),[234] she stood there in the Great Hall of the Goetheanum in a role, however, that was in no way to new to her—or Rudolf Steiner's—destiny.

In Stuttgart at the time of her Bodhisattva lectures, Elisabeth Vreede lived with the architect and archaeologist, Professor Ernst Fiechter, who was a knowledgeable partner in conversations on mathematics. Although Vreede's thoughts were on serious issues, she did not abandon her humor with the Fiechters. In a free hour she thought about the situation in Dornach and wrote on the day of her second Stuttgart lecture, possibly following a description of a preceding conversation:

Concerning the Esoteric Executive Council:
An exoteric Contemplation

Once upon a time, there was in the Executive Council that was so composed: There was a president who did not want to preside; a secretary who did not want to "secretary." The latter would not have been so bad, but the president did not want to preside when the sitting members did not want to sit.

Then there was yet a Secretary–Treasurer who carried out his duties as Secretary-Treasurer; and in addition, the duties of the secretary, and now and then also the duties of the president, and after that of the Executive Council carried on like a bottle that remains floating in the water by its cork.

Then there was yet a sitting member who could not sit (meet)—because there was no sitting—and who wanted absolutely to sit because it was her duty—and made a fuss and wrote cheeky letters to the president who didn't want to preside, because she the sitting member, could not sit in this way.

That this Executive Council was an esoteric and not an exoteric council is clear from the report above. —E.V.[235]

Elisabeth Vreede: lecture manuscript, July 9, 1930

The work in the "periphery" and the difficulties continued: the activities for the founding of a World School Association and the Camp de Stakenberg in Holland; the medical, pedagogical and curative educational initiatives, and the foundings. These were valued very little in Dornach but led Elisabeth Vreede and Ita Wegman together again and again. Elisabeth Vreede wrote to Professor Schüler on May 14, 1932: "One should differentiate between 'what the Goetheanum has to give and what comes forth from the Goetheanum as Society leadership.'"[236] Without doubt the professional work and events "in the periphery were part of the Goetheanum, even when they were in no way carried or even accepted by the whole Executive Council. In a letter to Gertrud Kalbfuss on May 2, 1932, Vreede stressed that this whole council existed "only in the spiritual realm," and it will "achieve its reincarnation only from there."[237]

In the General Meetings, Elisabeth Vreede often fought completely alone. Elisabeth Knottenbelt wrote, "One could only admire the courage with which she stood ever again before an assembly in which the majority were hostile toward her."[238] "She was a courageous fighter, but when she fought, it was never personal but always an objective striving. When she became incensed, it was out of a sense of justice. Her being often had an abrupt and self-willed effect on others, but one did not notice that within her heart was bleeding, suffering" (Madeleine van Deventer).[239] George Adams-Kaufmann called Vreede "incorruptible," but also "unrelenting," and wrote a personal recollection of her: "Where others remained silent, she raised her voice, without worrying about how it would be accepted. She detested all careful weighing of the effect of her deeds. When she had to choose between cleverness and truthfulness, she did not have to think about which she needed to choose, even when perhaps an existing rift would only become greater."[240]

In the spring 1932 General Meeting of the General Anthroposophical Society, Elisabeth Vreede spoke directly after Albert Steffen. She fought for—as almost the only voice against the overwhelming majority of those present—those people against whom others (the

Elisabeth Vreede after her lecture; Camp de Stakenberg, 1930

followers of Albert Steffen and Marie Steiner) certified that they were using "incorrect" anthroposophical methods. She stood up for those people who were in actual fact excluded from working at the Goetheanum. According to Lili Kolisko, who took stenographic notes, Vreede commented:

> We have here now a large assembly of people, but we could think of just as many more people at least who feel painfully that they are pushed out of here again and again. They say, I know also that my work was valued by Rudolf Steiner, and I am treated in such a way that one says of me that my methods are bad, that I conduct a false science, etc. That is what increasingly drives people away. And the more that one feels happy here in a certain manner, just as much does one make accessible what should also be there. There are many; there are many directions. I am truly not speaking for single individuals. I have been here many years and see that many people are here [in the Great Hall], but I see also that many are *not* here—people whom one otherwise met. They say: Why should I let myself be treated with such a lack of understanding? Out of love to the Goetheanum, which many of the people helped to build and for which they suffered and helped carry—out of this love, they now *remain silent*. They no longer speak; they stay away. And because that is the case, I feel it is my duty to speak for these people who also belong to us and who want the good....
>
> None of us are perfect—that we know well—but no one is completely bad either.... And if we would unite all our positive forces, then we could achieve something totally different from what exists now. In the seven years [since Rudolf Steiner's death]—this one must admit—a part of the anthroposophic movement has been shut out of the Anthroposophical Society.... And I would like to hope that in the next seven years before us... also magnanimity of heart could be shown toward others, about whom one first had formed bad ideas; that one could give to oneself the task of finding the good also—what, for instance, Dr. Steiner has also valued in the people. If that could happen, then I think we could become a much larger and more powerful movement in the next years. I feel I have the duty to express this, as unpleasant as it might be. It is

> not merely in the *unity* that the highest is attained, when this unity goes so far as not to want to see the other.
>
> Perhaps what I wanted to say is said in an unformed manner, but it is what lives in my heart—and from which I have the impression that it must be brought out. I remember how Rudolf Steiner carried *all* human beings and did not separate them and lead them according to their methods. My whole hope is that this could be continued.[241]

With this stance, however, Vreede stood again with a lost cause at the General Meeting; she had to suffer scorn and mockery. Nevertheless, she did not let anyone dissuade her; she maintained steadfastness courage unequaled by anyone.

Again and again, there were breaks from these troubles. In October 1931, half a year before the General Meeting quoted from above, Elisabeth Vreede accepted an invitation to travel to Egypt. There she studied the pyramids and the spiritual history of the land of the old mysteries; she was fifty-two years old. Ernst Bindel, who had invited her, had brought to her in Dornach samples of stones from the pyramids in Giza, Medum and Daschur; they were carefully selected and labeled. Two years later she wrote a significant article about the meteor shower of October 9, 1933,[242] that had impressed her deeply, "in a time of difficult troubles and the dark future,"[243] in Dornach and Germany. Up to that time, Elisabeth Vreede traveled to Silesia to give astronomy lectures that were met with great approval. To Gertrud Zaiser, however, she said in reference to the Goetheanum, "I no longer have any skin."[244]

At the General Meeting of 1934 Dr. Vreede defended herself yet a last time, but she was made a laughing stock to a great extent. With the decision of the majority (and against the decision of the German Work Association, as well as the national societies of England and Holland), those assembled gave the further continuation of the Executive Council activities, "in the sense of the Christian Conference," to Albert Steffen, Marie Steiner and Guenther Wachsmuth. Ita Wegman lay ill in her wood-framed house in Arlesheim prior to being brought to Lake Thun, in her last journey in the Executive Council car. She had asked Madeleine van Deventer to write an open letter to Albert Steffen to be red aloud at the General Meeting. This then did happen.

Herr Dr. Steffen!

Again the General Meeting approaches. Again the emotions of the members will be whipped up. Again surely decent people, whom Dr. Steiner valued and loved, will be attacked with the aid of these whipped up emotions; their reputations undermined and the human beings systematically shattered. And you, as President of the Anthroposophical Society, allow it to happen. You think it is good that people correct one another. What is reduced to rubble, however, you ignore.

Now a group of seven people bring a motion. With this motion, Herr Steffen, they want to give you, besides the rights of the president, yet other rights that go far beyond [the realm of the president]. I do not see anything good in this. It is a distancing of oneself still more from Dr. Steiner's principles and is a tendency to make the Goetheanum accessible only to a certain group of people and to shut out the others. This has already been the case for years more or less and I cannot, as member of the Executive Council, agree that this condition, which is being insistently carried out, be legalized.

I support the decision of the Groups of the Work Community, the national societies of Holland and England, because they are right to defend against the one-sided running of the Goetheanum.

As concerns my work in the Goetheanum that has to do specifically with the healing arts, I am declaring to the Executive Council that I am not at all willing to accept the changes that could be made in the Sections. I will dedicate myself to the task that Rudolf Steiner assigned to the Sections, along with all of those who want to work with me and within themselves feel the will to heal. Then we will have possibilities, under the protection of the spirit of Rudolf Steiner, to dedicate ourselves to this healer-profession far away from the quarrels and disagreements that are causing havoc now in the Goetheanum. Out of this will to heal, we consciously avoided all the quarrels; and we remain consciously in the Goetheanum, the place Rudolf Steiner created, not only for a

Dr. E. Vreede, Dornach (Schweiz)

Leiterin der mathematisch-astronomischen Sektion
am Goetheanum, Dornach,

spricht am Donnerstag, dem 10. November 1932, 20 Uhr,
im Rahmen des Kurses von **Dr. med. König** über das Thema:

Anthroposophie und Astronomie

im Lyceum, Hindenburgplatz.

Unkostenbeitrag 30 Pfg.   Erwerbslose und Minderbemittelte frei.

Lecture announcement in Liegnitz (Silesia), November 10, 1932

small chosen group of people but for us all. And with those who have a feeling for this manner of work we want to attempt in unity and mindfulness of the Christian love, to deepen, continue and spread the knowledge that Rudolf Steiner gave so richly to us. We want to do this without worrying about the confusion within the Anthroposophical Society.

Dr. I. Wegman[245]

The possibilities for Elisabeth Vreede to hold lectures at the Goetheanum were increasingly cut over the next few months. As *persona non grata*, she was not allowed to use a lot of the rooms. Also her Section notices were further hindered, "because they were no longer included in the *News for Members*, and they were systematically torn down from the bulletin board."[246] Elisabeth Vreede wrote, "Thus, also the fulfillment of the task that Rudolf Steiner gave me, on which I have worked to the best of my ability for over ten years, is being brought ever more to a standstill." And she spoke of a gradual decline and finally complete deprivation of rights that was immediately imminent.[247] Elisabeth Vreede had to move her Easter lectures with Lilly and Eugen Kolisko into the Mathematics–Astronomy room after the Terrace Hall was no longer available to her. So she spoke on Easter Sunday, April 1, 1934 (a few days after the dramatic General Meeting), about, "Memories of Rudolf Steiner." Eugen Kolisko continued on Easter Monday with, "Sun, Moon and Earth: A cosmological-anthroposophical Contemplation." Then Lili Kolisko closed with, "The Formative Forces in the three Kingdoms of Nature," and showed slides. The permeation of natural science with Christ for which Rudolf Steiner planned, hoped, and strove was actualized in the work of these people, despite all the darkness of the Society's condition as a whole.

Elisabeth Vreede wrote to Ita Wegman in Wengen in Bern Oberland in the weeks of Wegman's slow convalescence.[248] She invited her to participate "after her recovery" in a Meeting in The Hague at the end of June to discuss the continuation of the national societies of Holland and England, as well as of the German Association that did not go along with the official course of the Goetheanum. The majority of the members in Holland, England, and the Anthroposophical Association of Germany stood behind Ita Wegman and Elisabeth Vreede; and had impressive leaders in Willem Zeylmans, D. N. Dunlop and Eugen Kolisko. In The Hague the first steps were to be taken toward a merger of the two national societies and the association. Ita Wegman stayed away. In her reply of June 20, 1934, she stressed that during the past weeks of her illness she had thought a lot about the future organization of the national societies, as well as of the Medical and Mathematics–Astronomy Sections, and she pleads for an intensive, continued anthroposophical work, for regular conferences and meetings together, and yet, "One thing I hope does not happen is the formation of a new Society."[249]

Ita Wegman considered that a "free form" is appropriate for the work together ("And it speaks thus in my heart, and seems to me that it is spiritually approved"), yet not the attempt to create a new organization of the Anthroposophical Society beside and beyond Dornach. She invited Elisabeth Vreede to come to Wengen for a visit; to recover from Dornach, and for further conversations. Ita Wegman wrote about herself in this connection: "The wonderful nature—first in Hondrich above Spiez, and now here in the Antlitz der Jungfrau [Countenance of the Virgin]—does wonders for me. I feel as if life has been given anew to me."

~

Ita Wegman avoided the meeting of the "United Independent Anthroposophical Groups," the merger in The Hague, and the first large conference together in Stuttgart at the end of June and beginning of July.[250] After her recovery, she traveled to Palestine and southern Italy and came back to Arlesheim first in November 1934, half a year after the last General Meeting. She sought her own way in the given situation, and was decreasingly willing to continue with the confrontation with the actual leadership of the Goetheanum. Wegman went inward; in November 1934 she said she wanted in the future to concentrate

Wengen 20/6 34
Hotel Belvédère

Liebe Dr. Vreede,

Herzlichen Dank für Ihre Einladung zur Zusammenkunft in Holland. Ich wäre gerne gekommen aber so weit ist es mit meiner Gesundheit doch noch nicht.
Ich bin noch hier zur Erholung.
Von Herzen hoffe ich dass Sie zusammen eine richtige Lösung finden werden für die Gestaltung der Landesgesellschaften und Arbeitsgruppen. Ein Ding hoffe ich das nicht geschieht und das ist die Bildung einer neuen Gesellschaft.
Ich habe nachdem ich wieder besser wurde viel darüber nachgedacht welche Möglichkeiten da sind um unsere Arbeit durchzuführen. Es sind viele Möglichkeiten da: die Konsolidierung der Landesgesellschaften (auch Deutschland soll eine 2te Landesgesellschaft bilden), dan deren Zusammenschluss mit frei bleiben wollenden Arbeitsgruppen (3 B die medizinische und Ihre Section). Die Generalsecretäre und die Sectionsleiter kommen 4× im Jahr zusammen entwe., der in London, Haag, Stuttgart oder Arlesheim und besprechen die Arbeit und die gemeinsame Tagungen. Dieser Zusammenkünfte können beliebig

erweitert werden durch Einladung an diejenige
Menschen die durch wichtige Arbeit oder
durch Empfehlung sich ausgezeichnet haben.
Diese freie Form kömt mir als die geeignetste
vor. Und es spricht so in meinem Herzen
und es kömt mir vor alsob es gütig bejaht
wird. —
Diese Paar Worte nur um Ihnen zu zeigen, dass
ich mit meinen Gedanken bei Ihnen bin.
Die wunderbare Natur, erst in Hondrich oberh. b
Spiez, und jetzt hier im Anblick der Jungfrau
tut Wunder an mich.
Ich fühle wie das Leben mir neu geschenkt
worden ist. Haben Sie keine Lust mich
mal hier zu besuchen und einige Tage auszu
ruhen? Viele Möglichkeiten der Einquartierung
sind hier: Hotels, Pensions, bei einfachen Berg,
führern.
Mit meinen besten Wünschen für das Gelingen
der Zusammenkunft bleibe ich mit herzlichen
Grüssen Ihre Ita Wegman

Letter from Ita Wegman to Elisabeth Vreede, June 20, 1934

completely on her Class tasks; to strengthen Arlesheim spiritually; and to take part little, or not at all, in anything else.[251] Elisabeth Vreede found Ita Wegman's way understandable, but not right, and she found herself to be even more alone there. Also she (Vreede) did not think about a new founding of the Society; she hoped, however, that it would be possible to intensify the common activity and develop it organizationally. Vreede herself took on the "correspondence position" of the "United Independent Anthroposophical Groups," and stood in the midst of the work, in its social center, in the next years. In Arlesheim she set up her own lecture room for meetings and contributions of the "Groups," because her Section room had a different purpose; was too small; and would soon not be available to her. Ita Wegman denied herself this intention almost completely and went her own logical, determined way. Elisabeth Vreede had to accept this like much else, even though since 1925 she had drawn much aggression in the Executive Council and the Society to herself that was, to a great extent, meant for Ita Wegman. In November 1934, Vreede took part in a Folk Psychology Conference in the Independent Waldorf School in The Hague together with Willem Zeylmans van Emmichoven and Herbert Hahn, who accomplished significant works in this field. Herbert Hahn wrote to her in Arlesheim two days before Christmas, "I feel we have to thank your loyal custodial task and your unfailing enthusiasm for all of Anthroposophy to thank for much, much more than we can grasp at this time."[252]

The most eagerly wished and intended withdrawal from the fighting at the Goetheanum was made difficult for Ita Wegman. Yet in December 1934, few weeks after her return from Palestine, a paper written by Hermann Poppelbaum (and anthroposophists from Hamburg) was published. It was titled "Out of the History of the Anthroposophical Society since 1925." Poppelbaum's pamphlet could not only be gotten in the Goetheanum, but it was also sold (in the open market) with the consent of the Dornach Executive Council (and with the proceeds going to the benefit of the Goetheanum: "*Net proceeds for the Goetheanum*"[253]). It described Ita Wegman's alleged attempt to take over the Goetheanum as Rudolf Steiner's successor and as a leader of the Dornach School for Spiritual Science after his death. It said that Wegman is supposed to have, since March 30, 1925, set up a power-empire with the international bases that work against the Goetheanum. According to Poppelbaum, she was endangering the existence and substance of the anthroposophic movement and the Society, through her will for power-occupation, as well as her scientific and business "un-methods." These are supposed to be part of a comprehensive strategy and to have manipulative, suggestive effects on the members. Poppelbaum was not a member of the Dornach Executive Council; he got his information about the Dornach meeting secondhand. Ita Wegman was shocked, and yet answered him thoughtfully on February 12, 1935:

> I have read your abusive pamphlet against me and am amazed how it is possible that a human being who is a student of Rudolf Steiner can judge another human being, who is also a student of Rudolf Steiner, so one-sidedly and can consider the events from such a thoroughly one-sided standpoint. The tone and opinion of your paper is so extraordinarily trivial, so loveless, that I will not occupy myself with it any longer. I will not defend myself against such accusations. The way they were brought is absurd. I know you from earlier and would rather keep that image of you in memory than to engage in an unpleasant fight. Sometime you will see that things look different from what you have one-sidedly heard.[254]

Poppelbaum's accusations and interpretations were indeed "absurd." Wegman responded in detail to only one of his many false representations:

> The purpose of my letter is not that I wish to write about me, but I must strongly reject the nerve with which you claim that Dr. Steiner let me persuade him to take Fräulein Vreede onto the Executive Council. Do you really believe that Rudolf Steiner acted out of personal sympathies when he appointed the Council? There were totally different grounds. The appointment of the Council was made on the basis of laws more worthy than what you so

Rudolf Steiner

thoughtlessly write: 'He took Fräulein Vreede out of the special wish of Dr. Wegman.' Now this is a huge error. I do not want to go without saying this because it involves Dr. Steiner, and I will never allow that.

Elisabeth Vreede herself spoke about "trivializing Dr. Steiner's intentions and a flagrant misunderstanding of what Steiner had created with the "esoteric" Executive Council.[255] She asked Eugen Kolisko to answer Poppelbaum in a document and to write his own independent history of the Anthroposophical Society since Rudolf Steiner's death. Also Kolisko was deeply affected by Poppelbaum's presentation of ("an indescribable document of lies").[256] He found himself in the situation of not being able to write such a document quickly, due to the burden of his profession. At the end of January 1935, however, he wrote to Elisabeth Vreede from England that he sees, in the meantime, the absolute significance of an early response and wants to work this out quickly after his return to Stuttgart. In the meantime, however, Vreede had begun her own work on documentation, with the hope that it would be supplemented by Kolisko. On January 25, she wrote to a close friend, "The task is difficult because I wrote *for me* and *against others*; Frau Dr. Steiner, however, allows Poppi to write for himself."[257]

At the beginning of March 1935, Elisabeth Vreede wrote in a letter about the "complete destruction of the Section I built up with ten years of arduous work."[258] At the same time preparations had already greatly progressed for her approaching expulsion from the Executive Council, her School Section and the General Anthroposophical Society. Vreede knew this. Elisabeth Vreede was one of the few—in contrast to Ita Wegman and her circle—who understood Karl König's vehement letter to Albert Steffen; a letter that resulted in König's expulsion from the Society three months later.[260] Even Vreede was unhappy about König's tone, but she saw the inner state of this doctor after all the attacks on him in the meantime, and she communicated this to him. As a result, he wrote to her from Pilgramshain on February 25, 1935:

> I do not have the slightest intention to retreat, not even one-half step. If one wants to expel me, I will know how to defend myself. For years one has scolded every human being possible in the most terrible way. Now I speak the unvarnished truth (in German if one is polite, one lies), and then such a storm breaks loose.
>
> It is too bad that also all the "friends" become so meek and fearful and crawl into a moral mouse hole.
>
> You do not know how grateful I am for your letter. It was, within the flood of others, the only courageous one. I am happy that you see that I could not have acted differently.[261]

On the other hand, Vreede clearly distanced herself from Karl Ballmer by letter. Ballmer sent her longer letters—one right after another—in March 1935. These were in close connection to the Dornach Executive Council crisis and the prepared removal and expulsion petition. Ballmer was outraged over these petitions and had reacted with great joy over König's open letter to Steffen. He himself had written to Marie Steiner and Albert Steffen, whom he had labeled as erring teachers of Anthroposophy, and whom he had seen as having played a substantial role in the "destruction of the Christmas Conference."[262] Ballmer asked Vreede about the history of the Statutes of the Anthroposophical Society ("Who is responsible for the text of the legally registered Statutes?"[263]) and their final editing after Rudolf Steiner's death. On the basis of these Statutes, per Ballmer, Elisabeth Vreede and Ita Wegman can in no way be voted off the Executive Council through a General Meeting; for there is proof that the Statutes "contradict the clear will of Rudolf Steiner."[264] According to Ballmer, the only way to block a successful step by the Goetheanum would be a legal action on the part of Vreede and Wegman. ("It is my conviction that after the undoubted result of April 14, Rudolf Steiner's General Anthroposophical Society will cease to exist."[265])

> Since the situation in Dornach is such as is shown in the last *News Sheet* with the petitions to the General Meeting, I am convinced that it is only a matter of a legal action by Dr. Vreede and Dr. Wegman. I have tried to picture the legal aspects of this matter and

"Executive Council's Idylls" (1925–1935)

Elisabeth Vreede with children

have the opinion that this process can with one-hundred-percent certainty be won by the plaintiffs.... If the leading anthroposophists in their delusion no longer know how to protect the spirit, then one must confer the spiritual will of Rudolf Steiner to an objective court. I am aware that my neutral view corresponds completely to Rudolf Steiner's will.

On the occasion of a broken marriage (Frau Häfflinger), there was much confusion in Dornach. The one person wanted to take over the care of the children, because the father reneged on his obligations. Others made sentimental, good suggestions, and so on and so on. Dr. Steiner intervened neutrally and said to Frau Häfflinger, 'Take your husband to court!' It is a matter of just such cool wisdom at the present time.[266]

Ballmer went on to say that he had already written to the President of the County Court of Dorneck-Thiersrtein, Halberthür, and had heard back from him that the General Meeting could not be forbidden officially. However, he wrote also, "It could also be mentioned that as far as the Statutes are not in agreement with Dr. Steiner's will, this issue would have to be handled by an orderly court trial. Whether or not this process would meet with success, we naturally cannot predict."[267]

Elisabeth Vreede protested decisively against this action and the whole tone of Ballmer's letter. Already with Ballmer's first letter of March 16, she had made a note in the margin: *"Here is a lack of love as an organ of knowledge."* On March 30, 1935, the tenth anniversary of Rudolf Steiner's death, she wrote Ballmer that she did not share in any way his judgment of Albert Steffen and Marie Steiner. "One cannot describe Herr Steffen as a Judas, or Frau Dr. Steiner as a 'character' and then want to work for better relationships in the Society." Vreede's letter goes on:

> It is not just because I did not like the mere *How* of the presentation, but rather *what* comes to expression in such a *How* can always be only one-sided.
>
> Certainly, there can be truths found through thinking, but these must be placed side-by-side with other truths that are seen from another side. And in order to find these, love, the truly

universal human love, must be formed into an organ of knowledge, in the sense that Rudolf Steiner spoke of it. My feeling about Dr. König's letter is somewhat similar, although I can understand that the one-sided publication in the News can ultimately lead to a kind of rage. In spite of this, an esotericist should always see the other side of things; then he or she cannot simply formulate his or her views so extremely. And I wish absolutely to see you as just such a person striving for the true esotericism.

I am also convinced that not very much can be accomplished for the spiritual with the legal system.[268]

In addition, concerning the Statutes of the General Anthroposophical Society, she told Ballmer:

> Dr. Wachsmuth and a representative of the authorities formulated the Statutes registered according to commercial law during Rudolf Steiner's illness. Dr. Steiner saw them and—as was told to me upon asking indirectly—he probably found them not to be good, but added that one could change them later and then improve them. Dr. Wachsmuth has often maintained that the Swiss authority himself brought in all kinds of democratic principles, while he (Wachsmuth) wanted to try, based on the principles of Dr. Steiner, to remove the necessary legal aspects. Yet, Dr. Steiner signed them along with others, if I am not very much mistaken. That was in February 1925. In any case, they were never brought before the members for approval or rejection like the Principles were. That was also most likely never what Dr. Steiner had intended; these should serve only for dealing with the authorities. Now, where members suddenly experience that they are accepted or excluded (or expelled) according to the circumstances, they have indeed a right to know how they came about. There may well be aspects that can be contested, but I think that should be considered only in a *spiritual* sense.

Ballmer wanted in no way to let Vreede's conclusion stand. He also did not share her articulated reservations toward Karl König's action. He wrote her again. "This letter [Karl König's] is, according to form and the issue, a totally excellent and well-thought-out document of the spiritual conflict, struggle.... This letter by Dr. König has much of Rudolf Steiner's spirited temperament. In ten years one will not even remotely judge this letter as containing rage."[269]

~

At this time, Elizabeth Vreede had completed her own objective document of justification against Hermann Poppelbaum, "*Zur Geschichte der Anthroposophischen Gesellschaft seit der Weihnachtstagung 1923*" (Concerning the history of the Anthroposophical Society since the Christmas Conference 1923). She sent it in manuscript form to Ita Wegman, among others. Wegman's request for corrections, of March 22, reached Vreede after it had been typeset and was ready to print, and so was no longer considered.

[Ita Wegman]:
I forgot to say to you yesterday, what I also discussed with George Kaufmann, whether it would not be possible to add as a last sentence to your historical document that there is still much that needs to be put in the proper light, which is not possible in this document; for instance, several events within the Executive Council meetings. I mean with this the Alexander issue, the esotericism of the First Class. Your document would gain significance thereby. I don't think I have to start with this because this is too personal, and yet, in these two issues lies the kernel of the drama."[270] Ita Wegman was right in this, as Elizabeth Vreede was indeed quite aware. Albert Steffen also answered Elizabeth Vreede on March 27—albeit in his own way: "I have received your brochure and have passed it on for others' information. In looking at it, I hit upon many incorrect points. Because I do not have the time, however, I must reserve the right to deal with this material and corrections at a later time."[271] On the envelope of his letter to his Council colleague, he wrote the address as, "Arlesheim (near Basel)." Vreede's humor was still not broken; she scribbled beside it: "Should it not lie yet *much* farther from Dornach?"

Many other people reacted to her publication with joy and relief, among them the Cologne art dealer Goyert, but also Karl Ballmer and

Arlesheim, den 22. März 1935.

Liebe Dr. Vreede!

Ich vergass gestern Ihnen zu sagen, was ich auch mit George Kaufmann besprach, ob es nicht möglich wäre, in Ihrem Geschichte-Dokument noch als Letztes den Satz einzufügen, dass noch manches zurechtzusetzen sei, was in dieser Schrift noch nicht möglich gewesen ist, wie z. B. einige Geschehnisse innerhalb Vorstandssitzungen. Ich meine hiermit die Alexander-Frage, die Esoterik der Klasse. Ihr Dokument gewinnt dadurch an Gewicht. Ich glaube nicht, dass ich damit anfangen muss, weil diese Geschichte zu persönlich ist, und doch liegt in diesen zwei Dingen der Kernpunkt der Dramatik. - Was meinen Sie?

Mit freundlichem Gruss

Ity Dr. I. Wegman.

Letter from Ita Wegman to Elisabeth Vreede, March 22, 1935

Arlesheim, den 28. März 1935.

Liebe Dr. Vreede!

    Seit einigen Tagen wollte ich mit Ihnen sprechen; leider musste ich mich wegen heftigen Neuralgien im Kopf hinlegen. Weder sprechen noch arbeiten war mir möglich. Inzwischen geht die Zeit herum, und ich hatte doch einiges so gern mit Ihnen besprochen, was die Denkschrift betrifft.

    Es ist doch notwendig, einige Dinge zurechtzusetzen, und ich habe Ihre Hilfe dabei nötig. Wie gross ist der Hass Frau Dr. Steiners gegen mich, und um diesen Hass zu befriedigen, muss das Werk Rudolf Steiners zerstört werden.

    Können Sie morgen, Freitag, eine Zeit bestimmen, um zu mir zu kommen?- Ich muss mich noch hüten, sonst würde ich auch gerne zu Ihnen kommen.- Ich wäre Ihnen sehr dankbar. Ihre Schrift ist sehr gut und wird schon aufklärend wirken.

                        Mit freundlichem Gruss

                              Dr. I. Wegman

Letter from Ita Wegman to Elisabeth Vreede, March 28, 1935

Valentin Tomberg. In spite of her explicit criticism of his contributions, Ballmer wrote on March 27, about her small, thirty-eight-page comprehensive document: "It makes a quite excellent impression on me. It is both, according to the *What*, as well as to the *How*, a significant document that will have an important role to play." In the same letter Ballmer stated: "The History of the Anthroposophical Society is a right interesting story."[272] Valentin Tomberg reported from the Baltic States of the positive reception of Vreede's publication in the circle of friends, and said of himself: "On my behalf, may I say that I appreciate in this book especially the fact that it was written more from pain than out of indignation; more as defense than as attack."[273]

Tomberg's characterization was right. Vreede had defended Ita Wegman and herself in the issue of the Council's meeting in view of Wegman's highly controversial article and "Leading Thoughts"; her connection to the First Class;[274] her activities in the "periphery," but also in connection with the World School Association; the Dornach conferences; the founding of the "Anthroposophical Work Association in Germany"; and more. Still, Elizabeth Vreede did not want to be mixed in with Ita Wegman or belong to her "party." ("...I figure, out of the forced deliberateness, ever again as a supporter of Dr. Wegman."[275]) Moreover, Ita Wegman did not agree with all of Vreede's actions.[276] On the other hand, the events of the last few years had brought them together in an increasing connection and created a destiny in common. Ita Wegman became softer and more open, and once again approached Vreede more—after years during which she lived and worked totally from her interconnection and love to Rudolf Steiner and was unapproachable; and at the same time, she was devoted to the setting up of the international medical institutions and therapeutic services for those in need of special help.

~

Vreede's history presentation was published with a print run of 2,000 copies and found a certain distribution. Yet, the General Meeting of April 14, 1935, with its motion for expulsion came ever closer. At the beginning of April Vreede wrote to Fritzanton Krücke, the second husband of the widow Theodora Kunert (the mother of Willfried Immanuel). She wrote of her idea for an examination commission instead of a member vote.[277] This commission should be comprised of people who were neutral, such as Friedrich Rittelmeyer, Margareta Morgenstern, Friedrich Doldinger, Emil Leinhas, Graf Holzer-Poditz, Gottfried Husemann, and others. In spite of Fritzanton Krück's efforts, it did not come about, because many who were chosen were not willing to collaborate, or their neutrality had long since gone by the wayside. On April 2, Elizabeth Vreede wrote in a letter: "As concerns the General Meeting, I hope for a miracle that could bring it about that we still remain together."[278]

Preserving the unity of the General Anthroposophical Society appeared to Elizabeth Vreede to be urgent, but she herself could do no more for this unity. Already in January, in a discussion in a small group in Arlesheim, she had proposed to make public particularly some of Rudolf Steiner's esoteric manuscripts for Ita Wegman. Bringing them out would have brought a sudden change in the power situation in the General Anthroposophical Society, because the real position and spiritual circumstances of Ita Wegman would have been brought to light.[279] Ita Wegman, however, was not willing for this step and rejected it with a noble attitude, as Werner Pache recorded in his diary on January 20: "*Vreede believed that all that was still possible to do to prevent this [the expulsion motion] was to publish the documents. Dr. Wegman believed that whatever comes, we must suffer through, so that the truth may reveal itself.*"[280]

At the end of March, ten years after Rudolf Steiner's death and three weeks before the General Meeting of the General Anthroposophical Society, there came out instead a further document in Dornach that presented the fivefold scope of Vreede's formulation. It was titled "Memorandum about Issues of the Anthroposophical Society during the years 1925 to 1935," published by twelve anthroposophists, and could be ordered through the Goetheanum Office. All of the objections that Popplebaum had raised three months before

Nur für Mitglieder.

Zur Geschichte
der
Anthroposophischen Gesellschaft
seit der Weihnachtstagung 1923.

E. Vreede.

Publication, 1935

were intensified yet again and systematically built up in this piece. The "Memorandum" was already announced on March 17, 1935, in the *News (for Members)* parallel to an extensive printing of the Dismissal Expulsion motions. ("Both Council members, Dr. Ita Wegman and Dr. Vreede, due to their disregard of the Society through actions that bear the character of self-expulsion, shall no longer be recognized as members of the Executive Council. Dr. Ita Wegman and Dr. Vreede are to be dismissed as members of the Executive Council of the General Anthroposophical Society. Further activity of either in the sphere of the General Anthroposophical Society seems to the General Meeting to be impossible."[281]) It also included an explanation of the motions,[282] as well as a corresponding editorial by Marie Steiner:

> Each of us must ask ourselves: Does our task lie in the direction of comfortable tolerance in which, in order to avoid the fight and to maintain an outer appearance of brotherhood, we allow things to run simply the way they are? Is it to be a comfortable tolerance from which the ideal striven for of a wakeful, pure spirituality is sacrificed, so that every new attempt of a Society dedicated to the study of spiritual knowledge on a strictly ethical basis meets with failure? Or is our task to bring our full moral forces to bear for Rudolf Steiner's greatest wish for the movement he created? His deepest wish was that one may be able to say that there was once a Society dedicated to the study of spiritual research, which did not tolerate idle play with esotericism wherever it wanted to arise; and which did not allow those who claim the power to control for themselves, thus easily opening the way for charlatanism to get a foothold in its midst" ("actuality"[283]).

In a certain way, with this, everything was finished, was over. When an anthroposophist from Holland asked Elizabeth Vreede to send him the book "Memorandum," she replied, *"I am ashamed, out of reverence for Rudolf Steiner's Anthroposophy, to hand this on."*[284]

Elizabeth Vreede did not take part in the General Meeting on Palm Sunday, April 14, which decided her expulsion from the Executive Council and removal as Section leader. Fritzanton Krück read

"Executive Council's Idylls" (1925–1935)

schwerte Arbeit zu verwandeln. Niemand dachte daran, daß ein Zusammenwirken der Vorstandsmitglieder einmal unmöglich werden könnte, und erst nach vielen bitteren Erfahrungen lernte man einsehen, daß sogar die Berechtigung, ein solches Zusammenwirken fordern zu dürfen, nicht mehr vorhanden war. Nur völlig unorientierte Mitglieder konnten in späteren Jahren aus ehrlichem Gewissen diese Forderung noch stellen.

Nicht weniger tief und schmerzlich hatten andere Mitgliederkreise den Tod Rudolf Steiners empfunden. Sie bildeten sich aber eine andere Ansicht über die zukünftige Leitung der Gesellschaft, und zwar hatten sie darüber sehr bestimmte Meinungen. Auch sie erkannten den nunmehr aus fünf Mitgliedern bestehenden Vorstand als die Leitung der Gesellschaft an. Mit allem Nachdruck betonten sie dessen esoterischen Charakter, wiesen aber hin auf den Unterschied zwischen der Leitung der Gesellschaft und der Leitung der Hochschule. Rudolf Steiner selber war Vorsitzender der Gesellschaft und Leiter der Hochschule gewesen; nach seinem Tode übernahm der Vorstand die Leitung der Gesellschaft und es sollte, nach der Auffassung der Mehrzahl der Mitglieder, auch die Hochschule als Zentrum der anthroposophischen Arbeit und besonders als Pflegestätte der Esoterik vom Vorstand geleitet werden. Gegen diese Auffassung wandten sich die anderen Mitgliederkreise, indem sie die Anerkennung Frau Dr. Wegmans als Leiterin der Hochschule forderten. Durch die Art, wie sie selber diese Anerkennung vollzogen, galt ihnen Frau Dr. Wegman auch als die eigentliche Leiterin der Gesellschaft, wenn sie auch nicht dem Namen nach Vorsitzende sei. Die Sonderstellung, die hiermit Frau Dr. Wegman eingeräumt wurde, sollte ihr auch das Recht geben, in wichtigen Fragen allein zu entscheiden, und die anderen Vorstandsmitglieder sollten sich der als Nachfolgerin Rudolf Steiners betrachteten Persönlichkeit als Mitarbeiter unterordnen und dabei mithelfen, die von ihr anzugebenden Ziele zu verwirklichen. Daß gewisse Mitglieder damit rechneten, auf diesem Wege selber die Arbeitsziele der Gesellschaft zu bestimmen, wird sich aus dem tatsächlichen Verlauf der Ereignisse ergeben.

Auch auf dieser Seite erwartete man also ein harmonisches Zusammenwirken des Vorstands, und zwar schon deshalb, weil man aus dessen esoterischem Charakter sogar die Verpflichtung ableitete, durch ein-

9

"Memorandum," with Ita Wegman's marginal note

her letter aloud to the gathering. The letter spoke of the loss of the consciousness for the Christmas Conference and the destruction of its most important organ: the esoteric Executive Council that Rudolf Steiner instituted in 1923/24 through an "occult act." Once again, for the gathering, Elizabeth Vreede quoted Rudolf Steiner in view of the Christmas Conference. ("It may be done in the hope that, even if not a complete understanding, at least an inkling of the yet unspoken depths might awaken in the last hour."):

> Then with this, that I myself [Rudolf Steiner] am President of the Society, the anthroposophic movement became one with the Anthroposophical Society. That made it necessary that at Christmas in Dornach an outer, exoteric Executive Council was not instituted, but rather an Executive Council that is to be considered an esoteric Council. In all that it does, it is responsible only to the spiritual powers. This Council was not elected, but formed. All the things that are usually done at a Foundation Meeting were handled differently at Christmas. And this Council is what I want to call an Initiative Council—a Council that sees its tasks in what it does. Therefore, Statutes that sound like other Statutes were not worked out at the Christmas Conference. Rather, it was simply stated what relationship shall exist from human being to human being; between the Council and other members; the relationship of individual members with other members, and so on.
>
> What the intentions of the Council will be is not written as a Statute, but is actually a narrative of what one wants to do, that then took on the form of a Statute. Everything was different from what is found in other societies. And what is essential is that now an esoteric character has come into the whole Anthroposophical Society. The whole movement, now that it flows through the Society, must have an esoteric character. One must take this absolutely in earnest. For the Executive Council at the Goetheanum only those impulses of pure human work from the spiritual world will be deemed decisive, or definitive. Not paragraph 1, paragraph 2, and so on, but what is true spiritual life shall be supported unconditionally, without having to intend something else.[285]

Vreede closed her letter to the members with the sentences:

Perhaps it will be possible for a few of you to sense from these words what viewpoints were decisive for my actions during these twenty years—for my real actions, not for those fictionalized intentions and deeds attributed to me.... May this General Meeting succeed to lift itself in the spirit to that nouveau from which these words of our Teacher speak.

The General Meeting did not rise to this "level," but just the opposite. Elizabeth Vreede found the speech that Ludwig Polzer-Hoditz gave in defense of Ita Wegman to be quite good. There was no such speech for her.

During the deciding vote, Elizabeth Vreede was in her Rudolf Steiner Archive at the Goetheanum. Later that same day she saw a light in the reading room of the carpentry studio between 10:00 and 11:00 p.m. The next morning all lecture manuscripts had been removed from the Archive. Shortly afterward she received a letter from Marie Steiner. In it Rudolf Steiner's widow wrote that she herself is the owner of the Archive according to Rudolf Steiner's intentions. As a result, it is not appropriate that the Archive should work as a center for strife and a place of agitation against the leadership of the Goetheanum. The Archive was originally set up against Rudolf Steiner's will, "but he gave in." Now however, per Marie Steiner, she must intervene: "It is difficult for me to have to say this, as I have no personal animosity toward you, and would have gladly spared you this." At the end of her letter Marie Steiner wrote politely:

> There is nothing left to say than to express once again my regret that we were unable to come to an understanding. We have all suffered greatly from this and will suffer much going forward.
> With these feelings, greetings with thoughts of better days."[286]

The previous evening, Marie Steiner had arranged for clearing out the Archive, as well as changing the lock on the door. Elizabeth Vreede had not expected such a drastic action. Only after reading Count Ludwig Polzer-Hoditz's speech did some things became clear to her. "The man-of-bad-fortune said there were more and more

Rudolf Steiner-Archiv am Goetheanum

Dornach, den 2den Febr. 1933

Beste Dr. Zeylmans,

Zooals U wel zult weten, kan het Archief geen voordrachten naar andere plaatsen uitleenen; er zou dan altyd alles onderweg zyn. Om U met de bestudeering van het rasprobleem te helpen, zend ik U hierby - als groote uitzondering! - eenige bladen uit onze registers, waarin U in hoofdzaak de cyclusplaatsen vindt, die op deze vragen slaan. (Als in het Arenson-register beteekent XIII,6,7 : Cyklus 13,Voordracht 6, blz 7. Enkele aanwyzingen zyn wat obscuur, maar in't algemeen zyn het òf cycluasen, òf zgn. Einzelvorträge, die vroeger in die groote kleurige Hefte uitgegeven werden en nu ten deele herdrukt zyn.) Daarmee heeft U althans de gedrukte plaatsen, die terstond te bestudeeren zyn.

Verder is er over rasontwikkeling en -ontstaan gedrukt te vinden in: Gäa-Sophia Bd. III ("Wanderung der Rassen" 1904); "Die Welt als Ergebnis von Gleichgewichtswirkungen" (Dornach 14 Nov. 1914); Nachrichtenblatt 1925 (2de jaarg. Nr. 24-28,Voordracht Bern 9 Jan. 1916). Over het maleische ras speciaal vond ik allen wat in een voordracht van Keulen, 27. Dec. 1907 (niet gedrukt), wat ongeveer ook in de cyclus over de Volksseelen staat.Voorts in cyklus IV,6,16.- Over rassen in 't algemeen (alles niet gedrukt) : 3 Mei 1909 Berlyn, 28 Oct. 1904 Berlyn ("Der trojanische Krieg"), April 1906 Berlyn (Luciferische Wesenheiten), 21. Oct. 1906 Berlyn, 10.Juni 1909

Letter from Elisabeth Vreede to Willem Zeylmans van Emmichoven,
February 2, 1933

Budapest, 13 en 15 Febr. 1915 Stuttgart. In latere jaren
heeft Dr. Steiner zeer weinig meer daarover gesproken. Enkele
van deze voordrachten zyn, geloof ik, in de Haagsche Bibliotheek.
Als ik in Februari kom - (ik zal in Rotterdam spreken en M.Stibbe heeft
me ook voor de Haagsche School gevraagd) moet ik de registerbladen in
elk geval weer meenemen, en ook het andere, dat U nog van my heeft!

Met hartelyke groeten

Uwe

L. Vreede

letters, then pamphlets, and finally books written in the ten-year-war, and they now fill libraries and archives."[287]

With this the Rudolf Steiner Archive at the Goetheanum was actually closed—after long work. Albert Steffen had, as Chairman of the Council, used the Archive for many years.[288] Other members too found joy, help, advice and support with critical issues[289] in the Archive, in accordance with what Rudolf Steiner said at the Christmas Conference about Elizabeth Vreede's social work. "The Archive is Fräulein Vreede's work. You may not take it from her!" Those were his last words about the Rudolf Steiner Archive at the Goetheanum, spoken a few days before his death.

Vreede's place of work was taken from her with the expulsion from the Council and her removal from the Section leadership. On April 18, 1935, four days after the General Meeting, she had a furniture truck pick up her personal possessions from the Section hall and the Archive and the planetarium. At this time she was fifty-six years old and was passing through an important point in her biography—her third Moon node. Thirteen months before, on March 28, 1934, she left the last of the General Meetings of the General Anthroposophical Society that she would attend and the Great Hall[290] that she would never again enter. She left with this statement:

> *And I will just say this: No matter how things proceed, I will continue my work in the name of Rudolf Steiner and in the strength of the power with which I serve him!*

5

"May soul live in this house" (1935–1943)

The Final Years

> "But that for which we must strive with the refutations is, that with the others, in as far as they are capable, an insight might arise, so that they notice the errors that were made. And I feel just as strongly that we have the spiritual duty not to let the now-truly-misled brothers fall; not to make the break complete."
> —ELIZABETH VREEDE [291]

Elisabeth Vreede (undated)

At the beginning of 1935, before the last General Meeting, Elizabeth Vreede spoke from time to time about how deeply the events in Dornach affected her. She spoke of the terrible experiences of the last years and the experience of that destructive will in her own person.[292] Vreede was determined to remain in the Anthroposophical Society; yet, she found the whole process more than hard. She was of a sturdy constitution and good health, and a good balance of incarnation, and was highly intelligent, which allowed her to see through much. All of this (and the entire strength of her individuality and destiny) helped her not to break on the given situation, which showed the elements of a mystery. Within the Executive Council Vreede had represented most clearly the quality of social collaboration, on which Rudolf Steiner had built everything. However, neither Ita Wegman nor Marie Steiner nor Albert Steffen really wanted such collaboration. They remained in their separate domains, in a heightened self-awareness of each in their respective special tasks.

To Guenther Wachsmuth, Vreede was a thorn in his side from the very beginning; business would run faster and smoother without her. Now the connection was severed in the time before Easter 1935, in the twelfth year of its existence. It was an intention and a failure from the beginning. Vreede had held onto the original initiative the longest, not out of pride, but in the hope yet to be able to do justice to Rudolf Steiner's social instructions. "I have the particular conviction, Herr Steffen, that we all together have not yet realized the Christmas Conference, but also that, in working together, we can strive toward a realization."[293]

Vreede did not feel herself to be separated from the General Anthroposophical Society through the decisions made on April 14,

1935. She wrote in a letter[294] in the summer, "The tie that was bound through the Christmas Conference is stronger than a vote by the General Meeting." She continued to work together with the United Independent Anthroposophical Groups, and built within it a "study group of the Mathematical-Astronomical Section." The relationship with the friends in Holland, England, and Germany remained as close as ever. The will to continue working in the future in the sense of the spiritual intentions of the Christmas Conference had not in any way suffered from the decision of the majority.

In July 1935 Elizabeth Vreede translated the important publication, *Entwickelung und Geisteskampf 1923–1935* (Development and spiritual struggle 1923–1935), by Willem Zeylmans van Emmichoven into German. The complete title of Emmichoven's work, as published in Stuttgart, was (translated literally): "*Development and Spiritual Struggle of the Anthroposophical Society in Holland and the Friends' Groups, in Their Relationship to the General Anthroposophical Society, 1923–1935. With an Appendix 'Fable convenue, or History?' Several necessary Comments on the 'Memorandum 1923–1935.'*" Zeylmans calmly and clearly presented themes of the Society conflicts since 1923. He brought out central motifs, among which were the understanding of the leadership in Dornach and all the issues of "center" and "periphery." He belonged also to those who were expelled, with whom Vreede met often and discussed the future.

Elizabeth Vreede rejected—as did Ita Wegman—the idea of organizational forms that go further or the forming of a second Anthroposophical Society, although she in no way took the route of withdrawal, as Wegman did after her illness struck. Ever again suggestions from the circle of the United Independent Anthroposophical Groups came to her for her, together with Ita Wegman, to take a central leadership position. In August 1935, she received the manuscript "*Von der Notwendigkeit eines esoterischen Vorstandes in den Anthroposophischen Arbeitsgruppen*" (Concerning the necessity of an esoteric Executive Council in the Anthroposophical Work Groups) by Bruno Maggendorfer and anthroposophists from Hamburg. Several weeks before, Maria Stiefelhagen had already written to her in this direction. Maria Stiefelhagen was the manager of the Anthroposophical Study Library in Hamburg, and was highly valued by Vreede. Also Stiefelhagen proposed a closer joining together of the work communities "in the name of the Christmas Conference," under the *leadership* of Elizabeth Vreede and Ita Wegman, "which they have by virtue of their spiritual task given through Rudolf Steiner." ("It is a fact that Albert Steffen, Marie Steiner and Dr. Wachsmuth have withdrawn, and that Dr. Wegman and Dr. Vreede are still Executive Council members."[295]) Vreede and Wegman should call members they trust to serve on this Council, and thus determine the development for the future. Elizabeth Vreede, however, rejected this vigorously. On August 8, she wrote to Stiefelhagen in Hamburg: "Is it then so certain that it appears to the spiritual world that the Christmas Conference, the Executive Council, and so on, is shattered and now must be removed by *us*? Is it not perhaps that the bond that connects our Teacher with the Society through the Christmas Conference is so strong that not even such maya decisions as on April 14 can break it?"[296] Vreede stressed that the documentations from her and from Willems Zeylmans were necessary to correct the one-sided accusations.

> From everything that I experienced of Dr. Steiner during our struggle with the Theosophical Society, I know that, yes, we have the duty to present the injustice that was done, in order that the way remains open for a lifting of, or at least an insight into, this injustice. (This is not the reason for my joy about the excellent, objective, factual Zeylmanns pamphlet.) Dr. Steiner wrote at that time about the memorandum against *him*—yes, there was indeed such a memorandum! He wrote: "When things are brought forth, such as Dr. H.S. brought in his memorandum, these things, after having been brought forth, separate themselves from the one who brought them. Then they have an independent existence. In order to characterize *these* things, what preceded was written." We have this duty, too.

Vreede stated further that the making clear historically of the rejection of the inappropriate accusations would not have the purpose of determining that one is right and the other is wrong, not to declare the others error and confusion, but rather the purpose is to prepare future insights.

> But what we must strive for with the refutations is that, with the others, insofar as they are able, an *insight* might arise so that they notice the errors that were made. And I feel equally strongly that we have the spiritual duty not to allow the now-truly-misled brothers to fall and not to make the break complete.

The point, per Vreede, should be under no circumstance to make the separation complete or to establish fixed structures. She hoped that, in a span of about two years, insights would arise. "In the meantime, we may not do anything in regard to the Christmas Conference that cannot be undone! Thus, everything is still provisional. It will be difficult, but it must take place out of love precisely to the impulse of the Christmas Conference." Vreede stressed the necessity for a strong spiritual connection to one another, as well as the will to go through a real process of internalization, of making things inward. She mentioned, among other things, the lectures about the inner development of the human being that she was holding at that time. With this, Elizabeth Vreede went the same path that Ita Wegman took,[297] taking the tragedy of the situation totally within herself. She grasped the difficulty, the severity, and the partial cruelty as elements of development. She mentioned in her letter to Maria Stiefelhagen that also Ita Wegman would not accept the forming of an esoteric Executive Council within the Anthroposophical Working Community. "In this sense, I see it also as a sign of karma that, for instance, Dr. Wegman would never get involved with what seems so self-evident to you."

Elizabeth Vreede did not agree with Ita Wegman's withdrawal from the United Independent Anthroposophical Groups. However, her inner stance to the whole episode was to a great extent the same as Wegman's. Elizabeth Vreede did not want to leave or abandon

"May soul live in this house" (1935–1943)

Elisabeth Vreede (undated)

the Anthroposophical Society, and so therefore, also not the "misled brothers." She saw in the whole process "more illness than evil," as she wrote in the same letter—this illness, however, should be overcome and healed by the "good" where possible. She closed her guiding remarks with the following words: "Those are my opinions that I am expressing only on my own behalf, and with which I lived and wrestled for months. I find them often confirmed. We are not without guidance; we must only try to reach some clarity about these things."

In her own house Vreede forbade negative dinner conversation about the situation in Dornach. She was often in Holland and England—even for Class Lessons—and undertook further journeys: to Mallorca (where she occupied herself with the life and work of Raimundus Lullus); and to Italy, Greece, Palestine, Egypt, and Ireland. A travel companion wrote, "What she could relate on the spot from Dr. Steiner's lectures remained full of life, as if one had been there in person—very different from all the other lectures of Dr. Steiner's that one has read!"[298] In June 1936, Elizabeth Vreede observed, along with Lili Kolisko, a total eclipse of the Sun in Turkey. This was on the 8,200-foot-high Ula Dagh, the "powerful mountain" above the Sea of Marmara, the Bithynian Olympus, a dormant volcano. In Oslo on October 2, 1913 (more than twenty-one years earlier), Vreede had heard Rudolf Steiner's presentation of inner experiences during an eclipse of the Sun. It is to be found in his second lecture about *The Fifth Gospel*. At that time Steiner described the experiences as follows:

> To the inner eye, the whole area around the human being looks as follows during a partial or full solar eclipse. Everything looks different. I want to leave aside the aspect presented by everything produced by human skills and industry. It needs some strength of character, and full awareness of the fact that all these things had to develop, to behold without flinching the spirits arising from industrially produced objects devoid of art. I will not go into this but merely tell you that at such a time nature shows itself full of light

The Total Eclipse of the Sun 19th June, 1936

by

E. VREEDE

IT is not given to everyone to witness a total eclipse of the Sun, for the phenomenon, if not exactly rare, is very local in character, being only visible on each occasion over a narrow strip of territory. In Europe, for example, save for the eclipse of June 29, 1927, there has scarcely been another total eclipse of the Sun during the present century.

It was therefore a fortunate event in my life to be able to observe in its total phase the solar eclipse of June 19th this year. Several important phenomena, as is well known, can only be observed during a total eclipse, and some of these have not yet found an adequate scientific explanation. For me, however, it was not a question of finding "explanations" but of witnessing the pure phenomena, and perhaps from contemplation of them being able to penetrate a little more deeply into their inner nature.

A suitable and not too remote locality appeared to be the "Bithynian Olympus," a mountain of about 7,500 feet in Asia Minor not far from the Sea of Marmora. Most of the larger scientific expeditions went to Siberia, or even farther afield to Japan, so as to have a longer period of totality. On the said mountain one could at least reckon on a duration of 77 seconds, with a fair prospect of good conditions. (This particular eclipse was of comparatively short duration, with a maximum of little more than two minutes.)

An eclipse of the Sun always begins at a place on Earth where the Sun is rising. Such is the moment at which the shadow of the Moon first touches the Earth. Thenceforward the shadow passes across the Earth with great velocity from west to east, across a strip of land about sixty miles in width. The shadow therefore quickly

The Present Age, *September 1936*

in a way normally seen only after extremely difficult meditation work. All plant and animal life, every bird, every butterfly looks different. You note that the feeling of vitality is reduced. A deep conviction can arise that a life of the spirit connected with the Sun, the physical body of which may be said to be the Sun we see in the heavens, is intimately bound up with all life on Earth. The feeling arises that when the physical radiance of the Sun is forcibly darkened as the Moon moves between Sun and Earth, this is something entirely different from nighttime when the Sun is merely not shining. It feels as if the group souls of plants and animals were arising, while living physical bodies grow limp and feeble. Everything spiritual, representing group soul nature, seems to light up.[299]

After her return from Turkey, Elizabeth Vreede wrote an essay for an English magazine about her experiences in June 1936 on the Bithynian Olympus:

> In the early dawn we found ourselves together climbing up the last few hundred feet of the mountainside covered with juniper bushes and overgrown with violets. At the very moment when we reached the top the Sun was rising over the mountaintops to the east. There was as yet no sign of the eclipse; the Sun was rising in the radiant light of a lovely summer's day. No cloud was in the sky, and in spite of the snow that was still covering the highest summit of the *Ula Dagh*, the air was mild and warm.
>
> Very few minutes afterward, the shadow of the Moon began to creep across the Sun. From the right-hand side the lunar disk began to encroach upon the Sun, eating its way ever more deeply in. Most people have witnessed this phenomenon at one time or another at a partial eclipse. To a certain extent, even when the eclipse is only partial, one can experience the indescribable change that gradually comes over the landscape, not only in the quality of light but in the whole mood and feeling of the surrounding Earth. The daylight does not only lessen as at nightfall, but it grows pale and ashen gray, the color of a corpse, and an uncanny feeling of oppression, anxiety and doom increasingly comes over the Earth. The birds, which had been singing merrily until recently, are reduced to silence; the animals grow restless; and even the human heart cannot quite escape the feeling that increasingly takes hold of the entire Earth

around. I say advisedly "the Earth around," for the spectacle that now appears in the heavens is by no means so uncanny as is the pale and fading light down on the Earth. The visible surface of the Sun decreases, and the sky, too, grows darker, yet not in the same way as on the Earth. One feels a kind of estrangement between what is happening on Earth and in the cosmos. Above the ineffable laws of cosmic rhythm are finding their fulfillment, bringing forth eclipses in their periods with marvelous regularity in space and time. Beneath is the Earth, robbed of the sunlight out of due season, the victim as it were of an appalling misfortune, sick unto death and wretched—for such is the impression.

The feeling rapidly increases until the moment when totality sets in. Darkness is over the entire firmament; on the horizon only a narrow circle of light is still visible. Now to describe the last few seconds before totality: from the west we see approaching on the distant horizon a band of darkness, dirty reddish-brown in color, extending rapidly toward us, though without a well-marked outline. In it is the actual shadow of the Moon, coming toward us with great rapidity from the west, to envelop the whole surrounding world in darkness for a few short moments. And at the very moment when the shadow reaches us (though the exact moment would be difficult to tell), in the heavens to the east—that is, in the opposite direction—the miracle takes place: the light of the Sun suddenly disappears, the black disk of the Moon entirely covers up the Sun, and in the selfsame second, like a flash of lightning, the solar corona makes its appearance and beside it, the planet Venus. Both the corona and Venus shine with a silvery light, seeming to overcome the impending darkness with their clear transparent radiance, reaching far around the blackened orb of the Sun. So suddenly it happens that one feels tempted to describe it as a theatrical, melodramatic effect. Evidently some of the Turkish people who were present felt it, too, for when the seventy-seven seconds had passed by and the Sun gave its first light once more with equal suddenness, while Venus and the corona disappeared from sight, they clapped their hands as if in appreciation of the successful performance!

So now the eclipse was complete. For a few precious seconds we witnessed the marvelous corona, the only known solar phenomenon visible only during a total eclipse. The corona is highly luminous; it is by no means circular in form but rather horizontal, reaching out in bands of light to a great distance from the Sun and of intensely silvery appearance, so that beside it Venus on the right-hand side seemed only like a drop distilled and intensified from the same substance. No other stars were visible during the short time the eclipse lasted—neither Mars, which was situated between the Sun and Venus and probably overwhelmed by the corona light, nor Mercury, much farther away—near its greatest elongation—in the neighborhood of Aldebaran in the constellation of Taurus. I, at any rate, was unable to see either of these planets no matter hard I looked. Indeed the darkness, even during totality, was not so very intense. Immediately around the Sun, or perhaps I should say rather around the Moon, was a narrow strip of brighter light; it was as though the Moon had not quite succeeded in blotting out all of the Sun's light. (Within this circle of light one could see a few of the red protuberances, the so-called prominences or solar flames.) The light from this inner circle, taken together with the corona light, illuminated our surroundings in a dim twilight that no longer had the same death-like character as in the last few minutes before totality.

And now, no less suddenly than it had vanished, the light of the Sun returned. As in a lightning flash, the corona, Venus, and the surrounding darkness disappeared. A minute point of brilliant light appearing on the left-hand edge of the Sun rapidly increased to a tiny disc of light, which for a moment seemed to be rotating about the left edge of the Sun, and thereafter slowly increased in magnitude and intensity, repeating in inverse order the different degrees of partiality we had previously witnessed.

In these first moments of returning light a peculiar phenomenon occurs, which was visible also on this occasion. Against a rocky precipice to the north we saw a rapid play of wave-like shadows in periodic movement, wave upon wave of light and shade. For a few brief seconds only this phenomenon is to be observed. It is as yet quite unexplained. Down in the valley of Bursa, as was afterward related to me, the phenomenon was seen with great intensity, dark shadows speeding across the valley "like waves on the sea."

Thereafter, the daylight rapidly increased. But the remarkable thing was that, from the very first moment, the gradually returning light no longer had the uncanny quality that it'd had immediately before totality. Feebly though it is to begin with, the diffused light that gradually extends over the Earth feels normal and healthy. Gone is the nightmare of oppression that seemed to weigh upon the Earth. It is not only the gradual intensification of the Sunlight that calls forth this impression. It is also a radical difference in quality, an absolute polarity—formerly fear and anxiety, a sense of doom as at the end of the world; thereafter the brief and magnificent, no longer quite so uncanny interval of totality; and then at last the still feeble, yet apparently normal, Sunlight growing from moment to moment. Nature appears to awaken from its frozen fear, the customary life unfolds again, the birds begin to sing; even the cock finds it appropriate to confirm with full voice the returning light of day. From the first moment of returning Sunlight the whole feeling of oppression and embarrassment has disappeared. In this regard, the time immediately after totality is in no way to be compared with the time before.

Though it is a qualitative experience rather than an externally observable and measurable phenomenon, this fact presents at least as great a riddle as the chasing shadow-waves described above. Nay, more—looking back in quiet contemplation of the whole experience, one is even led to the conclusion that the two phenomena are not unconnected, and that the peculiar and inexplicable shiver that seems to overcome the returning light as it runs in rippling waves over the Earth is also to be taken, to begin with, as a purely qualitative phenomenon. So long as the eclipse is on the increase it seems as though heaven and Earth—the surrounding macrocosm and the immediate environment on Earth—were rent asunder, while in an intermediate realm between the two, positive evil was prevailing. Did not the ancient mythologies speak, for example, of a wolf or of a Dragon that was pursuing the Sun and in the moment of totality engulfed it? Witnessing a total eclipse, one can well understand that a truth lies hidden in this mythical picture, and that far more is taking place than the mere physical interposition of the Moon before the Sun. Nay, the experience is such that one might say: This placing of the Moon before the Sun, so that the centers of Sun, Moon and Earth are for a moment exactly in the line—in rhythmic intervals of time—occurring as it does with supreme regularity in rhythmic intervals of time—would be a thing of great beauty, harmony, and benign cosmic influence if only the Moon were transparent to the light. But as it is, the Moon is filled with opaque matter—matter capable of throwing a dark shadow. What is taking place on Earth while the eclipse works up to its climax—the deathly color of the light and so on—is not merely to be explained in an external way, for otherwise, the same phenomena would necessarily be repeated in inverse order when the total eclipse is over, which they are not.

It is rather like a memory of the Fall of the human being, which is brought to expression here in the life of nature. It is as though for a brief moment nature became capable of expressing something of a moral and spiritual character in a quite physical, sense-perceptible way. It is as though all that the Sun signifies, spiritually and physically, for humankind were to find expression in the momentary vanishing of its light, brought about by the fact that the Moon partakes in the nature of earthly things, namely in dark impenetrable matter, sending a shadow of darkness down to the Earth. The strange thing is that the worst moment in this respect is at the time when the shadow of the Moon is just approaching the place where one is standing, that is to say, the last few seconds or minutes before totality. Once the total eclipse is there, one is impressed far more—in spite of the surrounding gloom—by the feeling of majesty and wonder engendered by the celestial phenomena, the Corona, etc. It is as though the immediate juxtaposition in the cosmos of Sun, Moon, and Earth was to give voice to the great evolutionary relationship of these heavenly bodies to one another, which we experience with awe and reverence, in spite of the darkness due to the shadow of the Moon [compare Rudolf Steiner's *Outline of Esoteric Science*, "Cosmic Evolution and the Human Being"]. The rift between the heavens and the Earth seems reconciled and overcome.

Thereafter, once again the three move apart. The shadow has moved from the Earth or, to begin with, from the particular place on Earth where one is standing. Normal conditions make themselves felt once more; the cosmic illness is over. And as the cosmic world, represented by the Sun and Moon and Earth, recovers its normal balance, a momentary shiver passes over the Earth, comparable to the cool morning breeze so often felt immediately before dawn. It is a quivering, however, not in the air but in the light, which now begins to ray once more into

"May soul live in this house" (1935–1943)

Postcard transcription: "Bursa, June 19, 1936 / It was marvelous! The eclipse, the mountain, the surroundings, the weather! We were on the mountain several hundred feet higher than 6,500. Oh, how beautiful the Corona was. I had not imagined it this way—so silvery, radiant, transparent, shining intensively. It and Venus appeared suddenly. Mars was not visible (but the waiter at the hotel here had apparently seen it). This mood of the end of the world before and the joy afterward! On board. / Lily / House Vreede, Arlesheim, près Bâle, Swiss"300

the darkness. Quivering waves of light and shade run over every wall, over against the returning Sunlight. Thereafter, the balance is restored, and in the final period of the eclipse we feel all terrors vanished that the early period of the eclipse had seemed to show.[301]

~

At the end of 1937 Elizabeth Vreede received word that a free subscription to the weekly *Das Goetheanum* would no longer be available to her. She did not reply to the inquiry as to whether or not she would like to take a regular (paid) subscription. With May 1937 she no longer received the paper.

In January 1938 Elizabeth Vreede wrote a short foundational essay, *"Über die anthroposophische Arbeit"* (About the anthroposophic work), in the first issue of *Anthroposophischer Arbeitsberichte* (Anthroposophic work report). The current historic situation became ever more dangerous. In Germany the National Socialists reigned under Adolf Hitler and prepared World War II, as well as the murder of the European Jews. The Anthroposophical Society had already been banned for more than two years (since November 1935). Little was left of the developmental forces that Rudolf Steiner had united with the Goetheanum and his School. Vreede wrote:

> We know that the world always has the tendency, "to blacken what radiates out and to pull the lofty down into the dust." Yet we can ask ourselves, although a genius was always completely misunderstood, denied, and silenced, how was it with the powerful spirit of Rudolf Steiner? Quite often—may we forget it or not be so clear about it—how enormously much of what has been thought, written or done in the world, is thought, written or done in such a way as if Rudolf Steiner had never lived.[302]

Yet, per Elizabeth Vreede, the reality of the spiritual work exists. This spiritual work is a "quite concrete, real process" and changes, for instance, the aura of cities—even when the student of modern Spiritual Science was imperfect and incompetent. The anthroposophic

"May soul live in this house" (1935–1943)

The Vreede House, Arlesheim

movement has passed its thirty-fifth year of life, a turning point of life in which the spiritual becomes increasingly more effective than the physical. Concerning the anthroposophic movement, Vreede wrote further: "Therefore, it will become ever more able to ray out its spiritual forces into the world. And the effect of these forces will increase in maturity and strength to the degree that the purely spiritual will attain strength in the movement itself."

It continues further to be a matter in the current difficult situation of *the effect of the Anthroposophical in the world;* along with this, also of the inner spiritual work of the anthroposophists as relates to the reception of and the working through of the wealth of ideas that Rudolf Steiner researched and communicated to them—yes, with which he entrusted them. Vreede wrote impressively about the spiritual activity and spiritual freedom of the human being that leads into the future. She wrote, conscious of the almost hopeless situation, and yet with confidence in the nevertheless existing significance of the spiritual-scientific esoteric work. In the same year (1938) Elizabeth Vreede was in Germany for the last time, in order, through her international contacts, to help Jewish members of the Anthroposophical Society to emigrate. To Luděk Přikl, a Czech anthroposophist and publisher, she wrote upon his inquiry, of the whole anthroposophical situation:

> The battle was, for the most part, lost; the destructive spirit has won.... Since then, for my feeling, it is like in the mystery drama: "Since our precious leader has fallen—all our earthly striving is hopeless."... It fell first in its earthly effectiveness through the events at the Goetheanum during the ten years until 1935 (1925–1935).[303]

Per Vreede to Přikl, one should no longer occupy oneself with the anthroposophists in Dornach. "From them proceeded the destruction of Rudolf Steiner's work, without them having even noticed it." Vreede's letter showed a hardness like few of her writings otherwise. It gave testimony of her sadness and consternation concerning the

Central European situation and the failure of the Anthroposophical Society, both of which she saw as responsible, shortly after Austria joined the "Third Reich." Vreede had an alert spiritual consciousness her whole life. She followed current politics and the major course of events—Central Europe was close to destruction in 1938. Rudolf Steiner's essential work impulse was doomed to failure; and this not the least through the self-destruction process within the Anthroposophical Society itself.[304] All the rest, according to Vreede, will become devastating, in order then to find a turning point sometime:

> These [Austrian events] are, for me, a signal that it will continue yet further in the same style, with more or less terrible deviations. Yes, perhaps it is Europe's unavoidable destiny that only through such terrible catastrophes (concerning which Dr. Steiner always said that they would come) would it be able to come to its senses and thereby move forward.

Elizabeth Vreede's own destiny also stood within this destiny of the time. In 1938, she once again visited anthroposophical friends in Estland and traveled to Reval for lectures. A little more than a year later, World War II broke out at the beginning of September 1939.

In November during the first year of the war, Eugen Kolisko died in London while in exile. He was forty-six years old. Elizabeth Vreede was closely connected with him and his work, with his comprehensive effectiveness so highly valued by Rudolf Steiner. In Dornach and among leading representatives of the Anthroposophical Society in Germany, Kolisko was—as was also his friend Walter Johannes Stein—systematically denounced, if not destroyed. This was done in hate-filled talks and a strategic process that cannot be described to this day.[305] Kolisko's life ended in a suburban train in London, completely abandoned and alone.[306]

~

Elisabeth Vreede spent the war years at her house in Arlesheim; she lived separated from almost all of her friends and in increasing loneliness.

Eugen Kolisko

"*Haus Vreede*," with its foundation stone given by Rudolf Steiner, still had a character of protection and safety. It stood alone facing the second Goetheanum, from which Vreede was far removed inwardly.

In January 1940, Elisabeth Vreede spoke in the Basel-Bernoullian, at the invitation of the Dr. Ernst Marti, on *"Die Bildung des inneren Menschen durch Anthroposophie"* (The education of the inner human being through Anthroposophy). In May Ita Wegman left Arlesheim and moved to Ascona in Tessin, in their clinical branch—the Casa Andrea Cristoforo. Wegman had the impression that she must make a new beginning far away from Dornach and all that had happened. The beginning of the war in the presence of the military at the borders of Switzerland were merely the immediate cause of her leaving.[307] Ita Wegman's departure was not easy, and in Arlesheim and by Elisabeth Vreede it was received with alarm.

In the final years the relationship between the two former members of the "esoteric Executive Council" had cleared up and intensified. Much indicates that Ita Wegman opened up to Elisabeth Vreede about details of her collaboration and closeness with Rudolf Steiner; and possibly she also shared some of his notes and exercises with her. These documents show a special language in the content that allowed one to understand more deeply the mystery process of the Christmas Conference and the year that followed.[308] Ita Wegman's behavior after 1923 was often not understandable to Elisabeth Vreede—the unconditional, boundless relationship with Rudolf Steiner and much that went with it. Yet, in the last years, Vreede had achieved a different understanding for much, also for the tragedy connected with Ita Wegman's effect in the Anthroposophical Society that affected also Rudolf Steiner in a certain way. Count Polzer-Hoditz was absolutely right in his speech in defense of Ita Wegman on April 14, 1935, in the Great Hall of the Goetheanum.

> I must reject the outrageous moral slander that has happened through the years, especially against Dr. Wegman in public lectures, as directed toward Rudolf Steiner. It seems at times almost as if one has experienced some things that happened before the

Christmas Conference took place and feels it continuing to work; as if a mostly unconscious resentment or anger toward Rudolf Steiner's last years would make itself noticeable, and especially Dr. Wegman became a victim of this.[309]

Now, five years after the last General Meeting of the General Anthroposophical Society, Wegman set off and left Dornach, Arlesheim and her Clinic forever. This was a step that was not possible for Elisabeth Vreede out of inner reasons. She was also not in the position outwardly; she had no place at her disposal in which to settle. She had to be happy to have saved her house in Arlesheim from all the storms. This house, however, had "soul."

In Ascona Ita Wegman worked therapeutically and continued to work on her inner development far away from all the fighting. Elisabeth Vreede did the same in Arlesheim. What rayed out from Vreede became milder. George Adams spoke of a transformed anger and its metamorphosis into love,[310] in the sense of Steiner's lecture of October 21, 1909, in Berlin, which was of a fundamental significance for Wegman, as also for Vreede.[311] Madeleine van Deventer invited Elisabeth Vreede repeatedly to give anthroposophical talks in the Therapy House of the Clinic. After Vreede's death, van Deventer wrote about these presentations: "When one heard her lectures in her later years, one had the impression that, more and more, her memory became a seeing. The content of what she wanted to bring stood before her spiritual eye like a great Imagination that she could read, so to speak."[312] Comparable reports were given about Wegman's lectures during the last years in Ascona.[313]

It is not known how often Elisabeth Vreede saw and spoke with Ita Wegman in the time that followed (after Wegman's departure from Arlesheim). Wegman traveled sporadically back to Arlesheim, mostly for a few days to hold a talk, to pick up documents, or to help with legal proceedings in the clinic. It is very likely that Vreede visited Casa Andrea Cristoforo at least once, shortly before Christmas 1942.

"May soul live in this house" (1935–1943)

Ita Wegman, 1942

> Von R. Steiner aufgeschrieben während der Zeit seines Krankseins:
>
> Das Christus-Mysterium ist die Enthüllung des grossen Wunders, das sich zwischen Herz und Lunge abspielt. Der Kosmos wird Mensch, der Mensch wird Kosmos. Die Sonne trägt den Menschen aus dem Kosmos zur Erde, der Mond trägt den Menschen von der Erde in den Kosmos. Ins Grosse umgesetzt: was von der Lunge zum Herzen strömt, ist menschliches Korrelat des Herabsteigens des Christus auf die Erde. Was vom Herzen nach der Lunge kraftet, ist menschliches Korrelat des Hindurchführens des Menschen nach dem Tod durch den Christus-Impuls in die Geisteswelt. Insofern lebt das Geheimnis von Golgatha auf menschlich-organ-hafte Art zwischen Herz und Lunge.
>
> Durch Frau Dr. Wegman mitgeteilt 14.4.39

Elisabeth Vreede's handwriting[314]

Ita Wegman's illness at the end of February 1943, after a quick return to the clinic (for regulating official matters), and her death on the morning of March 4 in Arlesheim was completely unexpected. Vreede was present also at the time of the of Wegman's dying. "During the last hour before Ita Wegman's death, Dr. Vreede was in the next room, together with the rest of the doctors and several older coworkers with whom Ita Wegman was close. She could not and did not want to believe the end was coming" (Madeleine van Deventer).[315] Her departure from Earth was a great shock for Vreede, as well as for van Deventer.[316] However, she (Vreede) regained her composure at the deathbed. "She pulled herself together and spoke, with emotion in her voice, but in spirit-born composure, the Rosicrucian Verse."[317]

In the difficult days around March 4, 1943, Elisabeth Vreede was the unquestionable spiritual authority for the close-knit, internal circle of Ita Wegman's coworkers. One asked her to speak at the memorial for Ita Wegman on March 6 in the Therapy House of the Clinic. She did this in an impressive manner. "The soul of Ita Wegman could not be shaken—she, whom Rudolf Steiner called his friend, and with whom she was connected. Both of them were connected with Michael and the battle that he waged. She lived this battle in an exemplary way. She showed how it is when a human soul already lives completely in the spiritual" (Vreede).[318] Elisabeth Vreede stated these words in her address: "*Now the heart of our movement lies in the spiritual world.*"[319] To Ita Wegman's coworkers, this statement was immediately understandable, and it spoke a truth. In a historical perspective, however, there is a mystery connected with it. In her notebook of 1933, Wegman noted a conversation with Rudolf Steiner from the last period of his life: "Blossoms in the Christmas Conference. Renewal of the Anthroposophical Society after the high point was reached—why not a further continuation? Everything said that human beings could take in. Now, the heart in the spiritual world. The dead must be prepared for the new Earth incarnation, just as also the Third Hierarchy."[320]

From this, therefore, the formulation, "Now the heart in the spiritual world" came from Rudolf Steiner and showed the situation in 1924/25. Whether Vreede had read Ita Wegman's notebook, or whether Ita Wegman had told her Steiner's formulation, is not known. Elisabeth Vreede had experienced Rudolf Steiner and Ita Wegman, or rather Rudolf Steiner in his collaboration with Ita Wegman, in 1923/24 as *"the direct working spiritual principle"* of the esoteric Council and the Christmas Conference. After Rudolf Steiner's death on March 30, 1925, Ita Wegman was alone on Earth. However, she worked further out of an inner connection with him, in spite of all the opposition.

> She showed [per Vreede, in her memorial address of March 6, 1943] how it is when a human soul already lives completely in the spiritual. This strength in the spirit held out against the attacks of the opposing forces. It is difficult to understand what it means, when a soul like Rudolf Steiner passes over into the spiritual world and the other souls remain here; but here one understood this.[321]

First with Ita Wegman's death was, for Vreede, the total "heart or center point" of the anthroposophic movement in the spiritual world. Until then, Wegman had represented this mystery of the "heart or center point," even if only a few people understood it.[320] However, the "center point" that was transferred into the spiritual world has a yet greater reality and significance. Elisabeth Vreede also stressed this on March 6, according to Werner Pache's diary notes.[323]

Elisabeth Vreede spoke not only at the memorial for Ita Wegman in the Therapy House of the Clinic, but also at the Cremation ceremony in Basel, "after heavy inner wrestling" (Deventer).[324] This wrestling was because of the presence of Albert Steffen and Guenther Wachsmuth, both of whom Vreede saw again on this occasion for the first time in eight years. Ita Wegman's severe destiny path after March 30, 1925, as well as her early death were, for Elisabeth Vreede, inextricably connected with the social processes at the Goetheanum—and therefore, also with the people who came to the funeral in their dignified clothing, but did not show even a spark of consciousness

Elisabeth Vreede (undated)

of their injustice and complicity. Professor Ernst Fiechter, Priest of The Christian Community since 1938, celebrated the ceremony. Elisabeth Vreede spoke, after a sudden, passing feeling of weakness,[325] "inspired words" (Deventer) that were not written down. Also Werner Pache from Sonnenhof spoke. "With a noble passion and with effort his words came—words in which he, however, also had to reject the denial and unjust judgment expressed in the past years against Ita Wegman's personality and striving" (Deventer).[326]

A few weeks later, for the annual Easter Festival, Vreede again held a lecture in the Clinic. A few days afterward, on March 30, she spoke in a lecture there about the friends gathered around Rudolf Steiner in the spiritual world. She spoke now also of Edith Maryon, Alice Sauerwein, Count von Keyserlink, Louis Werbeck, Caroline von Heydebrand, and Eugen Kolisko with serene joy, per van Deventer. "There lay over this evening a breath from across the threshold." "The world of the dead was very near to us" (Deventer).[327]

In the weeks following Ita Wegman's death, Vreede tried very hard to awaken among various people an understanding for the significance of the individuality of Ita Wegman. "She made the effort in various circles, with special warmth, to show Ita Wegman's greatness of humanity to those who were close" (Fiechter).[328] Elisabeth Vreede knew which great and future-effective forces could go out from the individuality of Ita Wegman in the spirit world, provided that the Anthroposophical Society continued to exist and became conscious of the dead. For Vreede it was not so much a matter of a historical rehabilitation, as it was of the "central point or heart" of the anthroposophic movement in the spiritual world—and along with it, the destiny of those who remain on Earth. "Indeed, the heart of our movement passed over (into the spiritual world), but we feel that we must carry it further, and we will get courage through what is now in the spiritual world and gives us strength, the building-up force that is now set free." Elisabeth Vreede had said this already on March 6 in her memorial address in the Therapy House of the Arlesheim Clinic. Six weeks later she wrote in a letter about Ita Wegman and the mourning friends:

"From what one hears about the way her memorial is celebrated here and there, one sees a deep bond with her among the people in various countries—and it is wonderful to see that."[329]

Holland was occupied by the German army and suffered terrible treatment—"and we sit here and experience the entire terrible happenings only from afar"; Vreede wrote this in a letter from Arlesheim to someone in the humiliated country. "The difference to our country is so enormous that it would be almost overwhelming, if on the other hand, it would not spurn us to a greater obligation to work."[330] The year of 1943 was catastrophic. Ita Wegman said to Madeleine van Deventer[331] during the short time of her illness, "If no spiritual work [on Earth] is possible anymore in the near future, I will die." Right up to the end, she tried to follow the actions of the military: the events at the front and the development of the war. Germany mobilized all the military Reserves and was determined to continue the war to the point of the last catastrophe. The Reich Propaganda Minister Goebel asked in his rabble-rousing talk in the Berlin Sports Arena on February 18, "Do you want total war? Do you want it, if necessary, to be more complete and more radical than we can even imagine today?" He received frantic agreement (from the audience). On the same day the young members of the resistance of the "White Rose" in Munich were arrested and questioned; only four days later they were hanged. Hans Scholl, Sophie Scholl, and Christoph Probst died on February 22, 1943. At this time almost half a million people were already in concentration camps run by the National Socialists. Alone on March 4, the death day of Ita Wegman, a thousand Jews were deported from the assembly and detention camp Drancy to Auschwitz; close to nine hundred were killed immediately in the gas chamber.[332] Wegman's heart, readiness to help, and enthusiasm had always been directed toward the innocent who were suffering—the diverse sacrifices of the time. Now she herself was gone, possibly because she could be more helpful in the other sphere of existence than on Earth.

Elisabeth Vreede tried, in her way, to work further. She held a large lecture about the Polish astronomer and Cathedral Cannon Nicolaus

The Rose Cross of Rudolf Steiner and Ita Wegman

Copernicus at the beginning of May for the 400th anniversary of his death. She wanted to give more courses, but her own illness began on May 6 in Arlesheim.

~

Before this, Elisabeth Vreede was never really ill. Now she laid with a high septic fever in the modest little room of her house at "Auf der Höhe 1," and was treated medically by Madeleine van Deventer, Ernst Marti, and Werner Klein. Van Deventer had the impression that Vreede's life and health condition turned with the difficult cremation address for Ita Wegman. "She achieved in Basel an inner victory, but at the same time, it was as if here lay the beginning of the dissolution of her own life on Earth."[333] Visitors were very moved by Elisabeth Vreede's inner composure while bedridden.

> Without complaint, with a patience one would never have expected from this restless person, with a touching gratitude for every help her friends gave—with all this, she bore her lot. It was a deep experience for those caring for her and for the visitors who were allowed to witness this. She, who could flare up when she had to see things that violated her sense of justice, was peace and mildness itself in the time of her illness. (Ernst Bindel)[334]

Moreover, Madeleine van Deventer wrote as the treating physician, "She...carried the illness with great patience and objectivity. There was a strict clarity present in her own observation and judgment of her symptoms. Her soul, however, was filled with gratitude and the power of love.[335]

George Adams spoke once quite accurately of a "deep humility" that lay hidden under Elisabeth Vreede's fire and determination.[336] This humility became visible to many people through her impressive surrender to, and saying yes to, her destiny in the last years of her life and during her illness. If she was alone on her sickbed, she felt herself surrounded by a world of geometric forms.

After a first improvement of her condition in the beginning of August, Elisabeth Vreede wished to be moved to Ita Wegman's last therapeutic place, to the Casa Andrea Cristoforo in Tessin where there were strong healing qualities that could help with convalescence. The Arlesheim doctors around Madeleine van Deventer were worried about this transfer. Elisabeth Vreede wanted, with all determination, to go to Ascona. "It was as if through immense effort of will, her forces really grew stronger" (Deventer).

At this time, Dr. Hilma Walter worked in the Casa; she had worked closely together with Wegman and Rudolf Steiner. Also during these weeks a person, whose talent and work Vreede valued enormously, was working on the property of the therapeutic Institute LaMotta in nearby Brissago. The painter Liane Collot d'Herbois worked there on the frescoes for Ita Wegman's urn Chapel.[337] Liane Collot was a close friend of Ita Wegman, but also a friend of Elisabeth Vreede, in whose home she often stayed when she visited Ita Wegman at the Arlesheim Clinic. Vreede had an eye for Liane Collot's special art and her way of being, but also an eye for her accurate knowledge. There were few people with whom she could speak about cosmic connections the way she could with this painter. Collot lived in "Light" and "Darkness," in the primordial qualities of creation, and bore within herself an impressive wisdom, an ancient mystery knowledge of the cosmos that had experienced a new birth in the light of Anthroposophy in the twentieth century. She practiced a form of the mystery art.

Vreede's decision to go to Ascona was, in the end, not motivated by particular people—not through Walter or Collot. It was based on other levels of will and destiny. Only four days after her arrival at the Casa Andrea Cristoforo, she suffered a difficult relapse and fought for over three weeks with this illness that had taken hold of her. On August 27, Ernst Fiechter wrote a final testimonial letter for her. Her life, per Fiechter, had become a "battlefield," even though she was predestined to a peaceful, but extremely spiritual trial. He wrote further, "Now I can feel and understand much of what you experienced. How near the witch Bitterness draws and poisons the whole human being! And yet we want to strive, from the deepest insight and love, that it not happen—*so that the Good continues to exist.*"[338]

"May soul live in this house" (1935–1943)

Liane Collot d'Herbois: Fresco in the Motta Chapel (detail)

In all the years that lay behind her, Vreede had tried, in this sense, to live in a wonderfully significant spiritual manner. Four days after Fiechter wrote his letter (on August 31), she passed into the spiritual world—into the sphere of those stars and spirit beings to which she had dedicated her life of knowledge. Her life on Earth was sixty-four years and six weeks long, almost exactly the same amount of time that the life span of her teacher measured.

According to Rudolf Steiner, the place and time of a person's death stands in direct relationship to that person's individuality. Steiner died on March 30, 1925, in his Goetheanum studio in Dornach. Ita Wegman, his friend and coworker, was brought back from Ascona to Arlesheim to her wood-framed house that Steiner had designed for her. On the other hand, Elisabeth Vreede crossed the threshold into the spiritual world in the Casa Andrea Cristoforo in Ascona, beyond Arlesheim and the Vreede House that Rudolf Steiner had built and christened. She died in the Therapy Center in Tessin that Ita Wegman built up and that Wegman left shortly before her death in favor of Arlesheim. The life paths of both had crossed and connected in diverse ways in the twentieth century, right up to the signature of their deaths.

Almost none of the friends could come to the cremation ceremony in Lugano. Madeleine van Deventer (along with Ernst Marti and Margareta Kirchener-Bockholt) held the main address in a largely empty room. She recalled, however, (in her address) the many for whom—on Earth and in heaven—Elisabeth Vreede meant something. No notice of her death was put into "What is Happening in the Anthroposophical Society," the news in the weekly *Das Goetheanum*. There was also no notice for Ita Wegman. Yet both of them went into the spiritual world with the conviction that the Anthroposophical Society would continue to exist and would grow further in the future.

"*May soul live in this house*" *(1935–1943)*

Elisabeth Vreede (death), Casa Andrea Cristoforo, Ascona

Ex Deo nascimor
In Christo morimor
Per Spiritum Sanctum reviviscimus.

From the Godhead humanity is born
In Christ death becomes life
In the World-thought of the Spirit the soul awakens.[339]

Appendices

Ceremony for beginning construction of second Goetheanum, 1926; Elisabeth Vreede next to Ita Wegman (fifth and sixth from left)

Elisabeth Vreede:
The Christmas and Michael Impulses

Lecture at the Opening of the Second Goetheanum

Dornach, October 2, 1928 [340]

Dear Friends,

We have been here together in our Goetheanum for three days; and we experience all of the power of this building, this creation by Rudolf Steiner, which could still be created from his spirit after his death. And we experience renewed again the greatness of the spirit that managed so to inspire people and instill enthusiasm that he could work so strongly in this physical world beyond his death. And when we consider from what small beginnings the movement has grown, which then was able to build out of itself this Goetheanum, even the first Goetheanum, then we are reminded of the words that resounded in our ears from the mystery drama: the words about the small seed that mysteriously expanded to the proud stature of the giant oak.

We see this small seed as having been planted a long time ago (1902), which is nevertheless only a short time in world evolution. And if we look back at that time we see, in a brief overview, how from this small seed has grown what Rudolf Steiner then summarized in the laying of the Foundation Stone of the Anthroposophical Society about five years ago and still lives in this building.

We see there a number of people around Rudolf Steiner who eagerly listened to what he had to give; people who bore within themselves a strong yearning for the spiritual world. They were people who desired knowledge of the spiritual world, of the connection between cosmos, Earth, and the human being; people who were permeated with a yearning to know the Christ-being. We know today that it was, so to speak, a karmic group of people who were together earlier in the spiritual world and had now found themselves together on Earth.

Rudolf Steiner spoke in the presence of these people in the most varied places. Moreover, it was only through the fact that he went from place to place and held his lectures—the individual lectures and the lecture cycles—that the movement gradually grew from a small kernel of devoted people to a larger Society that was, however, still closed within its own circle at any rate. The first people who heard the first communications of the spirit were not especially sophisticated, and so they did not have a special desire to carry the spiritual insights out into the world. However, for Rudolf Steiner that was naturally different. He gave public lectures constantly at that time—lectures that had nothing sectarian about them. The titles of the lectures give witness to this, the records of which we can still enjoy in the existing written materials.

Then came the wonderful time, of which we are now especially reminded, when the mystery dramas were performed—the time in Munich where the mystery dramas were created one after another over a four-year span. And you all know well that, from these mystery dramas, at the very beginning when they were first performed, the idea arose among the members for the creation of their own house. This building that was planned at that time was to be dedicated to and serve the words of the mystery dramas, but also the words of the spiritual researcher. Already quite soon Rudolf Steiner brought the expression "School for Spiritual Science" for this building. The building was then started. After the laying of the Foundation Stone that took place here fifteen years ago, one began quickly and eagerly to erect the first Goetheanum. And it was *a new phase* that began there in the anthroposophic movement. It was a phase wherein simply from out of the necessities of the world the anthroposophic movement had to go out of itself more than before; it had to deal with the outside world more than it was obliged to do before.

~

One could sense that, as one was able to participate in erecting the building here. It was an impression (excuse me for mentioning something personal here); one who came to the beginning of the work on this building and saw how people worked on this building—where precisely the columns were erected, while over in the carpentry a hundred workers were occupied—that person could sense all that played into the Society, what flowed from outside simply because one erected, as an employer, a work in the outer world. At that time the feeling could arise in the soul that it is something new for the Society! Are we then so disposed as a Society that we can make ourselves noticeable in the outer world in this way? Thus one could feel at that time.

There occurred such contacts—I want to say—with the outside world that one could not imagine taking place in the preceding epoch, in the time of the lecture cycles and the mystery dramas. For example, a small strike came about because a few workers were there whom the other workers did not want because they were not members of organized labor. One demanded that they be fired, and when this did not happen, the work stopped. The foreman did not give in, and the members helping with the building gave up even less. They ran the machines, carried the wood, and cut it into short pieces. In short, the work went forward, even if not with skilled labor. The other workers came back after two days.

From what was said, it should be seen merely that one had to deal at that time with social problems that never before came into the awareness of the Society. It is not that Rudolf Steiner did not repeatedly point out these problems, but they were not yet in sight for the members.

Now World War I came. And after it came a further phase of the Anthroposophical Society about which not much needs to be said now. It came about that one wanted greatly to be active outwardly. The social movement did not spring from the necessity for a building to be built, but it was from free choice that one began to work in the outside world. This work was such that it was felt by many to be a contradiction to what had been done before. Dr. Steiner had emphasized this contradiction fully, without saying that this or the other is right; but quite to the contrary, that both should be done. People felt that the work was less esoteric than in previous years. It was not that Dr. Steiner's lectures and work, in the time when the threefold social organism was worked on, became any less esoteric! It was a time when the School (for Spiritual Science) courses were introduced at various places, when Dr. Steiner also held more scientific lectures for the outside world. He said about this: In the first place, there is still a gulf between the branch work (members-only work) and the public work. This gulf could absolutely be bridged or reconciled, but it must first, at least, be recognized. One can say that this wish of Rudolf Steiner's was not fulfilled to the necessary degree at first. And that plays over also into our building, into our Goetheanum. Later Dr. Steiner often stressed this.

Then came that awful time, the terrible moment of the burning of our first Goetheanum. One could sense, as the fire struck everything that was supposed to stand as a symbol for human beings, does it not lie with *us* that this terrible misfortune should come to us? Do we then have such a Society that brings the inner, the esoteric, properly to expression in this outer world—a society oriented in such a way that its intentions correspond to the one who founded the movement?

We know that the Christmas Conference took place a year later. With this Christmas Conference (as stated by Dr. Steiner), "an esoteric character should again enter into the Society."

This Society was founded, newly founded, from the spiritual world. It was actually not "founded" from the spiritual world. I would rather use a word from Dr. Steiner himself: to found is one thing; to gift is another. What comes directly from the spiritual world and is arranged according to its lawfulness, is actually *gifted* from the spiritual world; and things here on the physical plane are *established*. Thus it was with the "spiritual laying of the Foundation Stone." You find the word *foundation* expressed in the term *Foundation Stone*, but at the same time one finds it was gifted from the spiritual world.

And we see, on the other hand, how this Society should be founded according to the laws of public life, according to the justified demands of public life.

This founding itself was related to the Christmas Festival. For at every Christmas we commemorate that event that revealed itself from the Heights, as the Spirit of the Universe was born upon the Earth—a vessel was born for a new impulse. And it was not by chance that already years beforehand Dr. Steiner had planned this new founding of the Society for Christmas. Yes, our whole movement has something of Christmas in it. One can feel that our movement is like the Child at Christmas—still young and still, on the one hand, protected from the outer world; how, on the other hand, it was also loved and revered—loved and revered as a movement as also the Christmas Child was loved by those of a plain and simple nature who came to him.

All of that, I would like to say, became, with this Christmas Conference, an impulse of the new founding that should work further through future times. The outer world and the spiritual world came together there—each with its own lawfulness. And there we see an extraordinarily important meeting.

The outer world has its laws and its justified demands that spring from the circumstances of the time. The spiritual world has *its* laws that have a longer validity than those of the outer world. They are longer lasting, even though an evolution is taking place; so when both meet, a balancing is necessary because they have to order themselves according to the demands of the time. And to trace from the Statutes how this balance came about is actually a wonderful thing. I would now like to draw your attention to this.

I would like to say, just as when light and darkness meet, the colors shine forth, so just as here in this building the color shines from the windows from the light outside into the darkness in the building, so it is in our whole movement, in our Society. It was set up by Dr. Steiner so that the outer meets the inner, not only the *"outside"* outer world, but also *the* outer world that—as anthroposophical outer world—surrounds the Goetheanum. That coincides with what the spiritual impulses of the Goetheanum and the Society should be. That coincides with what the spiritual impulse of the Goetheanum and the Society should be.

Let us consider what approaches from outside as justified demands of the time in certain areas, for instance, as democratic demands. We bring that with us from life outside; it is justified in that area that one calls the rights life outside. With everything that has to do with management in the Society, people have the right for things to be handled democratically; equality must be taken into account in a fitting manner. You find it held fast in the Statutes, in the Statutes that Dr. Steiner also called "Principles."

You will, of course, not think that I am speaking of a rights area in the legal sense, but rather, the Statues are formulated from the spiritual and contain as much of the reality of the spiritual world as a whole lecture cycle.

―

Thus, you will find in these Statutes the democratic element that flows from taking into account the equality of human beings. For example, the right of members to participate in all events "under the conditions to be given by the Executive Council." And there is especially the famous paragraph 11: "The members can form smaller or larger groups at any place and in any objective field." You will see how one reaches back to this arrangement ever again when it is a matter of wanting to act democratically in this Society. On the other hand, another element is expressed in the Statutes. And that is what one could call the demand for freedom of the spiritual life. There we have a demand that comes partly, even though unconsciously, already from the outer world—from what should live already in the outer world—and partly from the spiritual world. Both of these realms meet together there.

You know that the freedom of the spiritual life is one of the three central points of the social question; and one must hope that the outside world will develop ever more understanding of this threefolding the social organism. For we know that if it should not be realized freely, it will come about through catastrophes. There already lives in people this demand for the freedom of the spiritual life. They are just not so clearly aware and admire in many ways what is cultivated as spiritual life within the life of the state, in the rights life. And because there was no clear insight that the spiritual life can thrive only in freedom, this demand was not so clearly put by the outside world, as was the case with the demand for democracy in the rights life.

On the other hand, it is something that is fully justified in the face of the spiritual world (and can be seen consciously from there) that freedom of the spiritual life must exist. And when you track our spiritual scientific endeavors, you will see in a wonderful way how the *free* spiritual life was realized, how the central point is the center for a movement that grew from the free spiritual life. What could be freer, in the deeper sense be called a free spiritual life, than what Dr. Steiner founded as the anthroposophical worldview in the course of the decades? That is that point of the threefolding program that we, so to speak, have in hand. Dr. Steiner said of it: It is the only thing that is possible for us to realize. Concerning the rights life we have nothing to say directly; and we cannot separate our economic life from the whole surroundings, if we do not want to create economic sects. However, in the spiritual life we are free, even though limits can naturally enter in through the outer world, as with the founding of our schools, and so on. We can always look up to the free spiritual life as an ideal.

Now it is true and will be clear to you that such a freedom of the spiritual life cannot be based on anarchy, but that, on the other hand, an element of management does play a part. The spiritual life does indeed need to be directed. And every action within a society also has a directorial or managerial character. I mean with this, not outer management according to state and rights principles, but rather what should also belong in the spiritual life of a directorial-like or management-like nature. And there we have something that resounds together, collides, one could say: a spiritual demand with something that is simply given through the conditions of the physical plane. So, to give a concrete example, when a conference such as ours comes about with lectures and performances, it is the result of a management of the otherwise free spiritual life. Dr. Steiner always knew how to separate the areas clearly, and he saw it as an impossibility to introduce democracy into the spiritual life. And one can ask how Dr. Steiner would have handled it now so that, on the one hand, the outer Society, the Society as such, would have been founded so that it is based on freedom of the spiritual life and, on the other hand, so that this freedom can be properly managed and or directed, so that also again here a harmony could be created between the inner and the outer?

I would like to speak about this precisely, because I think that one can experience an example of the work of the true spiritual research when one looks at how Dr. Steiner did that, as he held the Christmas Conference—how he joined together there the outer world and the inner world, the freedom and necessity like two parts of a whole. There one must point out something that can be looked at from a spiritual point of view—that means, not yet from the organizational aspect. He already founded the individual national societies, or rather let them be founded, and helped with this in various countries himself in the year between the fire and the Christmas Conference. Several national societies already existed, but Dr. Steiner also founded such societies in other countries, in his presence. And it was extraordinarily interesting to see how he went about letting these societies be founded. This was done in such a way that the autonomy of these national societies was counted on strongly. That comes from the fact that they were founded *before* the Christmas Conference, and Dr. Steiner stressed the point that the national societies had to be there first and that, based on these existing societies, something should then come into being here in Dornach. What should thus arise should not merely combine synthetically in the outer sense, but rather should become, beyond that, a spiritual reality that should work from here into the entire society. In the national societies the strictest autonomy should be the rule—first of all the branches in relation to the leadership of the national society (what has to do with the spiritual, not the managerial), and then, in turn, the national societies in relation to the General Anthroposophical Society that did not yet exist but came into being at Christmas.

Dr. Steiner said that these individual national societies should be such that they can develop an unrestrained individual life. It should be that from this country *this* can proceed and from that country *something other* can proceed, based on the national characteristic and historical karma of each country, along with the anthroposophical life that already prevailed through the years during which Dr. Steiner worked there. At the founding of a national society that already wanted to include in its Statutes an indication of the leadership in Dornach, of an approval that should be given by Dornach, it was said that one could not do that. This was not because the General Anthroposophical Society did not yet exist, but because one must take care that the national societies form themselves clearly from their own inner kernel. "The national societies themselves must in some way emerge from the Statutes. The national societies will be formed before the founding of the international society in Dornach. This international society shall first arise on the basis of the national societies."

Dr. Steiner expressed this in another place, so that he said the societies in each land should form themselves in such a way that one had something established. And what was totally established should build a bridge to what would come as something higher—not managerially, but in the spiritual sense, in the sense of an initiative, a spiritual founding that should proceed out of Dornach.

That is important to mention, because in spiritual matters the things that stand at the starting point work ever further, whether they are carried out consciously or unconsciously. For what is done unconsciously comes definitely from the depths of the human soul. However, when they are carried out consciously, they can be directed further. The fact that will always play into the Society's further development is that it did not form from people merely joining together arbitrarily and founding something here because they thought of "how one does it best." Rather, they freely declare themselves for a spirit that was already there, for which they have decided *how* it was there.

Thus, we find two things at the basis of the Anthroposophical Society: First is a freedom based on the element of trust. Trust must prevail between the center here and the life of the individual national societies elsewhere; otherwise, it will not work. The freedom consists in the national societies leading themselves the way they want. However, it must be so given, in turn, that a free trustful collaboration can happen with Dornach. That was expressed in the same place that I spoke of before. It was at the founding of the Dutch National Society five weeks before the Christmas Conference that the Statutes for its society were drafted. It was mentioned in those Statutes that the general secretary was to be elected, but that Dornach must later recognize the general secretary. Dr. Steiner pointed out that this goes too far—that the national societies should choose their general secretaries in complete freedom, but that one should see that they are people with whom Dornach, in turn, can work. No right to be involved in the selection should be exercised by Dornach, but only the right to object. The element of trust and the element of freedom are thus present.

On the other hand, however, a hierarchical principle is expressed that is always of the nature of the spiritual world, for there are hierarchies in the spiritual world. What is founded on Earth, when it is done consciously, can only be a reproduction of the spiritual world according to the manner of *how* and *why*. One could execute that in the details. The leadership of the national societies stands in this somewhat hierarchical relationship to their own societies. This is because Dr. Steiner did not want the democratic element to be predominant, with frequent new elections and such things. He wanted rather that, because our society is a spiritual society, something of the hierarchical principle should express itself in the making firm of the position of the general secretary or of the national Executive Council.

From what I said, it is clear that there the demands of the spiritual world met with the outer world, and in a wonderful way, Dr. Steiner always created a balance, so that one sees how, whether to the one or the other side, what is right shall happen.

Then there came the crowning of the past through the Christmas Conference in Dornach. Also there things were done according to this principle. I wish to give as an example the admission of members. A society is made up of its members. Spiritually it should be more than the sum of its members, but should build a spiritual reality; otherwise it would not be a society of spiritual substance. How can this be expressed? Now, the members are admitted by the national societies. Through this they show their autonomy. The society consists of the individual national societies. They have their members, with whom they must work through the national Executive Council, and the members are admitted by the national Executive Council, and the admission should then be confirmed by Dornach. Thus, in May 1923 in Oslo, Dr. Steiner explained exactly how this admission should occur—the way it was then later also followed. So that one sees how clearly Dr. Steiner presented it even then:

> It was wished, so that the international society could be a unity, that indeed the admission be taken care of by the national societies; that, however, the membership cards were signed at the central office in Dornach. It was done this way everywhere. It would first found a certain federalism, which is very much desired. On the other hand, however, it was to be documented that a large society proceeds forth from Dornach. For this, it is naturally necessary that trust exist from the side of Dornach toward the one who represents the national society with Dornach. That is what is important. The entire constitution of the society rests on the system of trusted people.

Now what the national society does autonomously should be spiritually confirmed from here, from Dornach. *Here* one proceeds, so to speak, from what the individual Societies, as members, bring to the Goetheanum. That is "acknowledged" here. The term *acknowledgment* was used and the admission of the members was confirmed through the counter-signature of the members' cards that Dr. Steiner signed personally.

Or let's consider another point where the demands of the spiritual world and the outer world come together: the publishing of the lecture cycles. You know the lecture cycles were printed because, as Dr. Steiner said, the members desired it. And one can, one wants to say, as a consumer of these cycles, fully understand this desire. And one can also feel that had the lecture cycles not been printed and had they existed only once, merely as spoken word, then our movement would have remained a wonderful thing, but it would have perhaps lacked the necessary earthly gravity. Today it is such that things have to be put into print. Now the outside world is interested in the lecture cycles. They could not bear it that something should be "only for members," and put the blame on bad intentions. Now, Dr. Steiner said at the Christmas Conference that he wanted to make these lecture cycles available to the public, but—because they are brought from the spiritual world—with the caveat that they should not be regarded the same as other books that one finds in the outer world and over which the outer world may judge. For this meeting together of two demands, the small notice was printed, which you know ("printed as manuscript for members of the First Class of the Independent School for Spiritual Science, Goetheanum").

It is then pointed out that the author of the lecture cycles can enter into discussions with only those people who have participated in the anthroposophic movement, in what proceeds from the Goetheanum or its leadership. Those who do not meet this condition of preparatory study will not be recognized as justified to make a judgment or discuss the material. Moreover, there is a meeting of the outer, physical world with what points to the esoteric character of our movement.

We come in fact, in that the term "First Class" is used, to the realm of the purely spiritual, the esoteric realm. There we come to a realm where totally different laws rule than the laws of the outer world. Laws rule there that everyone must submit to if he or she wants to go the path of esotericism. Therefore, the desire to take this path can spring only from free choice, from the wish to enter into the spiritual world, let us say, with help from *How to Know Higher Worlds* and so on. However, there prevails something that lies beyond the freedom of the individual. For what one can call the choice of the teacher is no longer up to the freedom of the human being on this path. When someone seeks a teacher of esotericism, it is not as a rule that one says, I will consider this one or that one, but rather karmic relationships prevail. It is accepted that one who comes from the outside world and has the impulse to go through a spiritual path of training will be led to a teacher. Karma plays a role there. One can understand this when one studies the lecture cycle *Karmic Relationships*, volume 3. When one has entered into the esotericism, when one has taken up the initiative to enter into it, one is subject completely to the spiritual law. No longer can the laws of the outer world—that are justified there—hold sway, because everything must be formed, developed, according to the laws of the spiritual world. Above all, the democratic principle falls away completely there.

What prevails there as a lawfulness might be the esoteric feature that goes through the movement, the esoteric quality about which Dr. Steiner said it should come through the Christmas Conference. It should be such, inasmuch as possible, that in every individual measure that must be taken, esotericism must prevail, so that these measures can be seen as directed by the spiritual world and not by the thoughts and other habits and demands that enter from the outer world (and are justified there).

Thus, Dr. Steiner said the following at the foundation of the English National Society—again before the Christmas Conference: "To the outside, the anthroposophic movement must be represented in a vigilant manner. Inwardly, it must work purely from its own kernel and do nothing other than what is in total agreement with real occult laws."

The wonderful thing that one could experience of Dr. Steiner was the way he handled this naturally, the way he knew how to do all things so that one saw that they were handled by the spiritual world. Experiencing that in him was an esoteric schooling in itself. And that is what played a role, for example, with his signing the membership cards (that I mentioned earlier). You know that the membership cards were re-issued, even for long-time members. They were signed by the group officials and then sent to Dornach to be signed by Dr. Steiner. This is also contained in the Statutes as the method. Dr. Steiner said of this that countersigning the cards was, for him, not a formality. One could easily imagine it to be so. One could say that a signature stamp would suffice, that one could do it differently. He said, "No, it is important to me that I sign these cards myself so that, at least for a few brief moments, my eyes rest upon the name of the person who is being admitted."

This is something that, according to the circumstances of the outer world, seems to be senseless, a waste of time and work. That process is, however, quite well justified with regards to the spiritual world. This signature can also be called a gift: the fact that his eyes rested upon it and that a connection was given between him and every individual member through this deed of signing the cards. That is a small thing that one can sense as being more than a small thing where Dr. Steiner achieved it, even though it costs so much time and effort, to let the spiritual prevail. Also such small measures as this show that the esoteric element can be carried out right into the managerial element.

It will have come to the awareness of many of us only after the departure of our teacher what it means to own a membership card signed by him. A person can say that the one who is now in the spiritual world took the effort to write his name on it.

That was the sense of the Christmas Conference in December 1923, where Dr. Steiner took on the leadership of the Society himself, not just in spiritual-esoteric matters as up to that time, but also in the outer sense. He took it upon himself and began to organize the Society so that this impulse, the Christmas impulse of which I have spoken, could work effectively. It was not a totally foreign, new impulse, as, above all, in a spiritual movement continuity must rule—that is also a demand of the spiritual world. It was closely related to that impulse that had already always played a role in our Society: the impulse connected with Rosicrucianism. Right after the Christmas Conference Dr. Steiner held lectures on the old Rosicrucianism. It was at the Christmas Conference where the human dodecahedron was placed beside the world dodecahedron. It was placed beside the outer Foundation Stone, which is also a dodecahedron and is here in the Goetheanum.

The founding of the Independent School for Spiritual Science was now announced. This name had already been connected with the Goetheanum for a long time. Now it was to become a reality. And again in a wonderfully clear way, the relationship of the Anthroposophy to this School was expressed. It was stated in the Statutes as follows: The Anthroposophical Society sees in the Independent School for Spiritual Science in Dornach a center of its working. This will consist of three classes.

We don't want to talk about this here. However, it was stated again that the goal of the Anthroposophical Society is the support and fostering of research in the spiritual realm; and that the Independent School for Spiritual Science is this research itself (paragraph [9]). I ask you to think about this often, because this paragraph 9 shows in a wonderfully clear manner the relationship of the School to the Society. The members will see that one will come back again and again to the laying of the Foundation Stone of the Goetheanum and to the Statutes, which instruct us about our spiritual principles.

Dr. Steiner said about this School for Spiritual Science that it must not be a matter of specialty but that the general or universal human should play a great role in it. It could not be a matter of continuing what was characterized earlier as what created a gulf between the esoteric and the outer work; and just as little of setting up a rivalry or competition with the schools of the outer world.

Rather, the universally human that wants to lead to the esoteric should be strongly emphasized. As the paragraph having to do with the Goetheanum as the School for Spiritual Science was dealt with in the discussion of the Statutes. Dr. Steiner said, "Not the intellectual qualities, but the feeling, or moral, qualities; the direct conceptual capability for the esoteric–occult must play a great role."

And the esoteric element that, in the sense of the Christmas Conference, should run through the Society came to expression to a strong degree in the next months. It was not merely in what was given as esoteric in the narrower sense, but also in the Karma Lectures and (especially) the cycle *Über karmische Zusammenhänge der Anthroposophische Bewegung* (On the karmic connections of the anthroposophic movement, now *Karmic Relationships*, vol. 3), and in lecture cycles that followed in other places. It was a powerful stream of real spiritual life that went through the movement at the time.

And then came what we had to feel was placed upon us, because our teacher—the founder of the anthroposophic Spiritual Science; the creator of the Goetheanum; the one who gave us the Christmas Conference—had passed into the spiritual world.

What we have experienced since then has shown strongly that our movement is based on human beings, that human beings have formed and must form the character of the Society and the School. And that is proper. Dr. Steiner always directed the Society in such a way that *human beings* were taken into account, and what came from these people for the founding of the anthroposophic movement. For it corresponds to an esoteric law that a spiritual movement cannot come into the world in any old way, but that it must be permeated with the forces and heart's blood of individual people who, according to their best forces, always realize what they are obliged to realize.

We see thus also in the Christmas Conference a starting point for working throughout long times ahead, because it can be further connected to what must be there at the starting point that is based in the whole of karma. However, also here we see that it is a matter of a balance between what comes, on the one hand, from the individual human beings—what they bring with themselves as karmic past, what sticks to each of us as human personalities—and what the general requirements are, which can be brought rightly so through the members or through the outer world. There enters in again the "principles," the Statutes, given by Dr. Steiner as what can make the balance possible between the impulses and initiatives of the individual and the guidelines given by Dr. Steiner. It is the balance that must be there between freedom and necessity; between the principle of trust and the authority; or, let's say, between the democratic principal and the hierarchical principle. It is clear that such a balance must take place again and again, and that we have in this balancing a movable element that is characteristic of life. Thus, things cannot proceed according to a schema.

What I tried to develop for you today is that it will be important to know and to implement the lawfulness according to which these things develop. And it is important that in this implementation a universally human, yes, an artistic feature must actually prevail. How one accomplishes it—to know and to bring about a balance between the lawfulness of the outer world and that of the spiritual world—there the artist is the right one who knows how to mediate artistically and to add something new. Above all, it was a matter of a great degree of tolerance. That is where the universally human should express itself and why it can never be that we can exist as a society without confrontations and surprises, because there is a living element in it. This playing into one another and colliding with one another of various laws or various worlds or various human individualities cause a play of color just like here in the windows in this room. It is not dead light and darkness beside each other, but a shining forth and a sparkling of color. That is where the further working, the continued living, comes in. And Dr. Steiner pointed out that the human beings themselves must actually be there with their inner human depths.

Now, where we are thrown back upon ourselves, it must be seen as meaningful that Dr. Steiner spoke of this. He said we must count on a direct conceptual capability for the esoteric–occult. It is not demanded of us that we should all be great esotericists, but if we now want to remain a movement in the way it was founded out of the spirit, then we must try to act according to spiritual laws that we perhaps, first of all, do not yet fully understand but only surmise. However, in spite of it, we strive to maintain the totally concrete connection with the true spiritual world.

I believe, my friends, that first later times will look back at us—I mean with this, after decades when most of us are no longer on the physical plane—then it will be said that people at that time had a difficult time, because they lived in a time of transition. You know that Dr. Steiner said often that every time is actually a time of transition, but what is important is *what* it is that is changing, or shifting, in a particular time. In which respect is "time of transition" now meant? We can say that we live in such an epoch and that we are obliged to work according to the demands and laws of the spiritual world, which we can learn about for the most part from the works of our teacher—works, the implementation of which, we must first surmise and feel out. And then we must have the courage to direct ourselves according to it and not to renounce acting according to these laws first sensed from our esoteric–occult conceptual abilities. If we gave that up, we would also give up the foundation of our society. When we try, however, to act according to what we can perhaps only surmise at first, it will be possible that we make mistakes. These mistakes will quite certainly bring their atonement with them in karma; perhaps not through punishments that are outwardly visible, but rather through what every individual can experience for himself or herself. Also that will be good—not only through what one can learn from it, but because it will be proof that the spiritual world looks after us, that it takes us into account. It will be proof that we are still connected with the spiritual world. If we are so closed that this could no longer occur that our mistakes would not quickly find their atonement but perhaps have to wait first for the next earthly life (that must occur in any case), then we would no longer be a Society that bears the Christmas impulse fully within it. However, to be able to connect ourselves with the spiritual world we will also need to strive earnestly for a connection with the world of the dead.

And also future times will be able to look at us and say: These people did not have it easy. They had to begin something that could not yet be striven for in the right way in the outer world at that time. It was first completely in the beginning of a new working and they had to take that into account in their Society activity. One will certainly be able to admit that. And in spite of that, I think it can already be said today—and there are most certainly people who can confirm it—that much of the work that was accomplished could be accomplished right after the departure of the teacher, thanks to the fact that now people, in their way and according to their abilities, sought and found the connection with the souls in the spiritual world. It is only a matter of one going this path courageously and not letting oneself become discouraged or scared off by mistakes. And then we will be able to experience yet one other thing. I believe I can say that the past years have shown that, when we try to connect ourselves in this way with the great departed one, we will find that, in what he did that had an effect in such institutions as those connected with the Christmas Conference or in what he imparted to us through his words, we will meet what stands there that builds a portal to him in the spiritual world.

Thus, we can find, through this portal, the connection that we need. Also anything further, the new, must be generated, will be able to result from what he wrote in this way into the world ether already during his life. The dead will then be able to accompany and collaborate on what is to happen further. If we fail to do this, if we create further without a connection to the original existence, then we would indeed be free in our decisions on the physical plane, but we would have lost the connection with the spiritual world. Then that will be able to continue, to continue developing—for there must be a connection. New developments must be added to what was laid as the foundation at the Christmas Conference. The fact that mistakes, or errors, can happen here as we now stand should not deter us, but it can even be encouraging if we want to take it upon ourselves courageously. This courageous understanding of what we have done wrong that would show that the results are not in line with the spiritual demands of our movement—this courageous taking hold of these things belongs to the Michaelic impulse that should come to the Christmas impulse. It belongs to the Michael impulse that one courageously tries to carry down the spiritual into the physical, even if it should lead to errors. And if one allows the mistakes to be corrected by the reality in this physical world, one progresses and can count on the fact that the force that comes in from the spiritual world will also collaborate to lead the errors to the good; that our insight comes from imperfections.

We need this courage of the Michaelic impulse especially now when, through the opening of the Goetheanum, we must bring the Goetheanum before the outer world to a yet totally different degree, without letting the outer world come in to us in an unjustified manner.

We have heard from Dr. Steiner that the human relationship to Michael is such that one cannot pray to him. Michael is a spirit that is not approachable through human prayers. One can, however, fight for him; can develop the enthusiasm; can let the way be pointed out from the one who has a "guiding gesture," who introduces the holy human-bearing world-will into the spiritual being. Then Michael, the messenger of Christ, also leads us to Christ himself. And there we experience actually something like a new Christmas, but a still deeper Christmas—a Christmas impulse imbued with will impulse. Then we grasp again in a new way that Christmas impulse that was laid in us in 1923; that impulse of which Dr. Steiner said in the beginning that, if it were not fulfilled here on Earth, then it would withdraw to another planet. Then we will hold ourselves to the vow that our teacher expressed at the Christmas Conference a year after the fire. I will read his words in closing:

> We become worthy through what is imposed upon us in the end that we were allowed to build this Goetheanum, when, in memory of it, we each make the vow, before the divine-best that we bear in our souls, to remain loyal to the spiritual impulses that had their outer form in that Goetheanum. This Goetheanum [the first] could

be taken from us. The spirit of this Goetheanum, if we want to be honest and upright, cannot be taken.... If this inner oath springs forth from the heart in an honest, upright manner, if we can transform the pain-and-suffering into the impulse of action, then we will transform also the sad event into a blessing.

Let us remain loyal to this vow, for loyalty is also a characteristic of Michael, who carries the past into the present in the right way and works from the present into the future.

If we remain loyal to this oath, we can also connect the Christmas impulse with the Michael impulse in the right way.

Elisabeth Vreede (undated)

Elisabeth Vreede: Isis–Sophia

Christmas Essay, 1928 [341]

The Christmas festival that is now approaching draws the attention of the seeking human being in two directions. Those directions are, on the one hand, into the human depths with its deficiencies and needs and, on the other hand, to the heights of the starry heavens in its majesty, from which the message of peace rang out to the shepherds and from which the Magi from the East saw the Star shine that led them to Bethlehem. We know that the two revelations refer to two different birth events that even lay months apart. That shall not occupy us now, but the whole contrast between the wisdom that comes to the shepherds in the field and that of the Magi who saw the Star in the East. Rudolf Steiner pointed out these two streams in his Christmas lectures in 1920 and connected them with the mystery of Isis–Sophia, which stands in the closest relationship to the development of mathematics and astronomy right up to today and into the future, in as much as this future allows itself to be fructified by Spiritual Science. For this reason our Christmas contemplation will be dedicated precisely to this mystery.

In ancient times a primal wisdom was spread out over the entire inhabited world. It was connected to a primitive, dreamlike clairvoyance. In the centuries that preceded the appearance of Jesus Christ this clairvoyance disappeared rapidly. As the Jesus child—or both of the Jesus children—was born, people could, in exceptional instances, receive direct communication from the spiritual world. That was the immense pain for the growing Jesus of Nazareth, that the human beings around him could no longer hear the voices that still resounded for the fathers, and that the lofty spirit powers no longer descended to the altars that still stood at the place of the cultus, but were deserted or even ruled by demons.

There were two human tendencies in earlier times. There were such human souls, to which the Magi belonged as a last echo, who saw the spirit-imbued starry world. They also experienced the minerals and plants in a colorful world imbued with images. They possessed a deeply spiritual astrology, an astrology that was not yet calculated but was seen and heard, for "stars once spoke to human beings." That primal wisdom lived in Hermes, the reincarnated Zoroaster pupil who bore the astral body of Zoroaster as part of himself, and from whom we have received such deep expressions as, for example, the creation of the primal being of all things: "The Sun is his father; the Moon, his mother; and the wind he carried in his belly." The stars and the mineral and plant worlds stimulated knowledge in these ancient people that was not intellectual but later transformed into our modern intellectual knowledge. In its original form it was imagination, pictorial knowledge. That is one side of the Divine Sophia; that side that is turned toward the outer world and lets the human spirit be stimulated to wisdom from this outer world.

It works differently in that stream that we see represented as the last remnant of what the shepherds represent. These people are connected with the depths of the Earth, with what ascends from the Earth as forces, as aura, as color-cloud and connects itself with the human soul, on the one side, and with the animal life on the other. That streams into the human souls, inspiring them and fructifying their will and, above all, their feelings. These human beings in this stream possess inwardness and piety, wisdom of the heart, just as the others, who possess the cosmic wisdom, had characteristics of venerability and majesty. The characteristics that prevail in the shepherds, who experienced the message of peace from the Heights, are of a seed-like nature. They belong to that part of the human will that can fully develop only after death. They are especially active in childhood in the incarnated human being. They then recede gradually during life, only to shine forth again at death. Only with specially gifted people are they present in the later years of life. There is no genius without the childlike nature being preserved into old age. Therefore, also the shepherds are childlike souls, receiving with pious and reverent hearts the message of the Angels.

In contrast, the cosmic wisdom of the Magi was an experiencing again of what the human being went through in the life in the spiritual world before birth. From the way one goes through the cosmic spheres, the way one builds the spirit-seed of one's new body according to the constellations of the stars and planets—of this there remains for the human being a capability that emerges first in later life when the person is "old and wise." Human existence before birth is connected to cosmic spaces. The spiritual ancestors of the Magi beheld the cosmic spaces. For them, the stars were not points of light, but out of the dark black heavens-ground, as seen also during the day—the blue color was not yet seen at that time—they sprang as a spiritual element. They were called by names—though mostly not understood—that are used to a great extent yet today. This spiritual element spoke to them of the destiny of the human being, and especially of the descent of the human soul to the Earth through birth. This ability existed especially in ancient Persia among the Iranian people; and it was *cultivated* into the sixth century before Christ, as *Nazaratos*, the reincarnated Zoroaster, was the teacher of Pythagoras in Chaldea. It was cultivated up to the point when, due to the receding of the old ability, astronomical calculation began. One can say that, just as in the child the ability to count emerges after the seventh year of life to the degree that the forming forces (for the physical) of earliest childhood recede into the inner being, so there awakened in humanity the ability to use mathematics and outer astronomy, and later also mechanics to the degree that the old pre-birth, imaginative abilities disappeared. The knowledge enkindled from outside transformed into a knowledge that ascends from the inner being of the human. The colorful outer world, the moving spirit throng on the dark vault of the heavens, disappeared from human sight. With the emergence of the blue color for the human earthly perception of the sky the old clairvoyance was over. Instead of it, the grey mathematics arises within, and it is applied to abstract astronomy that occupies itself with the stars as mere points of light. Then, almost two thousand years later, this led from the now-fully intellectualized depths (of the human), to the development of laws of physics and mathematics and their application to the starry heavens as void of the spirit. That is the path that the one stream of the Sophia, the primordial wisdom, took: from the outer to the inner, from beholding the mysteries of the stars to the bringing forth of the abstract geometry, kinematics, and things of that sort.

In contrast, those human souls, among who were the last descendants of the shepherds' souls, experienced the opposite of the starry heavens: the qualities of the Earth that showed themselves through an inner ability of perception. They came to know the characteristics of the climate and the Earth through the ascending atmosphere, also the aura of the fellow human beings and the animals—all that lives in the earthly warmth. Also this ability as such disappeared. It changed, because it could no longer convey the spirit, into outer sense perception that conjures before our eyes a nature void of spirit and soul. It drew up to the surface from the depths of the human being into the sense organs and became many centuries later the modern knowledge of nature, today's abstract sense conception that became modern natural science. The world of the natural scientist is also grey; behind all the manifestations of color and objects of the senses, he or she assumes that there are vibrations and atoms.

As Jesus Christ was to be born, there were still in the East the Three Magi, once the students of the great Zoroaster, who had retained the pre-birth abilities and were especially able to behold births, to behold from the star constellation the approach of incarnating souls. (Characteristic of this is that Cicero tells a Persian legend in which that the Magi foretold, from the stars, the birth of Alexander the Great as the future devastator of Asia and Persia.) At the beginning of our time the Magi see the Star in the East, and they follow it. It leads them to Bethlehem and remains above the house in which the newborn child lies.

We do not need to think, therefore, of a usual star or a new star, nor of a comet or planet as done by well-meaning people from time to time. What the Magi saw was certainly a particular special constellation that refers to the constellation of Virgo in connection with that of Gemini. From this experience the last force of the clairvoyant pre-birth abilities emerged in order to see the spiritual Star of the reincarnating Zoroaster and the path that this "Gold Star"—for that is the meaning of the name Zoroaster—took to the place of the birth. Just as the writers of the Gospels were able to describe the story of Jesus Christ from a last combination of all the forces of ancient wisdom, of the ancient clairvoyance, so, too, was the preparatory birth of the Solomon Jesus child perceived through a last announcement of ancient holy human forces. That these were still cultivated by a few karmically predetermined souls and were still present at such a late time was probably due totally to this unique event. The Magi knew that, with them, these abilities would finally disappear. For this reason, they offer to the newborn Jesus child—the gold of wisdom, the frankincense of the purified feeling, and the myrrh of the purified will—all that was and must be transformed to resurrect again as Christ-imbued. The offering of the primordial wisdom is symbolized in the gifts of the Kings from the East. This is the primordial wisdom that is so great, so powerful, that Rudolf Steiner said that the present day, with its knowledge, could turn red with shame.

That is the Sophia who then fell into the abyss, as the Gnostic document *Pistis Sophia* describes in such moving words. At the same time, she is the ancient Isis who mourned Osiris. Pre-Christian world destiny, experienced in cosmic images, connects with what came into the world with Christ, through Christ. Tragedy holds sway in this destiny; it does so right into our time.

We have already examined the Isis–Osiris legend earlier and have seen what relationship it has to our time. Osiris is killed by Typhon–Ahriman, torn into pieces and sought by Isis who then becomes the mother of Horus. During his lifetime and his reign Osiris was, for the Egyptians, a Sun God. They look to him as to the Being of the Sun. In this respect, he was a forerunner of Christ for them. However, Christ cannot be killed for the Earth the way Osiris was. He lives on in the aura of the Earth, although the Christ-bearer, the child born of the Virgin Mother at Christmas, ended his life on the cross. Christ is always there for the human soul. However, it is actually the Mother, Mary–Sophia, the Isis (of olden times) become Sophia, who has disappeared for today's human being! She is the one who was killed. And if we ask who has killed her, the answer is given in the Isis–Sophia saying that was also given to us at Christmas 1920.

> Isis–Sophia,
> Wisdom of God,
> Lucifer has killed her
> And carried her into widths of space
> On the wings of cosmic forces.

As we saw, until the time of the Mystery of Golgotha, Isis–Sophia worked in a twofold way: through the shepherds and through the stream of the Magi, as ancient earthly and heavenly knowledge. We find the last remnant of this wisdom still working in the first pre-Christian centuries. It is used in order to be able to penetrate more deeply into Christianity. Along with the description of Christ as "Sun of Justice," John the Baptist is seen as the Moon ("He must increase, I must decrease"). Thus, just as Christ must have twelve apostles because there are twelve signs of the zodiac, likewise the Baptist must have twenty-nine and a half disciples, because that's how many days the Moon needs to return around to the Sun. The commentator Clemens Romanus explained that it is a matter of twenty-nine male disciples and one female disciple. Her name was Helen and, as a woman, represents "half a man." One sees that here, as in late antiquity, human history is directed according to astrology. The starry sky with its laws is primary. The historical event can only be an expression of this lawfulness.

Everything that once lived so and then, as in the previous example, reached a certain degree of rigidity, or dogmatism, or sank to superstition, to the fantastic—all of that was killed. It was killed by that other side of Christianity itself that believed the old must be destroyed, in order for the new to be able to come. The battle of the Christian Church against the Gnosis is known, for with the Gnosis, it is a matter of these insights. Even Origen (AD 183–CA. 253), the Church Father who wanted to connect cosmic views to Christianity, was banned. Of the Isis of ancient times only a coffin remains.

Today we can recognize that a necessity lay in this struggle; it had to happen for the sake of our freedom. The human being would not have become free of the ancient cosmic dependence, if the ancient wisdom had not been torn mightily away from him or her. The Christ impact was there, but it lived first of all merely weakly and delicately in humanity. It was anchored in the human mind and heart. It did not live as yet in human knowledge, except through the Gnosis. And this itself had taken on luciferic characteristics. The Gnosis was more familiar with the heavenly world than with the earthly world. There were a few Gnostic sects with the opinion that Christ was not really crucified, because he did not really incarnate; it had to do only with an etheric manifestation! The Church had to go up against such a view that destroyed the healing deed of Christ. It did it thoroughly and with cruelty; it stamped out mercilessly everything that could remind one of the ancient wisdom. Yet today, the Churchmen of the most varied directions shudder at hearing the word *gnosis*.

However, what has died must resurrect. Even Lucifer will one day transform into the Holy Spirit. The old Isis–Sophia shall become the new Isis–Sophia. As the shepherds and the Magi, each in their own way, honored, in addition to the Child, the Virgin and presented her with the gifts, that was the beginning of the new Isis–Sophia, Mary-Sophia. What shepherd and Magi abilities have become today merely

build the coffin of the old Isis. We must seek this coffin today. We do not need to search for the Osiris coffin, because he, who was given to us in place of Osiris, is with us "until the end of the world." The coffin of Isis is not to be found on Earth. It is spread out in the heavens. It is the modern natural science, above all astronomy and mathematics, that emerges only from the soul depths and applies laws void of spirit to space void of spirit.

Thus we see how the evolution goes through a null point, a low point, so to speak, and must come to a turning upside down or inside out; it must come to a crossing. The force with which the depths of the Earth once spoke to human beings, with which the shepherds could still catch the announcement of the Angelic hosts, became ineffective and now has transformed itself in the human being into the beholding of sensory splendor spread out before one, the outer maya. It became the doctor's and the natural scientist's outer view of nature and lives as the foundation of natural science today. What astrology and astronomy were in pre-historic times and had directed itself to the outer world, to the heavenly spaces and starry expanses, then receded back into the inner depths and lives further as mathematics in those peculiar constructions that are indeed sense-free but are, first of all, unable to grasp the concrete spiritual.

Rudolf Steiner explained that a certain fusion of both force directions had taken place in ancient times, and indeed, with the Jewish prophets. They were people of the inner life, in whom the capabilities from after death were strong. These alone would not have led them to their prophetic gift. There also played a role with them—as exceptional human beings—the pre-birth capabilities, the Magi forces of foreseeing and prophesying; and thus they could interpret prophetically the future of their folk.

One could say that also today such a penetration exists. It is only that it cannot be beneficial as long as Isis–Sophia has not resurrected from her coffin. Natural scientific research does not stand still before the nature spread out, but dreams that behind it is matter and mathematics: atoms, ether vibrations, electromagnetic equations, and more things of that sort—all that lives within as that Magi stream that has become abstract, all that makes up the luciferic concept of the world in our age. In contrast, if the mathematics is allowed into nature, it becomes technology handled with the forces of the depths of the Earth, but in such a way that they succumb to the ahrimanic, to the sub-sensible. From every direction modern development calls to us: Seek the Isis–Sophia. Seek her coffin in the heavenly spaces and the underworlds. Lift its lid with the strength that Christ can give. Then the inner aspect that has become dry mathematics will "intensify itself to Imagination."

Therein lies the progress of the old Magi-wisdom. Just as the Magi—from the pre-Christian to the worshipers of Christ, the Three Wise Men from the East—beheld the heavens in powerful images, so will people in the future experience the offspring of those star imaginations when they transform the abstract mathematics. Precisely with the mathematical abilities will one understand the *Imaginations*.

And what became outer sense perception, which was once heart wisdom of the shepherds, must go yet further outward. It should not remain fixed on the surface of the body, but should leave the body and become body-free knowledge. Then it becomes *Inspiration*. A new ability to perceive will thus impart to people in the future the same things that the shepherds in the field once experienced. Human beings will again "hear the Angels sing." *All of nature* shall announce to us, "Glory to God in the Heights, and peace on Earth among people of goodwill."

The mere view of space has torn the Isis to pieces. She is poured out into the universe, appearing in beauty, in the beauty of the cosmos, but is dead. We must seek her in the sky. Basically, the people of the materialistic nineteenth century sought her in the sky. It is just that they knew nothing of the new Isis and did not know that she (the old Isis) became (the new) Sophia, and that she can be found only with the Christ-force. Thus, one developed the knowledge that basically is still prevailing knowledge today, which is spread out to an infinitely greater extent than one would at first suspect. This is the mathematical and mechanical view of the world that has seen its model, its pattern, in the spiritless knowledge of the starry heavens.

Let us examine this conception of the world of the nineteenth century! On the one hand, was the atomism that explained the nature processes as the movement of tiny particles? On the other hand, was the mechanical view in astronomy that came to a certain end after LaPlace wrote his *"Himmelsmechanik"* (Mechanics of the sky), and after Urbain Le Verrier discovered Neptune only through calculations based on this mechanics of the sky? At the same time, too, the "Unity of matter in the universe" through spectral analysis was presented.

Now the thinking was that when one could follow and calculate the movements—those that in the end occur in the human brain when a sense impression happens to the human—just as is the case of the movements with the celestial bodies, then one could know exactly how the human soul life and spirit work. In opposition to this expectation, Emil du Bois-Reymond had to hurl his *"Ignoramous et ignorabimus"* (We do not know and will not know). He explained that even when the ideal could be fulfilled, to calculate astronomically the movements of the tiniest particles of the brain, we can never know *why* these movements translate into soul experiences for us.

In *"Was hat Astronomie über Weltenstehung zu sagen?"* (What does astronomy have to say about the genesis of the world?), March 16, 1911, Rudolf Steiner pointed out that exactly what is valid for the human brain must also be valid for the entire starry heavens—namely, that one cannot determine from movements what stands behind them soul–spiritually.

> When we imagine the human brain—in the sense of Leibnitz and du Bois-Reymond—so enlarged that we can walk around in it and see the movements in it like the movements of the celestial bodies, and when we do not perceive similar images of these (celestial) movements in the movements of our brain, we do not need to wonder about that. We do not need to wonder when we are standing in such an enlarged brain, namely in the world structure, when we do not find the bridge between movements of the stars in the heavens

and the possible soul and spirit activities that cross through space and that would stand in the same relation to the movement of the stars as our thoughts, feelings and soul experiences do to the movements of our own brain mass.

Thus, it is no wonder that the astronomer can find nothing in the universe that is of a space-filling soul-spiritual nature, because this is not to be found from the mere movements. With this, one is shown one's limit. One should have asked much differently from the way Emil du Bois-Reymond did. One should have asked, "Is there a possibility to move forward in a different way, in order to find the space-filling soul–spirit beings?" The answer is Spiritual Science; and the insight that one thus attains is the new Isis, the Isis–Sophia!

First, then, when these forces of knowledge are lifted to a higher stage, is it possible to find something different in space and time than what one regarded as the most ideal realization of space and time in the nineteenth century: the astronomical ascertainable movements of the forces and atoms in space.

Mathematics from the Imagination; natural science that receives Inspirations—they can come only from human beings. Let us consider such simple truths as those concerning the connection of the three dimensions of our ordinary space with the structure, the function of the human form with its division into left–right, above–under, front–back, and we will see this human form itself as the archetype of mathematics. Such a mathematics that elevates itself to Imagination will also be able to penetrate the starry heavens. Rudolf Steiner said, "The modern astronomer sees of the starry heaven just the same thing as the modern anatomist sees of the human being. And just as insignificant as the corpse of the human being is, just so insignificant is the content of modern astronomy of the starry sky." Let us take, in contrast, what *An Outline of Esoteric Science* offers concerning the genesis of the world through the cosmic stages of Saturn, Sun, and Moon. Then we have no corpse astronomy. Rather, we then take the other side of Sophia, the new Isis, who is invisible to the outer eye, but who bears, for the Imaginative sight, the clearly readable pronouncement: "I am the human being. I am the past, the present, and the future. Every mortal should lift my veil" (January 6, 1918). However, in another place Rudolf Steiner said:

> One must understand how the Isis, the living, Divine Sophia, had to be lost for the evolution that drove the astrology into mathematics, into the geometry, into the mechanics. One will also understand, however, that when from this field of corpses—from mathematics, kinematics and geometry—the living Imagination resurrects, that this signifies the 'finding of the Isis.' The human being must find her if the Christ-force that the human being has since the Mystery of Golgotha shall become living, fully living in him or her. That means becoming permeated with light. (December 25, 1920)

We are also of standing before a new Christ Event:

> It is not because something enters only from outside that Christ will reappear in his spirit form in the course of the twentieth century, but because human beings find that force that is represented through the Holy Sophia.... We then look in the right sense to the manger today only when we go through, with a particular feeling, what moves through space, and then we look upon that being that was drawn into the world by the Child. We know that we bear it within us, but we must bring understanding to it. For this reason, just as the Egyptians looked from their Osiris to Isis, we must learn to look to the new Isis, to the Holy Sophia. (December 24, 1920)

We are again directed to the manger in which the shepherds found the Child. The image of the Child lying in the manger between the ox and donkey speaks quite deeply to human hearts.

Old views are fallen. We have gone through a field of corpses. We are striving for a new science, for the new enlivening of Isis, and to lift her veil.

Sei in Zeit und Ewigkeit
Schüler im Lichte Michaels
in der Götter Liebe
in des Kosmos Höhen

(Denken, dass von oben gnade-
voll goldenes Licht strömt,
– und sich eingehüllt fühlen
in diesem Licht)
dann spreche man

SHANTIH

$(((\quad)))$ Strahlen, die den
Kopf einhüllen.

Meditation from Rudolf Steiner (Elisabeth Vreede's handwriting)

Christ-Will
Working in the human
Shall wrest from Lucifer
And, on the grounds of Spirit Knowledge
Call to new life in human souls,
Isis–Sophia
Wisdom of God.

Bibliography

Abbreviations for literature references used in the Notes are in **bold** in this list. The list is alphabetized by abbreviations given for the literature information.

Quotations about Elisabeth Vreede

Bindel. Ernst Bindel. "Über Leben und Werk von Elisabeth Vreede" [On the life and work of Elisabeth Vreede]. In *Mitteilungen aus der anthroposophischen Arbeit in Deutschland* [News from the work in Germany], 1948.

Deventer. Madeleine P. van Deventer. "Elisabeth Vreede. Zur 33. Wiederkehr ihres Todestag am 31. Aug." [Elisabeth Vreede. For the 33rd anniversary of her death on Aug. 31]. In *Nachrichtenblatt der Wochenschrif Das Goetheanum* [In the news in the weekly Das Goetheanum], Aug. 22, 1976.

Deventer/Knottenbelt. Madeleine P. van Deventer and Elisabeth Knottenbelt (editor): "Elisabeth Vreede: Ein Lebensbild" [Elisabeth Vreede: A life description], Arlesheim, 1976.

Kolisko. Lilli Kolisko. "Eugen Kolisko. Ein Lebensbild. Zugleich ein Stück Geschichte der Anthroposophischen Gesellschaft" [Eugen Kolisko. A life description. Also a piece of the history of the Anthroposophical Society]. Gerabronn-Crailsheim, 1961.

Mitteilungen. *Mitteilungen aus dem anthroposophischen Leben in der Schweiz.* Sonderheft 7—Weihnachten 2003: "Besinnung Elisabeth Vreede (1879–1942)" [News from the anthroposophical life in Switzerland. Special issue, no. 7, Christmas 2003: reflection on Elisabeth Vreede].

Zaiser. Hedwig Zaiser: "Im Memoriam Elisabeth Vreede" [In memory of Elisabeth Vreede]. Undated typescript, unpublished. Archive at the Goetheanum.

Quotations from Lectures and Writings by Elisabeth Vreede

Archive. "Zur Geshcichte des Rudolf Steiner Archivs am Goetheanum. (Nachschrift Vortrag 28.4.1935)." [On the history of the Rudolf Steiner Archive at the Goetheanum (Notes of the lecture in Stuttgart on April 28, 1935)], unpublished. Archive at the Goetheanum.

Astronomy. *Geschichte und Phänomene der Astronomie (Aufsätze und Vorträge)* [History and phenomena of astronomy (esaays and lectures). Dornach, 1995.

Bodhisattva. In Elisabeth Vreede and T. H. Meyer: *The Bodhisattva Question: Krishnamurti, Rudolf Steiner, Valentin Tomberg, and the Mystery of the Twentieth-Century Master.* Temple Lodge, 2010. "Die Bodhisattvafrage in der Geschichte der Anthroposophischen Gesellschaft" (Vorträge 1930) [The Bodhisattva question in the history of the Anthroposophical Society (lectures 1930)].

"Erste Begegnung mit Rudolf Steiner (Aufsatz, 1934) [First meeting with Rudolf Steiner (essay 1934)]. In: Deventer/Knottenbelt.

Geschichte [History]. "Kurze Geschichte der ersten Woche nach Rudlf Steiner's Death" [Brief history of the first week after Rudolf Steiner's death]. Unpublished typescript, 1934. Archive at the Goetheanum.

Idyllen [Idylls]. "Vorstandsidyllen" [Idylls of the Executive Council]. Unpublished typescript, 1928. Archive at the Goetheanum.

In me ipsam. Unpublished autobiographical typescript, 1937). Archive at the Goetheanum.

Vorstandsberufung [Appointment to the Executive Council]. "Meine Vorstandsberufung" [My appointment to the Executive Council]. Unpublished typescript, Dec. 25, 1934. Archive at the Goetheanum.

Zur Geschichte [On the history]. "Zur Geschichte der Anthroposophischen Gesellschaft seit der Weihnachtstagung 1923" [On the history of the Anthroposophical Society since the Christmas Conference 1923]. Arlesheim, 1935.

Notes

1. Letter to Frl. Schünemann, Jan. 31, 1934. In Deventer/Knottenbelt.
2. Quoted from Deventer. According to van Deventer, Hedda Hummel, one of Rudolf Steiner's stenographers, noted Steiner's statement about Vreede in her autobiographical notes.
3. In Deventer/Knottenbelt.
4. Ibid.
5. *Ita Wegman and Anthroposophy: A Conversation with Emanuel Zeylmans.* SteinerBooks, 2012.
6. In Deventer/Knottenbelt.
7. In Mitteilungen [News].
8. In Deventer.
9. Compare Peter Selg, *The Culture of Selflessness.* SteinerBooks, 2012.
10. Sonderheft in Mitteilungen [Special edition of News].
11. In Deventer/Knottenbelt.
12. Deventer.
13. In Deventer/Knottenbelt.
14. In Mitteilung [News].
15. In Deventer/Knottenbelt—Werner Pache recorded in his diary concerning the cremation ceremony for Elisabeth Vreede on Sept. 3, 1943 in Lugano, that Margarete Kirchner-Bockholt called the natural catastrophe Steiner described for Vreede a volcanic eruption ("that in an earlier life she died from the eruption of a volcano"). Ita Wegman Archive.
16. Jacques de Molay (d. Mar. 18, 1314), burned as heretic on an island in the Seine River in Paris. Concerning the life history and the story of the suffering, compare, among others, M.J.-Krück von Poturzyn, *Der Prozess gegen die Templer: Ein Bericht über die Vernichtung des Ordens* [The process against the Templars: A report of the destruction of the Order]. Stuttgart, 1982.
17. In Bodhisattva.
18. Deventer.
19. Astronomy.
20. Compare Rudolf Steiner, *Understanding Healing: Meditative Reflections on Deepening Medicine through Spiritual Science* (CW 316). Rudolf

Steiner Press, 2013. And Peter Selg, "Die Medizin muss Ernst machen mit dem geistigen Leben." [Medicine must take the spiritual life earnestly]. And Rudolf Steiner, *Course for Young Doctors*. Mercury Press, 1996.

21. Compare Madeleine P. van Deventer, *Die anthroposophisch-medizinische Bewegung in den verschiedenen Etappen ihrer Entwicklung* [The anthroposophic medical movement in the various stages of its development]. Dornach, 1983. And Peter Selg, *Helene von Grunelius und Rudolf Steiners Kurs für "junge Mediziner." Eine Studie* [Helene Grunelius' and Rudolf Steiner's course for young doctors. A study.] Dornach 2003. As well as Peter Selg, *Die Briefkorrespondenz der junge Mediziner. Eine dokumentarische Studie zur Rezeption von Rudolf Steiners Jungmedizinerkursen* [Letters of the young doctors. A documental study of the reception of Rudolf Steiner's courses for young doctors]. Dornach, 2006.

22. Rudolf Steiner, *Anthroposophical Leading Thoughts*. CW 26. Rudolf Steiner Press, 1973.

23. Kolisko.

24. In his foreword, Wim Viersen wrote in 1995: "The following volumes of the series will be published (in literal English), vol. 1, History and Phenomena of Astronomy; vol. 2, New Star Wisdom and Astrology; vol. 3 (a), Anthroposophical Work and vol. 3 (b), Mathematics and Physics; vol. 4, Book Discussions, Reports, Supplements, Index" (*Geschichte und Phänomene der Astronomie* [History and phenomena of astronomy]. Dornach, 1996).

25. *Das Goetheanum. Weekly publication for Anthroposophy*, no. 35; Aug. 28, 2009.

26. Emanuel Zeylmans van Emichoven, *Who Was Ita Wegman: A Documentation*, vol. 3. Mercury Press, 1996.

27. The most extensive and impressive documental work about the crises of the General Anthroposophical Society in the first decades after Rudolf Steiner's death was presented by Lili Kolisko in 1961, on the basis of countless stenographic texts from meetings and conferences that she had prepared herself [as translated before, Eugen Kolisko. A Life Description. Also a piece of history of the Anthroposophical Society]. Lili Kolisko's works—also her historical work—were unrecognized in much of the Anthroposophical Society. She died on Nov. 22, 1976, 33 years after Elisabeth Vreede. A reawakening knowledge and consciousness of her life work and personality—whom Rudolf Steiner valued immensely—belongs, in my opinion, to the future requirements of the anthroposophical movement.

28. Rudolf Steiner, *Rosicrucian Wisdom* (CW 99). Rudolf Steiner Press, 2000.

29. Compare *Nederland's Patriciaat. Genealogien van bekende Geslachter* [Holland's aristocracy. Genealogies of known families]. 68th year. 1984. Published by Central Bureau for Genealogy. Gravenhage (Indication from Christoph E. G. ten Houte de Lange).

30. Madeleine P. Deventer, in Deventer/Knottenbelt.

31. In Deventer/Knottenbelt.

32. Rudolf Steiner, *Paths and Goals of the Spiritual Human Being*. Rudolf Steiner Press, 2015.

33. In Deventer/Knottenbelt.

34. Ibid.

35. Ibid.

36. Ibid.

37. He spoke about the fact that there could not be a uniform, abstract theosophy, but that each folk must develop this according to their own way; and that, especially in Germany, it must be connected with the great spirits of history: Goethe, Schiller, Herder, etc. With these words Rudolf Steiner described his own path that had to do with the usual traditions and dogmas in the Theosophical Society. He developed, as it were, the plan according to which he wanted to lead the German Section. That seemed to me to be simply "nationalistic," and I was peeved because I could not understand that (Deventer/Knottenbelt).

38. Auto-report of the lecture in Rudolf Steiner, *Philosophie und Anthroposophie. Gesammelte Aufsätze 1904–1923* [Philosophy and Anthroposophy. Collected essays 1904–1923] (CW 35). Dornach, 1984. In a Theosophical Congress report Rudolf Steiner wrote about his contribution in a brief summary. "In the Philosophy Section Rudolf Steiner spoke about 'Mathematics and Occultism.' He proceeded from the point that Plato demanded a preparatory training in mathematics of his pupils; that the Gnostics described their higher wisdom as Mathesis (a hypothetical universal science based on mathematics); and the Pythagoreans saw the foundation of all existence in number and form. He explained that they all did not have abstract mathematics in mind, but that they meant the intuitive beholding of the occultist (esotericist), who perceived the laws in the higher worlds with the help of a spiritual sense or feeling that imagined in the spiritual what music is for our usual, sense world. Just as the air arouses musical sense impressions through vibrations that can be expressed in numbers, so can esotericists, when they prepare themselves through knowledge of the mysteries of numbers, to perceive in the higher worlds a spiritual music that intensifies, by especially high development of the human being, to the point of sensing the music of the spheres. This music of the spheres is no fantasy; it constitutes a real experience for the esotericists. Through the incorporation of Mathesis into their own being, through the penetration of their astral body and intellect with the intimate sense that expresses itself in the relationships of numbers, people prepare themselves to allow hidden world manifestations to work upon them. In modernity the esoteric sense has pulled back from the sciences. Since Copernicus and Galileo, science has focused on the conquest of the physical world. However, it is on the eternal plane of the evolution of humanity that also this physical science can find access to the spiritual world. In the age of physical research, mathematics was enriched by Newton's and Leibniz's *Analysis of Infinity* through the differential and integral calculations. Whoever not only seeks to understand abstractly,

but to *experience* inwardly what a differential reality portrays, stamps into himself or herself a sense-free view. For in the differential, the sensory view of space itself is overcome in the symbol; the cognition of the human being can become purely spiritual for moments. This reveals itself to the clairvoyant through the fact that the thought-form of the differential is open to the outside, in contrast to the thought-forms that the human being receives through sensory view. These are closed to the outside. Thus, through the *Analysis of Infinity,* one of the ways opened up through which the higher senses of the human being opens toward the outside. The esotericists know what process takes place with the Chakra (Lotus Flower) that sits between the eyebrows when they develop the spirit of the differential within. If now mathematicians are selfless people, they can lay what they have attained in this way upon the universal altar of human brotherhood. And from the seemingly driest science, there can come about an important source for esotericism." (Rudolf Steiner, *Lucifer-Gnosis* (CW 34). Dornach, 1987).

39. In Deventer/Knottenbelt.
40. Madeleine P. Deventer in Deventer/Knottenbelt.
41. Quoted from Bindel.
42. In Deventer/Knottenbelt.
43. Ibid.
44. Ibid.
45. Rudolf Steiner, *The Principle of Spiritual Economy* (CW 109). SteinerBooks, 1986.
46. Rudolf Steiner, *Mystery Centers of the Middle Ages* (CW 233a). Garber, 1994 and *Rosicrucuanism and Modern Initiation.* Rudolf Steiner Press, 1994.
47. Rudolf Steiner, *The Principle of Spiritual Economy* (CW 109). SteinerBooks, 1986.
48. Ibid.
49. Rudolf Steiner, *Rosicrucian Wisdom* (CW 99). Rudolf Steiner Press, 2008.
50. Ibid. Compare also, "Das Prinzip des Rosenkreuzertums is, den Geist in die Welt einzuführen, fruchtbare Arbeit für die Sache zu leisten." [The principle of Rosicrucianism is to introduce the spirit into the world, to accomplish fruitful work for the cause] (Rudolf Steiner, *Rosicrucianism Renewed: Unity of Art, Science and Religion and the Theosophical Congress of Whitsun 1907* (CW 284). SteinerBooks, 2006.
51. Rudolf Steiner, *Rosicrucian Wisdom.* CW 99. Rudolf Steiner Press, 2008.
52. In me ipsam.
53. Andrej Belyj, *Verwandlung des Lebens. Erinnerungen an Rudolf Steiner* [Transformation of life. Memories of Rudolf Steiner.] Basel, 1977.
54. Rudolf Steiner, *Rosicruciam Wisdom* (CW 99). Rudolf Steiner Press, 2008.

Notes

55. Rudolf Steiner, *Bewusstsein–Leben–Form* [Conciousness–Life–Form] (CW 89). Dornach, 2001.

56. Bodhisattva.

57. Vreede indicated in her Bodhisattva lectures, among others, the fact that Rudolf Steiner, in an inspirational manner in his Esoteric Lessons, could speak from another individuality with whom he stood in concrete relationship. She showed this on an example from an Esoteric Lesson held during the time around the Düsseldorf Course, about which she said, "And so, during the cycle at that time in Düsseldorf, we had a session in a smaller circle, an Esoteric Lesson, just as they were held in those days. There Rudolf Steiner began with the words, 'My dear sisters and brothers, this Esoteric Lesson is of a nature that it does not stand within the responsibility of him who speaks here.' And then he described how Zarathustra was initiated by Ahura Mazdao, how Zarathustra stood before the great Sun being. He was himself Zarathustra in this moment. It was extremely impressive to experience how our great teacher, who had conveyed to us the outcome of his research, now showed us directly how an ancient leader and teacher of mankind could, through Inspiration, reveal himself, for whom the way had been prepared, so to speak, through all that had also formed the basis of teaching in that cycle" (ibid.).

58. Bindel.

59. Compare Rudolf Steiner, *Mystery Centers of the Middle Ages*. Garber, 1994; and *Rosicrucuanism and Modern Initiation* (CW 233a). Rudolf Steiner Press, 1994. Lecture of Apr. 20, 1924.

60. Rudolf Steiner, *Spiritual Hierarchies and the Physical World* (CW 110). SteinerBooks, 2008.

61. Ibid.

62. Compare to this, among others, Peter Selg, *Christian Morgenstern. Sein Weg mit Rudolf Steiner* [Christian Morgenstern. His path with Rudolf Steiner]. Stuttgart, 2008.

63. Compare to this process Rudolf Steiner, *From the History and Contents of the First Section of the Esoteric School* (CW 264). SteinerBooks 2010; and the presentations in secondary literature by Thomas Meyer, "The Beginning of the End of the Theosophical Society." In Elisabeth Vreede/T. H. Meyer, *The Bodhisattva Question*. Temple Lodge, 1993/2010. And Sergei O. Prokofieff, *Die Geburt der christlichen Esoterik im 20. Jahrhundert und die ihr widerstrebenden okkulten Mächte* [The birth of the Christian esotericism in the 20th century and the occult powers opposing it]. Dornach, 1997. And Hella Wiesberger, *Rudolf Steiners esoterische Lehrtätigkeit. Wahrhaftigkeit, Kontinuität, Neugestaltung* [Rudolf Steiner's esoteric teaching activity. Truth, continuity, new forming]. Dornach, 1997. And Peter Selg, *Ich bleibe bei Ihnen. Rudolf Steiner und Ita Wegman. München, Pfingsten 1907. Dornach 1923–1925* [I remain with you. Rudolf Steiner and Ita Wegman. Munich, Whitsun 1907. Dornach, 1923-1925]. Stuttgart, 2007.

64. Rudolf Steiner, *From the History and Contents of the First Section of the Esoteric School* (CW 264). SteinerBooks, 2010.

65. About the situation in these years, Vreede said in her lecture of July 9, 1930 in Stuttgart: "Many people, particularly those from countries outside Germany, had been pupils of Annie Besant before they found their way to Rudolf Steiner; and all of them actually looked up to her, filled with reverence. It was a time of the most difficult trials of the soul for the members of that period, and many soul-struggles were endured precisely because of the way Rudolf Steiner brought forward these teachings, leaving it to the freedom of each individual to draw his or her own conclusions. Truly difficult inner struggles occurred. Heart's blood flowed with regard to the question: Is Annie Besant right to present Krishnamurti as the World Teacher, as a Bodhisattva, or as the Christ—or is Rudolf Steiner correct?"

66. In me ipsam.

67. In Deventer/Knottenbelt.

68. Ibid. Lecture, July 27, 1912.

69. Ibid. Lecture, Feb. 17, 1912.

70. Ibid. Lecture, Nov. 18, 1912.

71. Ibid.

72. Letter to the parents on Apr. 2, 1912. In Estate of Elisabeth Vreede, in the Library of the Dutch National Society. The Hague.

73. Ibid.

74. Rudolf Steiner, *Cosmosophy*, vol. 2 (CW 208). Rudolf Steiner Press, 1997. Margarita Woloschin wrote, "It was, unfortunately, a garrison church that we visited; the congregation consisted only of soldiers with stubborn countenances. The Choruses were Sung by sleepy soldiers in a boring and pitiful manner." (*The Green Snake: An Autobiography.* Floris Books, 2010.)

75. Ibid.

76. Rudolf Steiner, *Wahrspruchworte* (CW 40). Dornach 2005 [Part was published as *Truth-Wrought-Words,* SteinerBooks, 2010].

77. Rudolf Steiner, *Der irdische und kosmische Mensch* [The earthly and cosmic human being] (CW 133). Dornach, 1989.

78. Rudolf Steiner, *Erfahrungen des Übersinnlichen* [Experiences of the suprasensory] (CW 143). Dornach, 1994.

79. Ibid.

80. *Der irdische und kosmische Mensch* [The earthly and cosmic human being] (CW 133). Dornach, 1989.

81. *Erfahrungen des Übersinnlichen* [Experiences of the suprasensory] (CW 143). Dornach, 1994.

82. Ibid.

83. In Deventer/Knottenbelt. Lecture Dec. 27, 1911.

84. At the annual Theosophical Meeting in Adyar, Anniee Besant said in her lecture to open the meeting on December 27, 1912, "The German general secretary, educated by the Jesuits, has not been able to shake himself sufficiently clear of that fatal influence to allow liberty of opinion within his section.... The only thing left for me to do, as President, in face of this unprecedented outrage of opinion within the Theosophical Society, is to cancel the charter of the German National Society.

"The annulment of the Foundation Document of the German Section was communicated in a letter from a brother of Elisabeth Vreede (Adrian?), who participated in the Annual Meeting in Adyar. Following this, Marie von Sivers wrote to Rudolf Steiner on January 19, 1913, "Early this morning, Miss Vreede came with a letter from her brother, who participated in the Adyar Convention. It contained the news that we are 'cancelled'; and Miss Vreede thought that the official announcement would come only a week later with the next ship. She dictated for me the following passage from the letter, 'One of the most important things that the Annual Meeting that just ended brought is the decision to cancel the German Section and to pass the charter on to Dr. Hübbe-Schleiden. Besides the fact that the Executive Council made this decision, two or three days later Mrs. Besant came with an accusation that contained not more and not less than that Rudolf Steiner is under the influence of the Jesuits.'" (Rudolf Steiner and Marie von Sivers, *Correspondence and Documents, 1901–1925* [SteinerBooks, 1988]).

Rudolf Steiner read the official wording of the expulsion aloud at the first General Meeting of the Anthroposophical Society in Berlin on February 2, 1913, and added thereby words about the Jesuit accusation: "There is hardly an accusation that can be uttered, which is less true; and yet, an accusation that is suitable to play a role in Germany and other areas when one wishes to throw suspicion on us. Because that is so, and because here really objective things are connected with the personal, I make an inquiry of you. I cannot now convey everything that could show you how this accusation was pulled from thin air and how untruthful and unreasonable it is. I ask you, do you want to hear in the next days a brief sketch, a short excerpt of my biography? I can in no other way give you the proof of how foolish and untrue such a claim by Mrs. Besant is. I do not want, however, to force this report on you. For that reason, I ask you to tell me whether, at a more appropriate time during these days, you wish to hear my memoirs, condensed and shortened as much as possible."

The members at the General Meeting accepted Rudolf Steiner's offer. Then he continued, "Mrs. Besant knows very well that with every accusation, something of it sticks. And now I put an end to it, because there is actually no expression that can sufficiently characterize what has happened. It is unheard of that I would have to resort to describing my biography as a remedy." In 1930 Elisabeth Vreede wrote, *"The force and indignation with which Rudolf Steiner threw these last words into the meeting still ring in my ears."* (In *Bodhisattva*). Two days later, on Feb. 4, 1913, Rudolf Steiner spoke about his biography.

85. Compare Rudolf Steiner, *Die Welt des Geistes und ihr Hereinragen in das physische Dasein* [The spiritual world and its extension into physical

existance] (CW 150). Dornach 1980. Compare also Elisabeth Vreede's essay "Über das Osterfest" (1943). In Astronomy.

86. Compare Rudolf Steiner, *The Effects of Esoteric Development* (CW 145, SteinerBooks, 1997).

87. Letter to Li Content, November 24, 1913. In Deventer/Knottenbelt.

88. Compare also in this connection Rudolf Steiner's biographical path that likewise took place without Christian religious instruction or tradition. In Oslo, Steiner said at the end of the second lecture on his research in *The Fifth Gospel* in an autobiographical formulation, "Although it called for a certain overcoming to speak about precisely this subject, the obligation toward what must be prepared in our time outweighed my hesitation. That led to my speaking about this for the first time especially to you. When I speak of 'overcoming,' take this word literally.

"Please take everything I have to say on this particular occasion as a kind of hint. It will undoubtedly be possible to put it in a better and more precise way in the future. You may find it easier to understand why I say it has been an 'overcoming,' if you permit me not to withhold a personal remark. I am fully aware that in the science of the spirit to which I am devoting myself it is initially extraordinarily difficult and requires much effort to gain things of this kind from the spiritual record. I would not be surprised if the word 'hint' I have used did turn out to be much more meaningful and significant than we need to consider for the moment. At the present time I certainly cannot say exactly what the spiritual record contains, for I experience all kinds of problems and difficulties when seeking to gain images relating to the secrets of Christianity from the Akashic Record. It is an effort to achieve the necessary density of the images and to hold on to them, and I feel it may be karma that I am given the duty to say what I am saying now. I am certain it would have required less effort if, like many people today, I had receive a truly Christian education in early youth. I did not have this. I grew up in an entirely freethinking environment, and my studies also went in that direction. My educational track was purely scientific. Because of this, I now have some trouble finding the things of which I am obliged to speak.... On the other hand, because I was not connected with Christianity in my young days, I am much less biased toward it. Having come to Christianity and to the Christ through the spirit, I believe I can claim freedom from bias and prejudice and therefore have the right to make statements on the subject. At the present point in world history people may feel able to place more reliance in the words of someone who has had scientific training and was not connected with Christianity than in the words of someone who has been connected with it from his or her earliest youth. Nor do I think Christianity will lose anything from being presented at a deeper level by someone who only found his way from the spirit" (Rudolf Steiner, *The Fifth Gospel* [Rudolf Steiner Press, 1995]).

89. For this turning point, compare Peter Selg, *Rudolf Steiner and the Fifth Gospel*. SteinerBooks, 2009.

90. Compare Peter Selg, *Rudolf Steiner and the Fifth Gospel*. SteinerBooks, 2009.

91. About the Leipzig situation for Christian Morgenstern and Rudolf Steiner, compare Peter Selg, *Christian Morgenstern. Sein Weg mit Rudolf Steiner* [Christian Morgenstern: His path with Rudolf Steiner]. Stuttgart, 2008.

92. Christian Morgenstern, *Werke und Briefe* [Works and correspondence]. Stuttgart Edition, vol. 2.

93. Compare Rex Raab, *Edith Maryon. Bidhauer und Mitarbeiterin Rudolf Steiners* [Edith Maryon: Sculptor and coworker of Rudolf Steiner]. Dornach, 1993; and Peter Selg, *Edith Maryon, Rudolf Steiner und die Dornacher Christus-Plastik* [Edith Maryon, Rudolf Steiner and the Dornach Christ statue]. Dornach, 2006.

94. Rudolf Steiner, *Damit der Mensch ganz Mensch werde. Haager Hochschulkurs* [So that the human may become completely human being. The School course in The Hague] (CW 82). Dornach, 1994.

95. Estate of Elisabeth Vreede in the Library of the Dutch National Society in The Hague.

96. Ibid.

97. The best descriptions of these Dornach crisis years come from Andrej Belyj, *Geheime Aufzeichnungen. Erinnerungen an das Leben im Umkreis Rudolf Steiners* [Confidential records. Memories of life around Rudolf Steiner]. Dornach, 1992. Belyj's brilliant presentations are misjudged by many people even today and are interpreted as expression of his own unstable soul condition; actually they let be known the psychopathological status of much that Belyj, as schooled observer and chronicler, recorded.

98. "One sometimes feels a little pain when one enters *anthroposophical settlements or where people are put together*," said Rudolf Steiner on July 1, 1924 in his *Education for Special Needs* (CW 317). Rudolf Steiner Press, 2014 (italics by Vreede).

99. Rudolf Steiner, *Wege zu einem neuen Baustil* [Paths to a new architectural style] (CW 286). Dornach, 1982.

100. Rudolf Steiner, *Wahrspruch Worte* (CW 40). Dornach [Part as *Truth-Wrought Words*. SteinerBooks, 2010.]

101. Archive.

102. "Fräulein Bruinier, who began to index the lectures, had to leave Dornach soon for health reasons. Miss Mackenzie never did much with the archive. I did most of the work" (Ibid.). Elisabeth Vreede mentioned in her historical description that Steiner was not in agreement with one of Elisabeth Vreede's coworkers (Isi Mackenzie) and was only mildly enthusiastic with the first suggestion of founding the Archive. "I will not say that Dr. Steiner was immediately enthusiastic, and that was quite understandable. I know now that one of the three people who wanted to participate very highly unsympathetic toward him (Ibid.).

103. Ibid. at this point in her notes Vreede added, *"I would like to say with a certain pride, however, that the Archive is the only place from which Rudolf Steiner himself had gotten the names"* (Ibid.).

104. Compare for this his exemplary presentations for doctors. In Peter Selg, *Vom Logos menschlicher Physis. Die Entfaltung einer anthroposophischen Humanphysiology im Werk Rudolf Steiners* [About the Logos of human physiology. The development of an anthroposophical human physiology in the work of Rudolf Steiner]. Dornach 2006, vol. 1. What Steiner said and about which he gave reminders here for medicine can also be given for further fields, such as, pedagogy and the natural and social sciences, among others.

105. In Mitteilungen.

106. In Deventer/Knottenbelt.

107. Ibid.

108. Archive.

109. Ibid.

110. Letter to Elisabeth Vreede on Apr. 14, 1935. Archive at the Goetheanum. Quoted from Owe Werner. In Mitteilungen.

111. Marie Steiner, quoted from "Nachrichten der Rudolf-Steiner-Nachlassverwaltung, Nr. 1" [News of the Rudolf Steiner Estate, no. 1].

112. Kolisko. In her historical presentation Lili Kolisko dealt also with Marie Steiner's intervention in the Stuttgart Archive of the Goetheanum that was founded and built up with great personal involvement by Eugen Kolisko, Walter Johannes Stein, and Carlo Septimus Picht in 1920. Marie Steiner took it away from Kolisko and Stein in fall of 1931 and transferred the responsibility to the new German business management (ibid.).

113. In me ipsam.

114. Compare Rex Raab, *Edith Maryon. Bildhauerin und Mitarbeiter Rudolf Steiners* [Edith Maryon. Sculptor and coworker of Rudolf Steiner]. Dornach, 1993.

115. In Deventer/Knottenbelt.

116. In me ipsam. Vreede's lectures appeared in printed form in 1922. Compare Elisabeth Vreede, "Die Berechtigung der Mathematik in der Astronomie und ihre Grenzen." [The justification of mathematics in the astronomy and its limits]. In *Aenigmatisches aus Kunst und Wissenschaft* [Enigmatic elements from art and science], vols. 1 and 2. Dornach, 1922.

117. In me ipsam.

118. For historical context compare, among others, Peter Selg, *Willem Zeylmans van Emmichoven. Anthroposophie and Anthroposophische Gesellschaft im 20. Jahrhundert* [Willem Zeylmans van Emmichoven. Anthroposophy and Anthroposophical Society in the twentieth century]. Arlesheim, 2009.

119. Rudolf Steiner, *Erziehung zum Leben* [Education for life]. CW 297a. Dornach, 1998.

120. Rudolf Steiner, *Soziale Leben–Soziale Wirklichkeit–Soziale Praxis* [Social life–social reality–social practice], vol. 2 (CW 337b). Dornach, 1999.

121. Ibid.

122. For Ita Wegman's consequential Munich decision, compare my monograph *Ich bleibe bei Ihnen. Rudolf Steiner und Ita Wegman. München, Pfingston 1907* [I remain with you. Rudolf Steiner and Ita Wegman. Munich, Whitsun 1907]. Stuttgart, 2007.

123. Rudolf Steiner, *Mantric Sayings: Meditations* (CW 268). SteinerBooks, 2015.

124. In Mitteilungen.

125. Rudolf Steiner, *Damit der Mensch ganz Mensch werde. Haager Hochschulekurs* [So that the human being may become completely human. The Hague School Course]. Dornach, 1994.

126. Compare Rudolf Steiner, *The Sun Mystery: and the Mystery of Death and Resurrection* (CW 211). SteinerBooks, 2006.

127. Compare Peter Selg, *Edith Maryon, Rudolf Steiner und die Dornacher Christus-Plastik* [Edith Maryon, Rudolf Steiner and the Dornach Christ-sculpture]. Dornach, 2006.

128. Rudolf Steiner, *The Sun Mystery: and the Mystery of Death and Resurrection* (CW 211). SteinerBooks, 2006.

129. Rudolf Steiner Archive, Dornach.

130. Compare Peter Selg, *The Figure of Christ*. Temple Lodge, 2009.

131. Quoted from Peter Selg, *Willem Zeylmans van Emmichoven. Anthroposophie and Anthroposophische Gesellschaft im 20. Jahrhundert* [Willem Zeylmans van Emmichoven. Anthroposophy and Anthroposophical Society in the twentieth century]. Arlesheim, 2009; compare also Emanuel Zeylmans van Emmichoven, *Willem Zeylmans van Emmichoven. Ein Pionier der Anthroposophie* [Willem Zeylmans van Emmichoven. A pioneer of Anthroposophy]. Arlesheim, 1979.

132. Quoted from Peter Selg, *Willfried Immanuel Kunert. Zur Lebens- und Therapiegeschichte eines Kindes aus dem 'Heilpädagogischen Kurs'* [Willfried Immanuel Kunert. On the life and therapy of a child from the curative education course]. Dornach, 2006.

133. Ibid.

134. Compare Rudolf Steiner, *Das Schicksalsjahr 1923 in der Geschichte der Anthroposophischen Gesellschaft. Vom Goetheanumbrand zur Weihnachtstagung* [The year of destiny 1923 in the history of the Anthroposophical Society. From the Goetheanum fire to the Christmas Conference] (CW 259); and Peter Selg, "Rudolf Steiner und das zweite Goetheanum" [Rudolf Steiner and the second Goetheanum]. In Peter Selg, *Vom Umgang mit Rudolf Steiners Werk. Ursprung, Krise und Zukunft des Dornacher Goetheanums* [Concerning the handling of Rudolf Steiner's work. Origin, crisis and future of the Dornach Goetheanum]. Dornach, 2007.

135. In a short report of October 1936 (nine pages, handwritten manuscript), Elisabeth Vreede described, among other things, Steiner's dissatisfaction

with verbal financial agreements at the Delegates' Meeting in July 1923 in Dornach: "Before Delegates' Meeting the actual initiators for the financial reconstruction plan were already Frau Dr. Wegman and Mr. Scott Pyle, with support from Dr. Wachsmuth—one spoke generally of the Wegman-Scott plan"—and the delegates attending the meeting already had the impression that the reconstruction was well underway. However, Dr. Steiner appeared to be extremely unreceptive to every merely verbal agreement in these negotiations. The assurance by the general secretary and the delegates that they would, after returning home, do everything they could to raise as much money as possible, even naming specific sums that one hoped to raise, left him apparently unsatisfied. From his words and his actions it was quite clear to me that he would deal with the reconstruction only if he received written guarantees for the necessary sums of money. He could not be satisfied with general, nonspecific agreements or promises no matter how honestly and earnestly intended they were." During a break in the meeting of July 21, Vreede called together many Dutch friends and conveyed to them her assessment, "that the Doctor wants written pledges and guarantees, thus, that we simply wanted to take upon ourselves the guarantee of 150,000 sFr, as has already been said." Vreede's plan was approved. Individual Dutch people (including Ita Wegman) pledged personally in writing 10,000 sFr each and shared this with Rudolf Steiner. "The meeting received through this a different mood. One sensed for the first time during these days that Dr. Steiner was satisfied. The other delegations followed suit during the course of the day. On the 22nd, at the end of the conference, the reconstruction was assured (unpublished, estate of Elisabeth Vreede in the Dutch National Society in The Hague).

136. Compare Emanuel Zeylmans van Emmichoven, *Willem Zeylmans van Emmichoven. Ein Pionier der Anthroposophie* [Willem Zeylmans van Emmichoven. A pioneer of Anthroposophy]. Arlesheim, 1979; and Peter Selg, *Willem Zeylmans van Emmichoven. Anthroposophie and Anthroposophische Gesellschaft im 20. Jahrhundert* [Willem Zeylmans van Emmichoven. Anthroposophy and Anthroposophical Society in the twentieth century]. Arlesheim, 2009.

137. For this, compare Emanuel Zeylmans van Emmichoven, *Who was Ita Wegman: A Documentation,* vol. 1. Mercury Press, 1995.

138. Compare Rudolf Steiner, *Freemasonry and Ritual Work: The Miraim Service* (CW 265). SteinerBooks. And Emanuel Zeylmans van Emmichoven, *Who was Ita Wegman: A Documentation,* vol. 4. Mercury Press, 2009.

139. Rudolf Steiner, *At Home in the Universe: Exploring Our Suprasensory Nature* (CW 231). SteinerBooks, 2000.

140. *Vorstandsberufung.* My appointment to the Executive Council.

141. Ibid.

142. Compare Emanuel Zeylmans van Emmichoven, *Who was Ita Wegman. A Documentation,* vol. 4. Mercury Press, 2009.

143. Compare ibid.

144. Rudolf Steiner, *The Christmas Conference: For the Foundation of the General Anthroposophical Society 1923/1924* (CW 260). Anthroposophic Press, 1990.

145. "And so I want also... to ask that you do not see this Executive Council as an administrative Council, but as one that will work esoterically directly from the substance of the spiritual life. It is also not elected but formed. It is formed according to the necessities of the spiritual world. The more understanding you can bring to the fact that this Executive Council has an esoteric character, the more the Anthroposophical Society can thrive." (Rudolf Steiner, *Die Konstitution der Allgemeinen Anthroposophischen Gesellschaft und der Freien Hoschschule für Geisteswissenschaft. Der Wiederaufbau des Goetheanum* [The Constitution of the General Anthroposophical Society and the Independent School for Spiritual Science. The reconstruction of the Goetheanum] (CW 260a). Dornach, 1987. "That an Executive Council was created from esotericism says a great deal" (Rudolf Steiner, *Esoteric Lessons for the First Class of the Independent School for Spiritual Science at the Goetheanum* [CW 270/1]. England).

146. Ibid.

147. Ibid.

148. Rudolf Steiner, *Mystery Knowledge and Mystery Centers* (CW 232). Rudolf Steiner Press, 1997.

149. Ibid.

150. Rudolf Steiner, *The Christmas Conference: For the Foundation of the General Anthroposophical Society 1923/1924* (CW 260). Anthroposophic Press, 1990.

151. Ibid.

152. Vorstandsberufung [Appointment to the Executive Council].

153. Ibid.

154. In 1935 Ita Wegman wrote about the development of the Christmas Conference in a draft of a lecture: "Because the Christmas Conference plays precisely now again such an important role, I want to tell a few things about how it came about. Everyone has a different opinion about the Christmas Conference and it's impulses. However, what I now bring our conversations that took place between Dr. Steiner and me, at which others were often present; yet quite a lot took place between only the two of us.

"After the burning of the Goetheanum, it was Rudolf Steiner's constant concern to reorganize the Society, or as he often expressed it differently, to 'galvanize' it. The Society was, as he said, half dead. The one group of members became complete intellectuals; the others screamed again and again for the good old times when the threefolding idea did not yet exist and the old esotericism flourished. Many of the latter had no glimmer of the idea of threefolding, or no sympathy toward it, as had the first people who felt drawn to Anthroposophy precisely through the threefolding idea. Much was undertaken for clarification purposes. Dr. Steiner expressed himself to me in the following way: 'The older members have had too much esotericism and have not digested it; the young members had too little.' The old Society had completely failed—the old Society that was developed by Dr. Unger and his group, but also by Frau Dr. Steiner. And Rudolf Steiner constantly sought solutions for how the change could be brought about. He was deeply saddened. The courses of 1923 in Penmaenmawr and Ilkley took place; and it seemed to me that from this moment on Rudolf Steiner had a solution in mind. He spoke of how the singeing fire that destroyed the old Goetheanum has revealed powerful Mysteries that only now gradually become clear to him in the immense connections.

"Mystery knowledge has become open; and this Mystery knowledge that was protected in the various early Mysteries should now become the teaching content of Anthroposophy. The Society must, however, be newly organized. Here Rudolf Steiner no longer said that the Society should be galvanized or be given incentives, impulses; he spoke rather of a new organization. Dr. Steiner spoke these words after the trip to England. Then Rudolf Steiner became greatly active inwardly. It was as if he could not go about the changes quickly enough or thoroughly enough. He held a series of lectures in Vienna on the work of Michael. There an evening for doctors was held in Haus van Leer to which, along with Dr. Glas, a number of Viennese doctors and other people were invited. Dr. Steiner sparkled with originality, and there was a crossfire between the doctors and him. He sat in the middle of the circle; he was earnest, then humorous, then came some Viennese joke that only the Viennese could understand, followed by a volley of laughter. The evening was unique. One could discover with astonishment that Rudolf Steiner was not only a great scientist and an extraordinary esotericist, but also a charming comrade. It was as if the Vienna Café, where one went for something to drink afterward, had become more animated with him there.

"Here I want to insert something that is important to know, through which perhaps certain people who now play a peculiar role can be understood. Also Dr. Husemann came from Stuttgart, bringing a number of books. He thought he belonged at the doctors' evening and that he had something to say there. He believed, totally hidden in his intellect, that Dr. Steiner actually could not lecture on medicine; he, Dr. Husemann, must do it. Now, sometimes it happened that Rudolf Steiner could read the thoughts of other people. And thus, when Husemann came up to him, Steiner greeted him in an icy cold manner and asked what he was actually doing there. Pointing to the books, he said Husemann could put those away; he would allow only Frau Dr. Kolisko's book on the spleen. Husemann was quite taken aback.

"After this evening, it was decided that the medical book should be written. Dr. Steiner said, 'I cannot do it with the other doctors, because they are so conceited about their ignorance. I can do it only with you, and then it will be good.' This decision was then communicated to van Leer who, as president of Weleda, was always looking yearningly for textbooks on anthroposophic medicine. After the stay in Vienna, one went to Holland. One wanted to breathe new life into and refresh the national Society, which was not thriving through a visit from Dr. Steiner and through a lecture cycle. A new general secretary was to be named. It was thought that this was to be Herr de Haan. Now, when Dr. Steiner heard about this, he did not say much. However, in the evening at the café after the lectures, as we sat together in Hotel Doelen, Dr. Steiner made us aware, in a very fine manner, of the merits of Dr. Zeylmans; of how the Dutch Society must consider itself fortunate to have a doctor with such comprehensive knowledge as a member. And through question and counter-question, the situation became so clear that de Haan understood completely that he was not the right one to lead the Dutch Society, and that Dr. Zeylmans should leave his private practice and dedicate himself fully to the leadership of the Society. That occurred with such tremendous self-evidence that one could now only regret that such natural solutions can no longer be done easily. It did occur as Dr. Steiner suggested, and Dr. Zeylmans was installed by him as general secretary.

"In Dornach the work progressed systematically further. The extraordinary lectures on the Mysteries were given; lectures that you indeed know and which actually fructified the entire anthroposophical knowledge. One day then I heard from Dr. Steiner what he intended. He wanted to try to give the Society an entirely different form through a new organization that he himself would lead and with an Executive Council that would stand with him and with which he could work, and which he would select himself. I want to insert here also, that for a while, Dr. Steiner spoke of what he would do if things did not work out the way he wanted. In that case, he would start over in a small way, with a small group of people, and form it esoterically, as a kind of order. They should then work outwardly without the weight and burden of a Society. This was, at first, the new organization he intended. He also told me about the Sections he wanted to set up; how he actually wanted to set up various sections, such as a Section for Music, but could not yet find the people he felt were suitable.

"Regarding this meeting, Albert Steffen commented that Rudolf Steiner had said that, if things were actually to be done in keeping with the old ways of working, Frau Dr. Steiner should be the vice-chairman. However, Steiner did not now want to work in the old way; rather, new ways should be adopted. Consequently, he chose Albert Steffen to be vice-chairman. For Frau Dr. Steiner he now had different, very important tasks. A few days later, Rudolf Steiner asked me what I would think if Fräulein Vreede were to join the Executive Council. It would be good for the continuity of the Anthroposophical Society to take her in because she had participated in so much. He would then admit Frau Dr. Steiner and Fräulein Dr. Vreede as members of the Executive Council. Rudolf Steiner told me from the beginning that I, as his secretary, should always arrange things together with him. *That is the true course that the preparations of the Christmas Conference took*" (Ita Wegman Archive, Arlesheim; italics by E. Vreede.).

155. Rudolf Steiner, *The Healing Process: Spirit, Nature, and Our Bodies* (CW 319). SteinerBooks, 2010.

156. Rudolf Steiner, *Karmic Relationships,* vol. 4 (CW 238). Rudolf Steiner Press, 1983. Lily Kolisko drew one's attention in 1961 to the fact that a part of Steiner's Dornach lecture of Sept. 5, 1924 was not printed (two years after the expulsions), including the quoted passage about the Executive Council, the totality of which is an obligation, an esoteric task (See Kolisko).

157. Vorstandsberufung [Appointment to Executive Council]. For this, compare also Ita Wegman's presentations in note 154.
158. Vorstandsberufung [Appointment to Executive Council].
159. Rudolf Steiner, *The Christmas Conference: For the Foundation of the General Anthroposophical Society 1923/1924* (CW 260). Anthroposophic Press, 1990.
160. Rudolf Steiner, *Die Konstitution der Allgemeinen Anthroposophischen Gesellschaft und der Freien Hoschschule für Geisteswissenschaft. Der Wiederaufbau des Goetheanum* [The Constitution of the General Anthroposophical Society and the Independent School for Spiritual Science. The reconstruction of the Goetheanum] (CW 260a). Dornach, 1987.
161. Rudolf Steiner, *Background to the Gospel of St. Mark* (CW 124). SteinerBooks, 1986.
162. Rudolf Steiner, *Anthroposophical Leading Thoughts* (CW 26). Rudolf Steiner Press, 1973.
163. In Mitteilungen.
164. In Bodhisattva. For the fundamental significance of humor for Rudolf Steiner's life and work, compare Heinrich Eppinger, *Humor und Heiterkeit im Leben und Werk Rudolf Steiners* [Humor and merriment in the life and work of Rudolf Steiner]. Dornach, 1985.
165. In Deventer/Knottenbelt.
166. Archive.
167. Zaiser.
168. Rudolf Steiner, *The Christmas Conference: For the Foundation of the General Anthroposophical Society 1923/1924* (CW 260). Anthroposophic Press, 1990.
169. Ibid.
170. Elisabeth Vreede wrote in 1934, "To Frau Dr. Steiner, Dr. Steiner, the Goetheanum, the Anthroposophy and the Anthroposophical Society belonged to her alone. The rest of the Executive Council members were only a bothersome addition that the Doctor had wished, but now since the leadership came to her through his death, they no longer had a role to play. She had also absolutely behaved in this manner in the Executive Council meetings with the Doctor (Geschichte [History]).
171. Zur Geschichte [On the history].
172. Oskar Schmiedel came to speak about this already at the consequential Dornach crisis meeting of Feb. 6, 1926; see Kolisko. Later (1943 and 1957) Schmiedel laid out in detail the course of the conversation with Rudolf Steiner in his memoirs ("Records"), which Emanuel Zeylmans published in the third band of his documentation *Who was Ita Wegman*, vol. 3 (ibid.).
173. Compare Peter Selg, "*Die Medizin muss Ernst machen mit dem geistigen Leben.*" *Rudolf Steiners Hochschulkurse für die "jungen Mediziner"*

[Medicine must take the spiritual world seriously. Rudolf Steiner's Course for Young Doctors]. Dornach, 2006.

174. Elisabeth Vreede, "Der Weihnachts- und Michaelimpuls." [The Christmas and the Michael impulse]. Lecture in Dornach, Oct. 2, 1928; see appendix in this book.

175. Rudolf Steiner, *Die Konstitution der Allgemeinen Anthroposophischen Gesellschaft und der Freien Hoschschule für Geisteswissenschaft. Der Wiederaufbau des Goetheanum* [The Constitution of the General Anthroposophical Society and the Independent School for Spiritual Science. The reconstruction of the Goetheanum] (CW 260a). Dornach, 1987.

176. Compare Peter Selg, *The Agriculture Course, Koberwitz, Whitsun 1924.* Temple Lodge, 2010.

177. Albrecht Strohschein, "Die Enstehung der anthroposophischen Heilpädagogik." [The origin of the anthroposophical curative pedagogy]. In M.J. Krück von Poturzyn, *Wir erleben Rudolf Steiner. Erinnerungen seiner Schüler* [We experience Rudolf Steiner. Recollections of his students]. Stuttgart, 1967.

178. Guenther Wachsmuth, *Die Geburt der Geisteswissenschaft Rudolf Steiners Lebensgang von der Jahrhundertwende bis zum Tode. 1900–1925. Eine Biographie* [The birth of Rudolf Steiner's Spiritual Science and his biography from the turn of the century until his death. 1900–1925]. Dornach 1941.

179. Christoph Lindenberg, *Rudolf Steiner: A Biography.* SteinerBooks, 2012.

180. Guenther Wachsmuth, *Die Geburt der Geiusteswissenschaft Rudolf Steiners Lebensgang von der Jahrhundertwende bis zum Tode. 1900–1925. Eine Biographie* [The birth of Spiritual Science. Rudolf Steiner's biography from the turn of the century until his death. 1900–1925]. Dornach 1941. (This passage was unchanged in the second edition in 1951, eight years after Elisabeth Vreede's death.) Lili Kolisko wrote in general about Wachsmuth's book, "This book is interesting because of what was not included in it" (Kolisko).

181. The Estate of Elisabeth Vreede in the Library of the Dutch National Society in The Hague.

182. Rudolf Steiner, *Die Konstitution der Allgemeinen Anthroposophischen Gesellschaft und der Freien Hoschschule für Geisteswissenschaft. Der Wiederaufbau des Goetheanum* [The Constitution of the General Anthroposophical Society and the Independent School for Spiritual Science. The reconstruction of the Goetheanum] (CW 260a). Dornach, 1987.

183. Quoted from Peter Selg, *"Willfried Immanuel Kunert. Zur Lebens- und Therapiegeschichte eines Kindes aus dem 'Heilpädagogischen Kurs'"* [Willfried Immanuel Kunert. On the life and therapy of a child from the curative education course]. Dornach, 2006.

184. Ibid.

185. Archive at the Goetheanum.

186. Archive.
187. Ibid.
188. Protocol. Archive at the Goetheanum.
189. Zur Geschichte [On the history].
190. Ibid.
191. Geschichte [History].
192. About a situation shortly after the arrival of Marie Steiner from Stuttgart, Vreede recorded in 1934, "With a very superior expression, she said to Frau Dr. Wegman, as we stood together at the deathbed: 'How do you know then that he is dead? He could be merely in meditation and will awaken again later!' She wanted to have a featherbed put on him to keep him warm, in case he would wake up again. Frau Dr. Wegman gave in and helped to cover him with a short featherbed. It was an unusual situation that I sensed. Frau Dr. Steiner acted with great certainty as an experienced esotericist; in contrast, Frau Dr. Wegman appeared to be the exoteric doctor who knows nothing about such things and bows to the great esoteric insight of Frau Dr. Steiner. The scene seemed to me to be the first triumph of Frau Dr. Steiner over her 'opponent,' who let her medical authority recede into the background—even though she may have had her own thoughts about it. In any case, my thought was—and it was in itself terrible—that if it should be as Frau Dr. Steiner suspected, we had actually already made this reawakening impossible because Wachsmuth had already trumpeted the news of the Doctor's death to the four winds. I could not imagine that the Doctor would return to the physical plane under such circumstances" (History). Vreede wrote further in her memoirs, among other things, "I saw one evening, as the Doctor was laid out, Frau Dr. Steiner go through the studio with Mrs. Pyle and look everywhere in the books and papers lying around. Apparently they were looking for a file with papers or documents that she [Frau Dr. Steiner] feared Frau Dr. Wegman might have taken for herself. I could sense the attitude from the whole manner in which this was done and the remarks that were made" (Ibid.).
193. Ibid.
194. Ibid.
195. In a letter from Marie Steiner to Eugen Kolisko on April 4, 1925, "I have clearly recognized that our Executive Council as it now is (orphaned in its childhood stage) is a nothing" (quoted from Kolisko).
196. Geschichte [History].
197. Compare Peter Selg, *Rudolf Steiner and the School for Spiritual Science*. SteinerBooks, 2012.
198. Zur Geschichte [On the history].
199. Compare Peter Selg, *Rudolf Steiner and the School for Spiritual Science*. SteinerBooks, 2012.
200. Geschichte [History].

201. "The admission process took place in the studio. I had to stand beside the Doctor. Dr. Wachsmuth led the members into the studio. Dr. Steiner asked a few questions of each person who was asking to be admitted. And if he or she could be admitted, Dr. Steiner spoke the following words: 'If you will to remain loyal to the Michael School, give me your hand (shake my hand). Give your hand also to Frau Dr. Wegman who will lead the Michael School with me'" (Ita Wegman, letter to Albert Steffen on Mar. 16, 1926; in Peter Selg, *Rudolf Steiner and the School for Spiritual Science*. SteinerBooks, 2012). Compare also the report from Wolfgang Moldenhauer, "On Sept. 5, 1924 I was admitted into the First Class by Rudolf Steiner. After a vow of loyalty connected with a handshake, he let me also shake the hand of Frau Dr. Wegman, co-leader of the Class, who was sitting next to him" (Ibid.).

202. Compare ibid.: "Before his illness, he gave me a small cross, set with small rubies as roses, that he wore on a red band around his neck. He put it around my neck himself after we performed a ritual" (Letter to Albert Steffen on Aug. 21, 1925. Ibid.). "And I received also directly his cross, that he took from his neck and put it around my neck himself and said, *'From this moment on we are there for the Michael School together.'* This I want to have expressed so that it stands correctly." Ita Wegman said this on Apr. 25, 1930 in a meeting of the Executive Council with the General Secretaries and the Delegates of the General Anthroposophical Society, after a special task in the context of the First Class had been denied her (Protocol. Archive at the Goetheanum). Wegman—deeply weakened and unrecognized—was even willing half a year later, in a meeting on Nov. 29, 1930, to bring the text of the ritual into the circle. "[Tomorrow] I will take with me the documents in which he [Dr. Steiner] actually said it to me. I want to read the ritual in which he said it" (Protocol. Archive at the Goetheanum). Whether or not Ita Wegman actually did this on Nov. 30, 1930, is not documented, and not very probable. Based on the documents of her esoteric estate, the "Act" indicated by Ita Wegman exists in the ritual of the great Rose-Cross Meditation "Urkräfte haltet mich" [May primal powers hold me] (Ibid.). (Compare Emanuel Zeylmans van Emmichoven, *Who Was Ita Wegman,* vol. 4. Mercury Press, 2009.)

203. Geschichte [History]. Concerning the background of Steffen's hesitation to see Ita Wegman as more than, or different than a "secretary," or to see her differently with respect to the Class, compare especially his statements about her esoteric failure in the Dornach meeting of Nov. 29, 1930 (Protocol). ("No, Frau Dr. Wegman, there is no offense to your honor, but you have failed as esotericist. With that, there is no offense to any human being, but it is simply stated that you have not reached a certain stage" [Ibid.].)

204. Geschichte [History]: This situation was referred to in the presentation of the Lesson in Lili Kolisko's historical documentation. "After her return from Paris, Frau Dr. Wegman dared to hold a Class Lesson also in Dornach. That was an event that I will never forget. Frau Dr. Steiner came with a number of members of her Section. It surprised me. I knew that she could not stand Frau Dr. Wegman's speech. I was certainly not prepared for the fact that during the Lesson, Frau Dr. Steiner interrupted Frau Dr.

Wegman and took her to task, which caused a huge disturbance. Then she got up and ostentatiously left the room, followed by the members of her Section. Whoever knows the strict laws of esotericism had to be deeply shaken by this unforgivable action. This was a blow not only against the personality of Frau Dr. Wegman; it hit the center of the spiritual movement" (Kolisko). Already at the beginning of April Marie Steiner expressed to Lili Kolisko her objection to Ita Wegman holding Class Lessons—Ita Wegman, who was not capable with her speech. "She does not agree that Frau Dr. Wegman should read the Lessons. She cannot bear the Dutch accent and the scratchy voice, interrupted by coughing and spitting.... Frau Dr. Wegman may have Malaysian blood in her veins, and so on." (Ibid.). Concerning the style of Ita Wegman's Class Lessons, compare, in contrast, Peter Selg, *Rudolf Steiner and the School for Spiritual Science: The Founding of the First Class*. At the crisis meeting on Nov. 29, 1930 of the Executive Council members, General Secretaries and Delegates, the Belgian representative Frau Muntz said concerning Ita Wegman's Class Lessons in her country: "Frau Dr. Wegman held Class Lessons for us in Brussels, and the impression they made with us was that the rendition was so beautiful and perfect and significant and honest (which Dr. Steiner, unfortunately, could not revise for us). She brought them in beauty, in all simplicity and all reverence, I would like to say. I am quite outraged that it can happen that one can say such things about her. I am totally outraged" (Protocol).

205. Kolisko.

206. How little was known, for example, of the historical destiny of Rudolf Steiner's and Ita Wegman's collaboration in the "esoteric Executive Council" Vreede illustrated in a retrospective on the Executive Council meetings after Rudolf Steiner's death. "As Frau Dr. Wegman again began to speak of wanting finally to begin reading the Class Lessons, [Marie Steiner] asked her suddenly, 'How is it that you are supposed to have been Alexander the Great? Do you have that from Dr. Steiner?' To this Frau Dr. Wegman answered, 'But yes, Frau Doctor!' The effect was extraordinary. Because of the whole situation that existed there, this answer could only be taken as fully earnest. It was also accepted as such. There was amazement, astonishment, and even a certain emotion there. Not one of the members of the Executive Council who were present—and all were present—showed doubt in the correctness of this answer through their words or behavior. Such was also not possible, purely humanly and objectively, in *that* situation. Then Frau Dr. Wegman said further, 'I can even show it to you from the Doctor in writing, if you wish'—upon which I said, 'That is not necessary; when *you* give us this information, we believe you.' With this I wanted to express that her words had naturally convinced us, but for the further history, this rejection was perhaps not right.... For me, it was first through Frau Dr. Wegman's Leading Thoughts letters, that dealt with Aristotle and Alexander the Great, that attention was drawn to this problem; such that it came to me as a possibility that the solution could also lie in this. I never spoke to anyone about this, and no one spoke with me" (Geschichte [History]).

207. Zur Geschichte [On the history].

208. Geschichte [History].

209. News Sheet of Apr. 26, 1925. Also printed in Ita Wegman, *An die Freunde* [To the friends]. Arlesheim 1986.

210. Zur Geschichte [On the history].

211. In me ipsam.

212. Quoted from Deventer/Knottenbelt.

213. Ibid.

214. Ibid.

215. When Vreede formed the intention to build a star observatory and whether she might have discussed her intention with Rudolf Steiner is not known. On Mar. 25, 1927, she informed Albert Steffen that, with his approval, the project could be realized soon, which also happened. "Then I want to inform you with this—since I will be away tomorrow—that the plans, which I mentioned once, to build a small star observatory have suddenly received a firmer form in the last two days. It appears that it is possible to do, if everyone in the Executive Council agrees. The finances were discussed with Dr. Wachsmuth (It is a matter of approximately sFr. 3,000!). Frau Dr. Steiner and I have looked at the possible site for the building. It is approximately in line with the Schuurman house. Frau Doctor is in agreement with this. I hope to be able to show you a small model by Sunday. It is a matter of a small house, 4.5 m x 4.5 m with a movable roof, without the usual cupola. Hopefully, you too are in agreement" (Archive at the Goetheanum).

216. Archive at the Goetheanum.

217. Astronomy.

218. Ibid.

219. Compare Peter Selg, *Willem Zeylmans van Emmichoven. Anthroposophie und Anthroposophische Gesellschaft im 20. Jahrhundert* [Willem Zeylmans van Emmichoven. Anthroposophy and Anthroposophical Society in the twentieth century]. Arlesheim, 2009.

220. In Feb. 1931 Wachsmuth wrote a six-page typescript about "Einige Gedanken zur augenblicklichen Lage der Gesellschaft" [A few thoughts about the present situation of the Society]: "As Rudolf Steiner returned from his last journey out of the country, he found waiting for him countless numbers of invitations for lectures in various large and small cities. He said at that time quite spontaneously that this could no longer go on this way; the Society has now grown to such an extent that in the future a totally different system has to be introduced. No longer would he travel to do every small lecture tour or single lecture. Rather, there would now be, per year, 4 or 5 large conferences in Dornach, but only *one* large conference outside of Dornach, which would be organized by the Goetheanum and would be held in a different city in Europe each year. On these Dornach conferences and those organized by the Goetheanum for outside of Dornach (for which the place changes each year), all productive forces of the Society should participate. They should meet there the audiences from

all the nations. Otherwise, one would no longer succeed and would only scatter the forces" (estate of Elisabeth Vreede, archive at the Goetheanum).

According to George Adams, Rudolf Steiner also planned a two-month lecture tour through America for the summer of 1925. He asked Adams to take care of arranging the passage by ship in a timely manner (communicated verbally to the author by Gene Gollogly, New York).

221. Rudolf Steiner, *The Christmas Conference: For the Foundation of the General Anthroposophical Society 1923/1924* (CW 260). Anthroposophic Press, 1990.

222. Zur Geschichte [On the history].

223. Idyllen [Idylls], IV. Vreede wrote about this process less humorously in a letter to Albert Steffen on July 22, 1928, "Even such difficult statements like that by Dr. Grosheintz about the overtaxing (of the forces) of the Executive Council appear in the Newsletter without my knowing at all who gave him permission to do that. I wish to stress that I, as member of the Executive Council, do not feel myself to be overtaxed" (quoted from Kolisko).

224. Idyllen [Idylls], IV.

225. Idyllen [Idylls], VII.

226. Zur Geschichte [On the history].

227. "On the occasion of the General Meeting of the General Anthroposophical Society on Feb. 25, 1928, it could be communicated that in the fall of this year at Michaelmas, the Goetheanum will honor its mission. It was announced that there will be artistic offerings (Mystery Dramas, choruses, eurythmy performances, and so on) and lectures. As President of the Anthroposophical Society, I believe I may say that lectures will be considered from members who, from the comprehensive field of Anthroposophy, have developed in their inner work something new that has not as yet been lectured about in other places. I have, with these guidelines, held to a statement by Rudolf Steiner. It goes, 'The Goetheanum wants to hear the new. With this, the inner activity and creative activity will be called upon.' And so with these lines, the invitation goes out to our members, to communicate their topic and a short summary of the content of their lectures, so that the program of the conference can be put together as soon as possible. This will be done from the viewpoint that all of the lectures together will build a whole. It is to be expected that the Executive Council will not be able to consider all of the entries or communications. The number of collaborators is great, and the length of the conference is, unfortunately, short" (*Das Goetheanum,* July 14, 1928).

228. Archive at the Goetheanum.

229. Zur Geschichte [On the history].

230. Ibid.

231. Elisabeth Vreede in the meeting of the Dornach Executive Council with the general secretaries and delegates of the national societies. Goetheanum, Nov. 29, 1930; literal protocol, archive at the Goetheanum.

232. Archive at the Goetheanum.
233. Quoted from Kolisko.
234. Ibid.
235. Quoted from Uwe Werner, "Elisabeth Vreede im Vorstandszusammenhang" [Elisabeth Vreede in connection with the Executive Council. In Mitteilungen].
236. Archive at the Goetheanum.
237. Ibid.
238. In Deventer/Knottenbelt.
239. Ibid.
240. Ibid.
241. Kolisko.
242. In Deventer/Knottenbelt.
243. Astronomy.
244. Zaiser.
245. Compare Peter Selg, *Spiritual Resistance*. SteinerBooks, 2015.
246. Zur Geschichte [On the history].
247. Ibid.
248. Compare Peter Selg, *Spiritual Resistance*. SteinerBooks, 2015.
249. Archive at the Goetheanum.
250. See the impressive conference report by Jürgen von Grones in Kolisko.
251. Compare Peter Selg, *Spiritual Resistance*. SteinerBooks, 2015.
252. Archive at the Goetheanum.
253. In addition, Lili Kolisko wrote, "It occurred to me how in 1922 Rudolf Steiner said, as it came to the rebuilding of the Goetheanum, that the second Goetheanum had to be built differently from the first one. One built the first Goetheanum with donated money from the members; for the second Goetheanum, the money from the insurance company had to be used—some of which was not given out of goodwill. What would Dr. Steiner have said about the fact that in 1934 one raised money for the Goetheanum through such an abusive document [against Ita Wegman and Elisabeth Vreede]?" (Kolisko).
254. Quoted from Peter Selg, *Spiritual Resistance*. SteinerBooks, 2015.
255. Zur Geschichte [On the history].
256. Letter to Elisabeth Vreede on Dec. 26, 1934; archive at the Goetheanum.
257. Archive at the Goetheanum.
258. Letter to Frau Kyber on March 2, 1935.
259. Compare Note 281.

260. For the assumptions, circumstances, and consequences of this letter, as well as its content, compare Peter Selg, *Ita Wegman and Karl König*. Floris Books, 2008.
261. Archive at the Goetheanum.
262. Letter to Elisabeth Vreede on Mar. 16, 1935, archive at the Goetheanum.
263. Letter to Elisabeth Vreede on Mar. 18, 1935, archive at the Goetheanum.
264. Letter to Elisabeth Vreede on Mar. 20, 1935, archive at the Goetheanum.
265. Letter to Elisabeth Vreede on Mar. 27, 1935, archive at the Goetheanum.
266. Ibid.
267. Ibid.
268. Letter to Karl Ballmer on Mar. 30, 1935, archive at the Goetheanum.
269. Archive at the Goetheanum.
270. Ibid.
271. Ibid.
272. Ibid.
273. Letter to Elisabeth Vreede on Apr. 3, 1935, archive at the Goetheanum.
274. "Dr. Steiner placed upon Frau Dr. Wegman a great responsibility for the Class Lessons. (One would not have that be true already for a long time and even yet today, so that the consciousness of it gradually disappears more and more among the members.)" (Zur Geschichte [On the history]). With reference to this passage from her document, Valentin Tomberg asked Elisabeth Vreede on Apr. 3, 1935, for more details. He had no doubt, per Tomberg, in Vreede's ascertainment, "but would like to know more about Wegman's relationship to the Class—not the spiritual side of the issue, but the exact outer facts (it does not need to be many), out of which could be seen that Frau Dr. Wegman—now and then, here and there, through this or that statement of Dr. Steiner's, or through this or that manner of handling in the presence of these or those witnesses (few—who? Many—how many approximately?) was given, in this or that sense, this or that responsibility." Vreede gave Tomberg more exact information on May 18, for which he thanked her on June 5: "The letter contained completely satisfying information about the question that interested me" (archive at the Goetheanum). Vreede's important letter of May 18, 1935, apparently no longer exists.
275. Zur Geschichte [On the history].
276. Thus Wegman rejected decisively, for example, the conference in the Goetheanum on the nature of the old and new Mysteries that Elisabeth Vreede organized for Christmas 1934, because it was seen as a counter-event to the official program, and correspondingly, was used in an agitational manner against Vreede (and Wegman). Compare for this Peter Selg, *Spiritual Resistance*. SteinerBooks 2015. For the background and founding of this conference compare, however, also Vreede's presentations in "Zur Geschichte der Anthroposophischen Gesellschaft seit der

Weihnachtstagung 1923" [On the history of the Anthroposophical Society since the Christmas Conference 1923]. Arlesheim, 1935 (Zur Geschichte [On the history].)

277. Letter of April 1, 1935, archive at the Goetheanum.

278. Letter to Herr Dohnal, archive at the Goetheanum.

279. Compare Emanuel Zeylmans van Emmichoven, *Who was Ita Wegman. A Documentation,* vol. 4. Mercury Press, 2009.

280. Transcription of Werner Pache's diary in the Ita Wegman Archive. Arlesheim. Compare Peter Selg, *Spiritual Resistance: Ita Wegman, 1933–1935.* SteinerBooks, 2015.

281. "Both Executive Council members, Frau Dr. Ita Wegman and Fräulein Dr. Elisabeth Vreede, who expressed their disrespect of the Society through their actions that bear the character of self-expulsion, will no longer be recognized as members of the Executive Council. Dr. Ita Wegman's and Fräulein Dr. Vreede's memberships in the Executive Council of the General Anthroposophical Society are rescinded. Further activity of both persons within the framework of the General Anthroposophical Society seems to the General Meeting not to be possible" (Petition I).

"The founders and representatives of the so-called *Vereinigten Freien Anthroposophischen Gruppen* [United independent anthroposophical groups] (D. N. Dunlop, George Kaufmann, Dr. F.W. Zeylmans, P.J. de Haan, Jürgen von Grone, Dr. E. Kolisko) have stopped being members of the General Anthroposophical Society" (Petition II).

"The General Meeting asks the Executive Council no longer to recognize as part of the General Anthroposophical Society the national societies and groups that have joined the so-called United Independent Anthroposophical Groups, without rescinding the membership of individual members of such groups" (Petition III). In *What is Happening in the Anthroposophical Society? News for Members,* year 12, no. 11/12, Mar. 1935.

That the Executive Council understood the expulsion of Ita Wegman and Elisabeth Vreede also as an expulsion from the Society membership was documented by Lili Kolisko. She reported on the preparation of the Expulsion Petitions on Dec. 29, 1934, in a meeting at the Goetheanum and reported, among other things, on the contributions by Günther Schubert and Guenther Wachsmuth. "Further, the vote would take place concerning the dismissing of both ladies as members of the Executive Council. At the same time, along with this membership, they would also lose their leadership positions of their Sections and the right to be members of the Anthroposophical Society. On this point Dr. Wachsmuth gives an interesting explanation: "The members of the Executive Council are not, in accordance with the will of Dr. Steiner, members of the Society and do not possess membership cards. When they leave the Executive Council, they leave the Anthroposophical Society at the same time'" (Kolisko).

In contrast to Wachsmuth, however, compare the facsimile of Ita Wegman's membership card signed by Rudolf Steiner in 1924. In Peter Selg, *Rudolf Steiner as a Spiritual Teacher.* SteinerBooks, 2010 (original in Ita Wegman Archive).

282. Compare "What is Happening in the Anthroposophical Society," *News for Members*. 12th year, no. 11/12, Mar. 17, 1935; and compare Emanuel Zeylmans van Emmichoven, *Who was Ita Wegman: A Documentation*, vol. 3. Mercury Press, 1995.

283. "What is Happening in the Anthroposophical Society," *News for Members*, 12th year, no. 11/12, Mar. 17, 1935. For the continuation of Marie Steiner's argument, compare Emanuel Zeylmans van Emmichoven, *Who was Ita Wegman. A Documentation*, vol. 3. Mercury Press.

284. Letter to Herr Rohn on May 6, 1935; archive at the Goetheanum.

285. Quoted from Kolisko.

286. Archive at the Goetheanum. Compare also Uwe Werner, "Über das Archiv habe ich nie gesprochen" [I have never spoken about the Archive]. In Mitteilungen.

287. Letter to a friend, Apr. 19, 1935, archive at the Goetheanum.

288. Elisabeth Vreede spoke about this in her Stuttgart lecture of Apr. 28, 1935, among other places. "Herr Steffen often borrowed lectures that he needed to read from the Archive. At first, he kept to a sequence that I had recommended, and I always sent the lectures immediately to his house. After a time, he stopped reading them in sequence, and so I no longer knew what he would need. Thus, I could no longer send them out on my own. Then we noticed suddenly that lectures were missing from the Archive. When I pressed my coworker in the Archive, Fräulein Ruthenberg, she said that she was convinced that Herr Steffen picks up lectures, as the ones taken have stamped on them: 'printed in Goetheanum.' A while later, she met Herr Steffen who told her, 'I was just by you. I picked up a couple of lectures. With that we had the confirmation. Herr Steffen had keys to the Archive given to him and went in with the guard and picked up the lectures. Now, we had only one or two copies of each lecture, so we told the guard that we want at least to know *what* was taken. Then the next day we found a note on the stand: 'this and this lecture taken.' The Archive experienced thus a rash of disappearances."

289. The historian Karl Heyer made of Elisabeth Vreede an inquiry critical of a text yet on April 15, 1936, after the closing of the Archives. Heyer had noticed that in the printed edition of the Stuttgart lecture cycle *Occult History* (published by Marie Steiner) that there were passages that did not correspond to the wording by Rudolf Steiner or the lecture notes of the Stuttgart Archive. In three places in the text in the printed cycle only Aristotle was spoken of, whereas it can be proved that Steiner had spoken about *Aristotle and Alexander* [among other things], "there arose in Aristotle the inspiration to substantiate the world script" (instead of as should have been, "in both of these there arose the inspiration to substantiate the world script"). Vreede confirmed the discrepancy for Heyer. He thanked her for that on April 19 and stressed that he had also only "written with the slightest hope that she might perhaps be in the position to give a less compromised explanation or clue for such [a difference]" (Archive at the Goetheanum).

290. Protocol, or Kolisko.

291. Letter to Maria Stiefelhagen on August 8, 1935, archive at the Goetheanum.
292. Two days before the General Meeting on April 14, 1935, Wilhelm Kelber, Priest of The Christian Community, and Grete Brüll, of the Anthroposophical Work Community of Nürnberg, wrote to the Executive Council in Dornach. Among other things, they wrote, "What brought us on the part of the Work Community *to detest* the brutality of the persecution that has been done for many years to the persons who were forced from the Anthroposophical Society today, and the lack of true reasons for this devastating fight—that lets us stand also today by those who were expelled. We will never recognize their expulsion, which is an unlawful violation through a majority. We look upon this expulsion with sadness and outrage. This would have to allow ever further such practices. We all have known for years the reasons that are given for the fight for which you are responsible. Almost all were repeatedly refuted. And even if they had all been correct, they would not justify your actions. Through a majority that was brought together through questionable methods, you have the power today to destroy the small group of human beings that supports the work of Dr. Steiner, and will continue to do so" (quoted from Kolisko).

   Already on April 10, 1935, Wilhelm Kelber had written to the Dornach Executive Council with an independent piece. He wrote, among other things, about the destructive work of Boos, Englert-Faye, Zbinden and others, whose aggressive and excessive attacks (against Ita Wegman, Elisabeth Vreede, Eugen Kolisko, Walter Johannes Klein, and others) in the General Meeting, and about their trips through Germany that was tolerated by the Executive Council against all human feeling. The documentation by Lili Kolisko and the available meeting records give comprehensive evidence. Kelber wrote, "They were usable for the attainment of the goals of destruction. I am not under the illusion, that I could still act effectively in the last hour against your conviction of the necessary destruction of the persons and streams that you find unpopular.... Not in opposition to you, but before the forum of the history of Rudolf Steiner's Society, I follow my conscience and make this protest. I hold this imminent, hardly to be prevented expulsion to be a societal-political act of violence by the stronger group; for the shameful end of the General Anthroposophical Society, prepared by human beings upon whom Rudolf Steiner laid the obligation to work with others, upon whom he wanted to found the Society, and did so" (quoted from Kolisko).
293. Letter to Albert Steffen on October 11, 1929, archive at the Goetheanum.
294. Letter to Maria Stiefelhagen on August 8, 1935, archive at the Goetheanum.
295. Letter from Maria Striefelhagen to Elisabeth Vreede on July 21, 1935, archive at the Goetheanum.
296. Archive at the Goetheanum.
297. Compare Peter Selg, *Spiritual Resistance*. SteinerBooks, 2015.
298. Charlotte Fiechter. In Deventer/Knottenbelt.
299. Rudolf Steiner, *The Fifth Gospel* (CW 148). Rudolf Steiner Press, 1985.

300. Elisabeth Vreede wrote to her Arlesheim "housemates" in detail about the solar eclipse. She did not write this onboard the ship on her return home, but in a long letter from the Istanbul Hotel on June 21, 1936. It read: "It was an unique feeling to make a pilgrimage up the Olympus in the early dawn with a walking stick made from a root selected along the way. The climb, with no path, took about three-quarters of an hour. Then we were on a hilltop where the astronomy camp was. Gradually, about a hundred people gathered out of the tents, both from hotels and several farms—people who had climbed up from fairly far away. There was a *'Feldhessenhügel'* [a hill] on which [the Turkish astronomer] Fatin Effendi and his staff stood, and the governor. The instruments were set up quite well apart, so that the specialists and the laypeople would not bother each other; the others were spread out on boulders, etc. I, too, sought out a leaning stone as my place of observation, and with the aid of the awnings and Dr. Röschl's binoculars I was able to follow the process very well. From time to time I glanced at the projected image a telescope made, which was available to everyone. That was naturally all *before* the total eclipse. As we arrived on the hilltop, the Sun had just appeared. It was a bright, radiant day. The partial eclipse began soon after. The choice of that place was brilliant; it was in the midst of the central zone.

Shortly before the total eclipse, Fatin Effendi himself made everyone aware that one should now look to the west to see the shadow of the Moon approaching. We had a very good view into the distance (right to the Sea of Marmara). The terrible corpse-pale light came now, like we saw in 1927, only now much stronger and more unsettling—the mood of the end of the world, the twilight of the gods. Everyone felt this way. The heavenly bodies became ever darker, but not from this terrible color that was on the Earth; only on the horizon was there a bright strip around that was suddenly interrupted by a pale red-brown darkness, which however, spread over the firmament without clear contours.... In that moment one had to turn around and look to the East—and there was lightning-like, immediately in full splendor, the Corona, this radiant silver form. And next to it was Venus, like a condensed drop of the Corona, unbelievably bright and radiant. One could say almost trivially: a theatrical effect. I did not see other stars; Mars that was between Venus and the Sun was outshone by the Corona. I would have liked to have seen Mercury as it stood directly by Alpha Tauri (*Alpha Tau*), but there was no other star to be seen in that short time. Around the Moon was yet a small, narrow bright strip, almost like a ring-formed eclipse or similar to our last lunar eclipse. And from this, totally horizontal to the left, a red tongue jutted out, as if there was a mouth there. I hold it to be a very large protuberance; I did not see anything else. But oh, how briefly the whole glory lasted—for it is glorious in the heavens, and all that is horrible and atrocious is only on Earth—17 seconds seemed more like 77!

There was no question of photographing it—for me, I mean. The astronomers were naturally photographing diligently, and five minutes after the total eclipse I saw a drawing of the Corona lying beside the instruments. Despite the fact that Fräulein Huber had asked to take the photograph, we both absolutely forgot to do it during the short period of the fascinating spectacle. Then, suddenly, the Sun returned. However, the peculiar thing is that there is not a reverse of the drama, with again the pale darkness becoming less terrible and then yet less, etc., but rather immediately, from the first second, all the terrible process was overcome. The Sun's rays were still weak, but were clear and golden as always. Nature is again normal—it is a miracle" (estate of Elisabeth Vreede in the Ita Wegman Archive).

301. Elisabeth Vreede, "The Total Eclipse of the Sun, June 19, 1936," in *The Present Age,* vol. 1, no. 10. Sept. 1936.

302. Archive at the Goetheanum.

303. Letter to Luděk Přikryl on April 9, 1938, archive at the Goetheanum.

304. Nine years earlier, in May 1929, at the General Meeting of the German National Society—in its controversial Executive Council of which he was still a member at the time—with a view of the historical situation, Eugen Kolisko said the following: "My occupation with the appropriate relationships has shown me that the current world situation as such, especially in Germany, that we must say that we stand there with a tremendous responsibility that was placed upon us because we have received Anthroposophy through Rudolf Steiner. We stand before the world with an enormous responsibility; and that is especially the case in Central Europe. Today, where we have the sorry example that Central Europe appears to be as if shut out from its actual mission, surrounded by hostile influences, one can then have the feeling that it is high time that we find the possibility to end the fruitless arguments within our Society" (quoted from Kolisko). In connection with this, compare also Kolisko's lecture "Die gegenwärtige Weltlage" [The current world situation], given on Oct. 13, 1932 to former Waldorf school students in Stuttgart; in Peter Selg, *A Grand Metamorphosis.* SteinerBooks, 2008. Besides Eugen Kolisko, also Friedrich Rittelmeyer pointed out repeatedly—in the crisis meetings of the Anthroposophical Society in Germany and in Dornach—the historical tasks that have to be coped with but that are neglected and lost permanently over the internal difficulties. At the General Meeting of the German National Society at the end of January 1931, he said the following: "I am especially concerned about all that happens outwardly and what must happen. I feel it terribly, extremely, how little we have managed to bring Anthroposophy really into the general public and into the spiritual life. And I see with horror how the three largest political powers—Bolshevism, Fascism and Catholicism—have promised death to us. I have made suggestions because more must happen" (quoted from Kolisko).

305. For the "settlement" with Walter Johannes Stein, his lectures, his pedagogical activity and his intentions, compare the statements of the Dornach General Meeting of spring 1932 (In Kolisko) (Concerning Vreede's objection, ibid.). Concerning devastating criticism of Eugen Kolisko, his anthroposophical work and pedagogical activity within the framework of the Dornach General Meeting of spring 1934, see Kolisko, as well as the literal record of the General Meeting (archive at the Goetheanum).

306. Compare Peter Selg, *Eugen Kolisko*. In *Anfänge anthroposophischer Heilkunst* [The beginnings of the anthroposophical art of healing]. Dornach, 2000.

307. Compare Peter Selg, *The Last Three Years*. SteinerBooks, 2015.

308. For these notes, compare Emanuel Zeylmans van Emmichoven, *Who Was Ita Wegman*, vol. 4. Mercury Press, 2009.

309. Quoted from Kolisko.

310. In Deventer/Knottenbelt.

311. Compare Rudolf Steiner, *Transforming the Soul,* vol. 1 (CW 58). Rudolf Steiner Press, 2005.

312. In Deventer/Knottenbelt.

313. Compare Peter Selg, *The Last Three Years: Ita Wegman in Ascona, 1940–1943*. SteinerBooks, 2015.

314. Concerning content and context of this passage from Rudolf Steiner, compare Peter Selg, *Vom Logos menschlicher Physis. Die Entfaltung einer anthroposophischen Humanphysiologie im Werk Rudolf Steiners* [About the logos of the human physical aspect. The development of an anthroposophical human physiology in Rudolf Steiner's work]. Dornach, 2006. About the origin of Ita Wegman's question of Rudolf Steiner, "What is the relationship of the blood process in the lung to that in the heart?" Compare also Peter Selg, *Die Briefkorrespondenz der "jungen Medeziner."* Dornach, 2005.

315. Madeleine van Deventer. In Peter Selg, *The Last Three Years: Ita Wegman in Ascona, 1940–1943*. SteinerBooks, 2015.

316. Ibid. Also Werner Pache wrote in his diary after Vreede's death: "I remember how deeply affected she was. As Deventer came from the death chamber and brought the news of the death that had just taken place, she said, 'Already?'" (Ita Wegman Archive).

317. Madeleine van Deventer. In Peter Selg, *The Last Three Years: Ita Wegman in Ascona, 1940–1943*. SteinerBooks 2015.

318. Compare Note 319.

319. Compare Peter Selg, *The Last Three Years: Ita Wegman in Ascona, 1940–1943*. SteinerBooks 2015. Van Deventer made notes of Vreede's talk in fragments: "We are a large, displaced collection, but under other circumstances it would grow much larger. It is already much larger, not here but in the spiritual world.

"The mortal shell is only a part of what unfolds in the spiritual world. We perceive this as a riddle, but what is liberated from the bodily is great and very powerful. Puzzling, when we think about short periods of illness. Much must be newly prepared, much in the spiritual world. Perhaps this process is necessary for great tasks in the world.

"The soul of Ita Wegman was connected with cosmic thinking. Not a thinking with the intellect, but rather a thinking that was connected with all of humanity. This came about because her soul had guarded itself against moving into intellectualism too early, for she was born on Java, and this allowed her to develop the inner heart forces. Karma intended that she quickly find her teacher at the beginning of the century; from this time onward, there was a spiritual connection between the two of them. Then she decided on studying medicine. During the period of that time that Dr. Steiner was holding his lecture cycle *Universe, Earth and Man* (CW 105) in Stuttgart, Ita Wegman was a student in Zürich. Then came the time when destiny sent Dr. Steiner to Switzerland, and the group continued to travel from Zürich. In the meantime, she had completed her exams. Then she had a practice in Zürich, in which she was already active in realizing the spiritual within the physical. When she founded the anthroposophical clinic in Arlesheim, Dr. Steiner turned to her and said, 'It would be good to work together with you.' Dr. Wegman found joy in this clinic, despite how difficult it was to be active practically. It was a happy opening for her, and that also please Dr. Steiner. This inner collaboration, for which there was a spiritual understanding, was what Dr. Steiner had liked about Dr. Wegman. Dr. Steiner said to her, 'You are a person with whom one can communicate as a human being. Otherwise, one would suffocate.'

"In Ita Wegman a lot came forward from the rich past, and at the same time, something was there that belongs to the future. The spiritual was her directive, and she acted accordingly. This is foreign to many people today.

"Everything I have said so far is concerned with the soul. Behind that, the spirit stands as an image, and it will be much more difficult to speak of that. There one steps into a territory where tragedy is to be found....

"When Dr. Steiner was very ill, she asked him, 'What will happen when you are no longer there?' Dr. Steiner answered, 'At that point, karma will prevail.'" Ita Wegman's soul was not rattled by this karma—she, whom Dr. Steiner called his friend and with whom he was connected. Both of them were connected with Michael and the battle that Michael led. She was an example for that battle. She demonstrated what it is like when the human soul is already living fully in the spirit. This force in the spirit held its ground against the onslaught of opposing forces. It is difficult to understand what it means when a soul like Rudolf Steiner's transitions into the spiritual world and other souls remain here; but here, one can come to understand that.

"For us, the decisive spiritual weight of our movement has now moved over into the spiritual world. This is important to consider. It means that it is important to consider what necessary decisions will be made in the spiritual realm. One might ask, 'How is it to continue?' Indeed, the decisive spiritual weight of our movement has moved over into the spiritual world, but we feel that we must continue to carry it and we must muster the courage to do so through what is in the spiritual world and gives us power, the power to build, which has now been liberated. What is connected with this life [Ita Wegman's] and death? The fact that we see that a soul is truly lived and led by the spirit.

"'We are born from the spirit'—this means that the human body comes from the spirit; 'In Christ we die'—which means that the soul meets Christ in death, and everything we can experience on Earth is an experience that comes through the Holy Spirit—'that we may be awakened in this'" (Ita Wegman Archive).

320. Quoted from Ita Wegman (Peter Selg, ed.). *Erinnerung an Rudolf Steiner* [Memory of Rudolf Steiner]. Arlesheim, 2009.

321. Compare note 319.

322. Most likely also Lili Kolisko belonged among these people. Compare in this connection Kolisko's comment in note 204 concerning the disruption of Ita Wegman's Class Lesson: "The blow was not just against the personality of Frau Dr. Wegman; it hit the center of the spiritual movement" (Ibid.), as well as the recorded thoughts by Lili Kolisko in 1961 in her "Closing Observations" about Ita Wegman, with whom she was in no way always in agreement in the 1930s.

323. "Her phrase at the ceremony after Frau Dr. Wegman's death: 'the decisive spiritual weight of our movement has now moved over into the spiritual world,' receives an even greater sense of reality" (Werner Pache, "Diary notes. Michaelmas 1943," Ita Wegman Archive).

324. Madeleine van Deventer, "Zur Zeit des zweiten Weltkriegs' [Concerning the time of World War II]. Unpublished typescript. Ita Wegman Archive, Arlesheim.

325. "As she was supposed to begin to speak, she had a moment of faintness that she quickly overcame." (Werner Pache, "Diary Notes, Michaelmas 1943," Ita Wegman Archive).

326. Madeleine van Deventer, "Zur Zeit des zweiten Weltkriegs' [Concerning the time of World War II.] Unpublished typescript. Ita Wegman Archive, Arlesheim.

327. Ibid.

328. Charlotte Fiechter. In Mitteilungen.

329. Letter to Bien Jurriaanse on April 19, 1943. In Mitteilungen.

330. Ibid.

331. Madeleine van Deventer, "Die letzten Erdentage" [The last days on Earth]. In *Erinnerungen an Ita Wegman* [Memories of Ita Wegman]. Arlesheim, 1945.

332. Danuta Czech, *Kalendarium der wichtigsten Ereignisse aus der Geschichte des Konzentrationslager Auschwitz* [Calendar of the most important events from the history of the concentration camp Auschwitz]. In Waclaw Dlogoborski and Franciszek Piper (eds.), *Auschwitz 1940–1945. Studien zur Geschichte des Konzentrations- und Vernichtungslagers Auschwitz* [Auschwitz 1940–1945. Studies of the history of the concentration and death camp Auschwitz], vol. 5. Oświęcim, 1999.

333. Madeleine van Deventer, "Zur Zeit des zweiten Weltkriegs" [Concerning the time of World War II]. Unpublished typescript. Ita Wegman Archive, Arlesheim.

334. Bindel.

335. In Deventer/Knottenbelt.

336. Ibid.

337. Compare Peter Selg, *Liane Collot d'Herbois und Ita Wegman*. Dornach, 2008.

338. Quoted from Uwe Werner, "I have never spoken about the Archive." In Mitteilungen.

339. Rudolf Steiner, *Mantric Sayings: Meditations 1903–1925* (CW 268). SteinerBooks, 2015.

340. Unpublished. Typescript in Estate of Elisabeth Vreede in the Holland National Society in The Hague.

341. In "Astronomy Circular," December 1928. Reprinted in: Elisabeth Vreede, *Astronomy and Spiritual Science; The Astronomical Letters of Elizabeth Vreede*. SteinerBooks, 2007.

Books in English Translation by Peter Selg

On Rudolf Steiner

Rudolf Steiner: Life and Work: (1919–1922): Social Threefolding and the Waldorf School, vol. 5 of 7 (2017)

Rudolf Steiner: Life and Work: (1914–1918): The Years of World War I, vol. 4 of 7 (2016)

Rudolf Steiner: Life and Work: (1900–1914): Spiritual Science and Spiritual Community, vol. 3 of 7 (2015)

Rudolf Steiner: Life and Work: (1890–1900): Weimar and Berlin, vol. 2 of 7 (2014)

Rudolf Steiner: Life and Work: (1861–1890): Childhood, Youth, and Study Years, vol. 1 of 7 (2014)

Rudolf Steiner and Christian Rosenkreutz (2012)

Rudolf Steiner as a Spiritual Teacher: From Recollections of Those Who Knew Him (2010)

On Christology

The Sufferings of the Nathan Soul: Anthroposophic Christology on the Eve of World War I (2016)

The Lord's Prayer and Rudolf Steiner: A Study of His Insights into the Archetypal Prayer of Christianity (2014)

The Creative Power of Anthroposophical Christology: An Outline of Occult Science · The First Goetheanum · The Fifth Gospel · The Christmas Conference (with Sergei O. Prokofieff) (2012)

Christ and the Disciples: The Destiny of an Inner Community (2012)

The Figure of Christ: Rudolf Steiner and the Spiritual Intention behind the Goetheanum's Central Work of Art (2009)

Rudolf Steiner and the Fifth Gospel: Insights into a New Understanding of the Christ Mystery (2010)

Seeing Christ in Sickness and Healing (2005)

On General Anthroposophy

The Michael School: And the School of Spiritual Science (2016)

The Destiny of the Michael Community: Foundation Stone for the Future (2014)

Spiritual Resistance: Ita Wegman 1933–1935 (2014)

The Last Three Years: Ita Wegman in Ascona, 1940–1943 (2014)

From Gurs to Auschwitz: The Inner Journey of Maria Krehbiel-Darmstädter (2013)

Crisis in the Anthroposophical Society: And Pathways to the Future (2013); with Sergei O. Prokofieff

Rudolf Steiner's Foundation Stone Meditation: And the Destruction of the Twentieth Century (2013)

The Culture of Selflessness: Rudolf Steiner, the Fifth Gospel, and the Time of Extremes (2012)

The Mystery of the Heart: The Sacramental Physiology of the Heart in Aristotle, Thomas Aquinas, and Rudolf Steiner (2012)

Rudolf Steiner and the School for Spiritual Science: The Foundation of the "First Class" (2012)

Rudolf Steiner's Intentions for the Anthroposophical Society: The Executive Council, the School for Spiritual Science, and the Sections (2011)

The Fundamental Social Law: Rudolf Steiner on the Work of the Individual and the Spirit of Community (2011)

The Path of the Soul after Death: The Community of the Living and the Dead as Witnessed by Rudolf Steiner in his Eulogies and Farewell Addresses (2011)

The Agriculture Course, Koberwitz, Whitsun 1924: Rudolf Steiner and the Beginnings of Biodynamics (2010)

On Anthroposophical Medicine and Curative Education

The Warmth Meditation: A Path to the Good in the Service of Healing (2016)

Honoring Life: Medical Ethics and Physician-Assisted Suicide (2014); with Sergei O. Prokofieff

I Am for Going Ahead: Ita Wegman's Work for the Social Ideals of Anthroposophy (2012)

The Child with Special Needs: Letters and Essays on Curative Education (Ed.) (2009)

Ita Wegman and Karl König: Letters and Documents (2008)

Karl König's Path to Anthroposophy (2008)

Karl König: My Task: Autobiography and Biographies (Ed.) (2008)

On Child Development and Waldorf Education

The Child as a Sense Organ: An Anthroposophic Understanding of the Imitation Processes (2017)

I Am Different from You: How Children Experience Themselves and the World in the Middle of Childhood (2011)

Unbornness: Human Pre-existence and the Journey toward Birth (2010)

The Essence of Waldorf Education (2010)

The Therapeutic Eye: How Rudolf Steiner Observed Children (2008)

A Grand Metamorphosis: Contributions to the Spiritual-Scientific Anthropology and Education of Adolescents (2008)

Ita Wegman Institute
for Basic Research into Anthroposophy

Pfeffinger Weg 1a, ch 4144 Arlesheim, Switzerland
www.wegmaninstitut.ch
e-mail: sekretariat@wegmaninstitut.ch

The Ita Wegman Institute for Basic Research into Anthroposophy is a non-profit research and teaching organization. It undertakes basic research into the lifework of Dr. Rudolf Steiner (1861–1925) and the application of Anthroposophy in specific areas of life, especially medicine, education, and curative education. Work carried out by the Institute is supported by a number of foundations and organizations and an international group of friends and supporters. The Director of the Institute is Prof. Dr. Peter Selg.

www.ingramcontent.com/pod-product-compliance
Lightning Source LLC
Chambersburg PA
CBHW022000220426
43663CB00007B/890